# FANTASTIC BEASTS Of The NINETEENTH CENTURY

## Dragons, Birds, and Incredible Sea Creatures

### Edited by Anton Seder

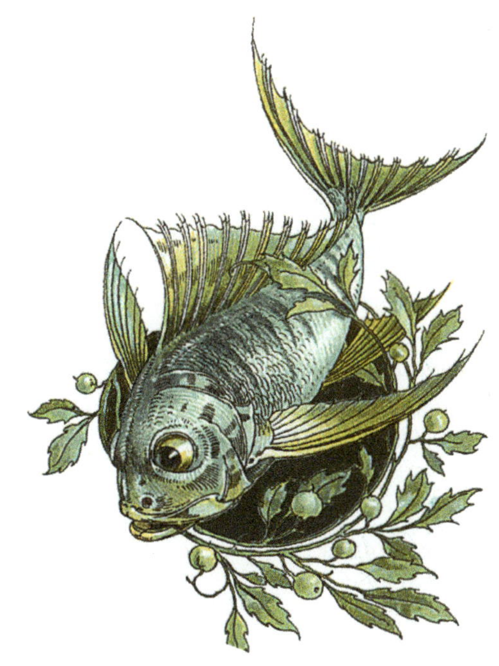

DOVER PUBLICATIONS
GARDEN CITY, NEW YORK

# Publisher's Note

Born in Munich in 1850, Anton Seder was one of the most influential German designers of his day, though few now know his name. At the age of 40, after more than two decades of professional design experience in the decorative and applied arts, Seder was awarded the director's chair of a new school in Strasbourg—The College of Decorative Arts. Looking to revive the Alsace-Lorraine region's artistic presence, Seder would bring together influences of French and German origin with Art Nouveau, Victorian, and Baroque styles in both his own work and that of his students. He was as active in publishing as he was in education, co-editing an Arts magazine of the region (*Das Kunstgewerbe in Elsass-Lothringen*) and producing numerous books on decorative and industrial design.

Originally titled *Das Thier in der Decorativen Kunst,* this collection incorporates animal motifs that were ever-present in design of the 1890s, both arranged in graphic patterns and expertly rendered in natural form. From his wonderfully depicted fish and birds to the imaginative and fantastic dragons, the portfolio of material here is sure to provide inspiration to the creative today, just as it did when Seder was active and teaching.

*Bibliographical Note*

*Fantastic Beasts of the Nineteenth Century: Dragons, Birds, and Incredible Sea Creatures* is a new work, first published by Dover Publications in 2017.

*International Standard Book Number*
*ISBN-13: 978-0-486-81956-3*
*ISBN-10: 0-486-81956-6*

Printed in Canada by Marquis Book
81956602    2024
www.doverpublications.com

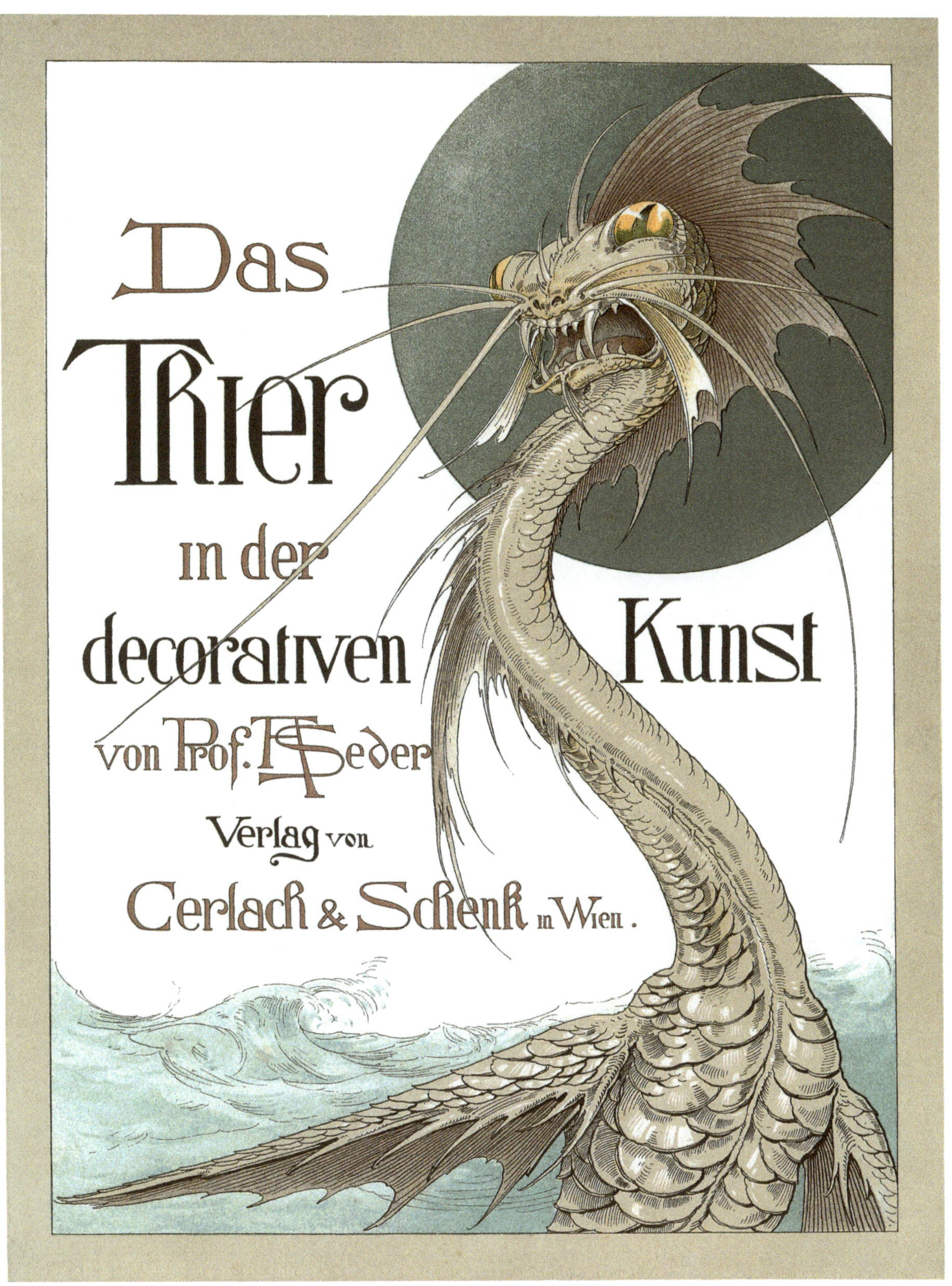


Das
Thier
in der
decorativen
Kunst
von Prof. A. Seder
Verlag von
Gerlach & Schenk in Wien.

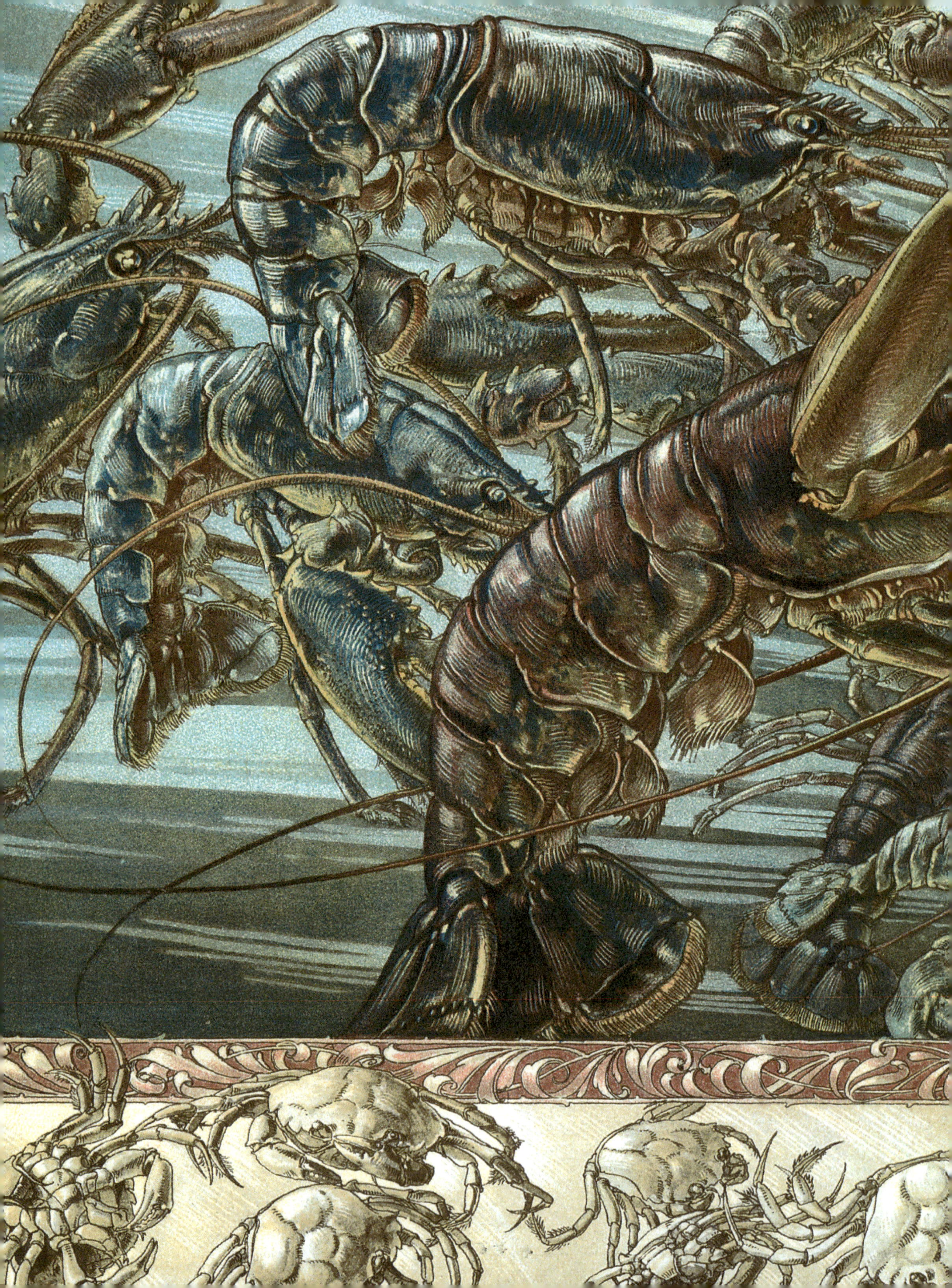

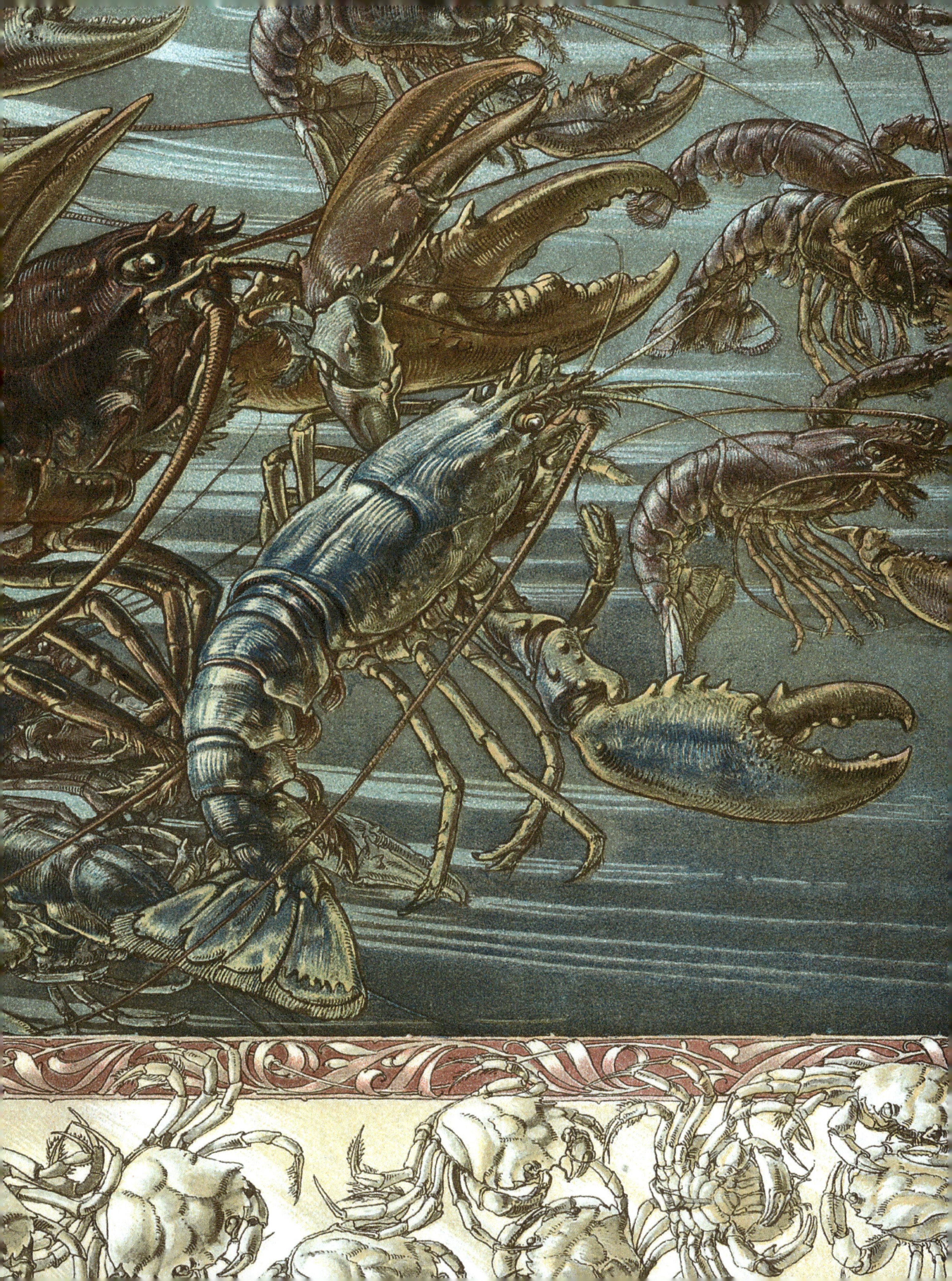

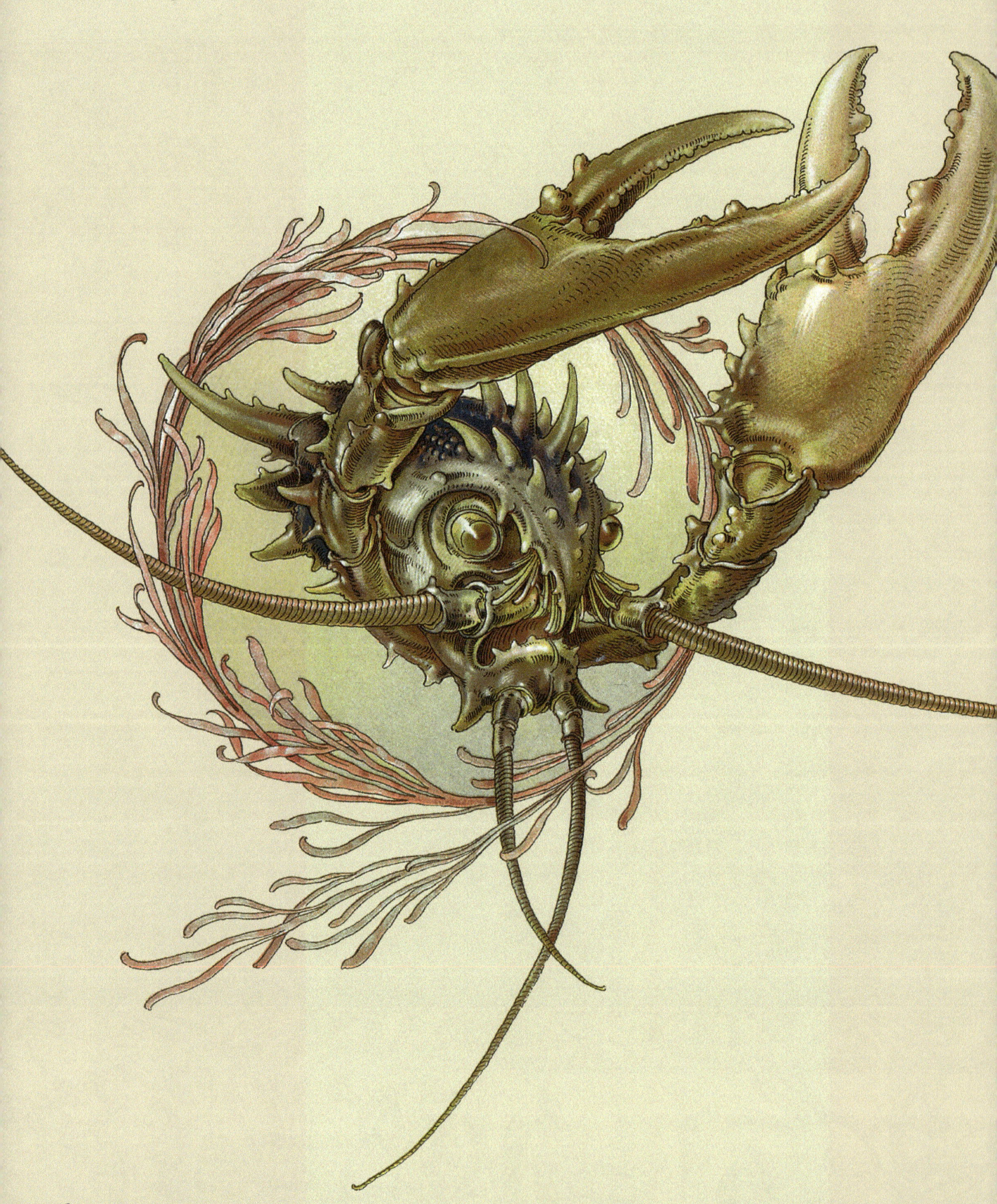

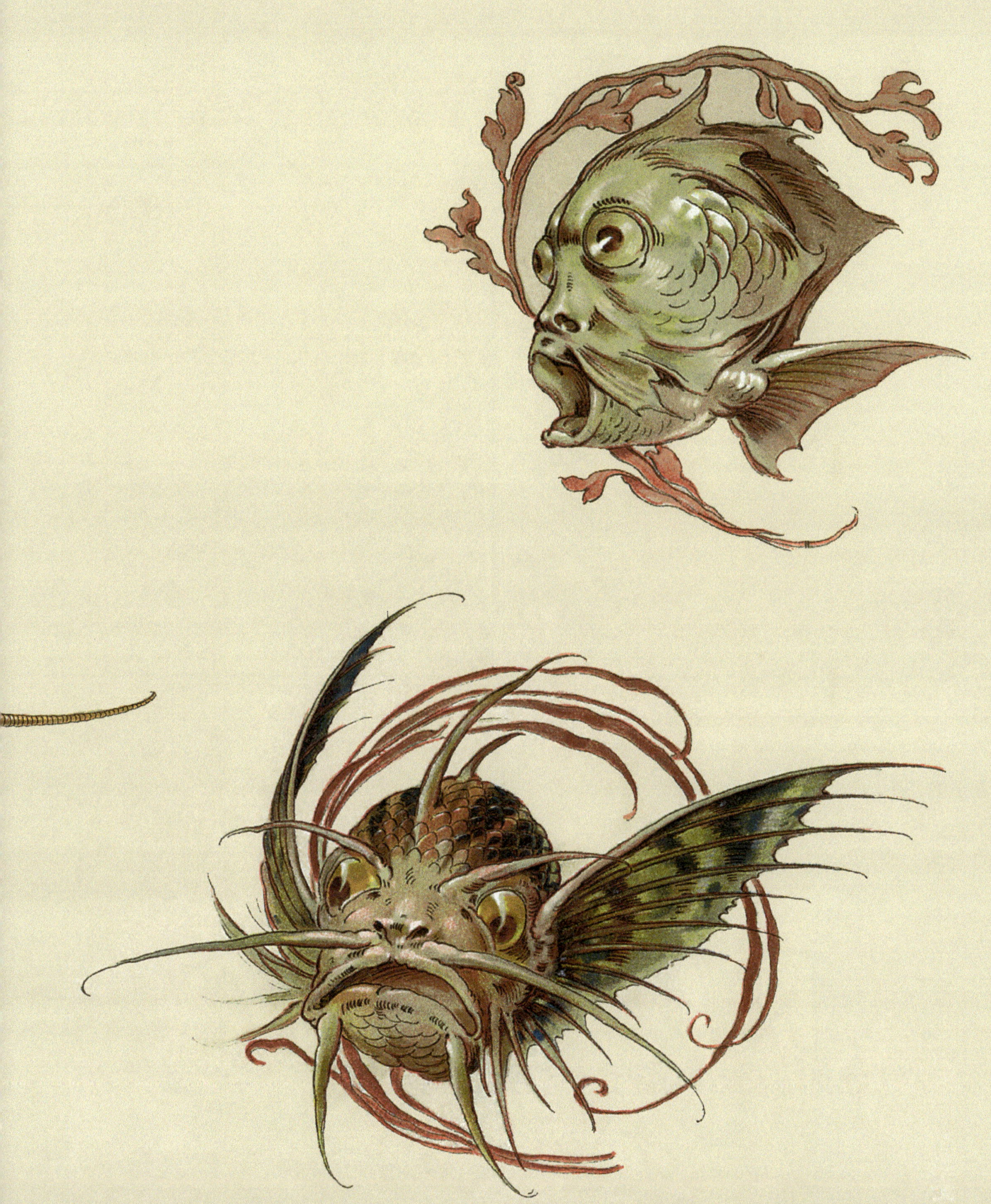

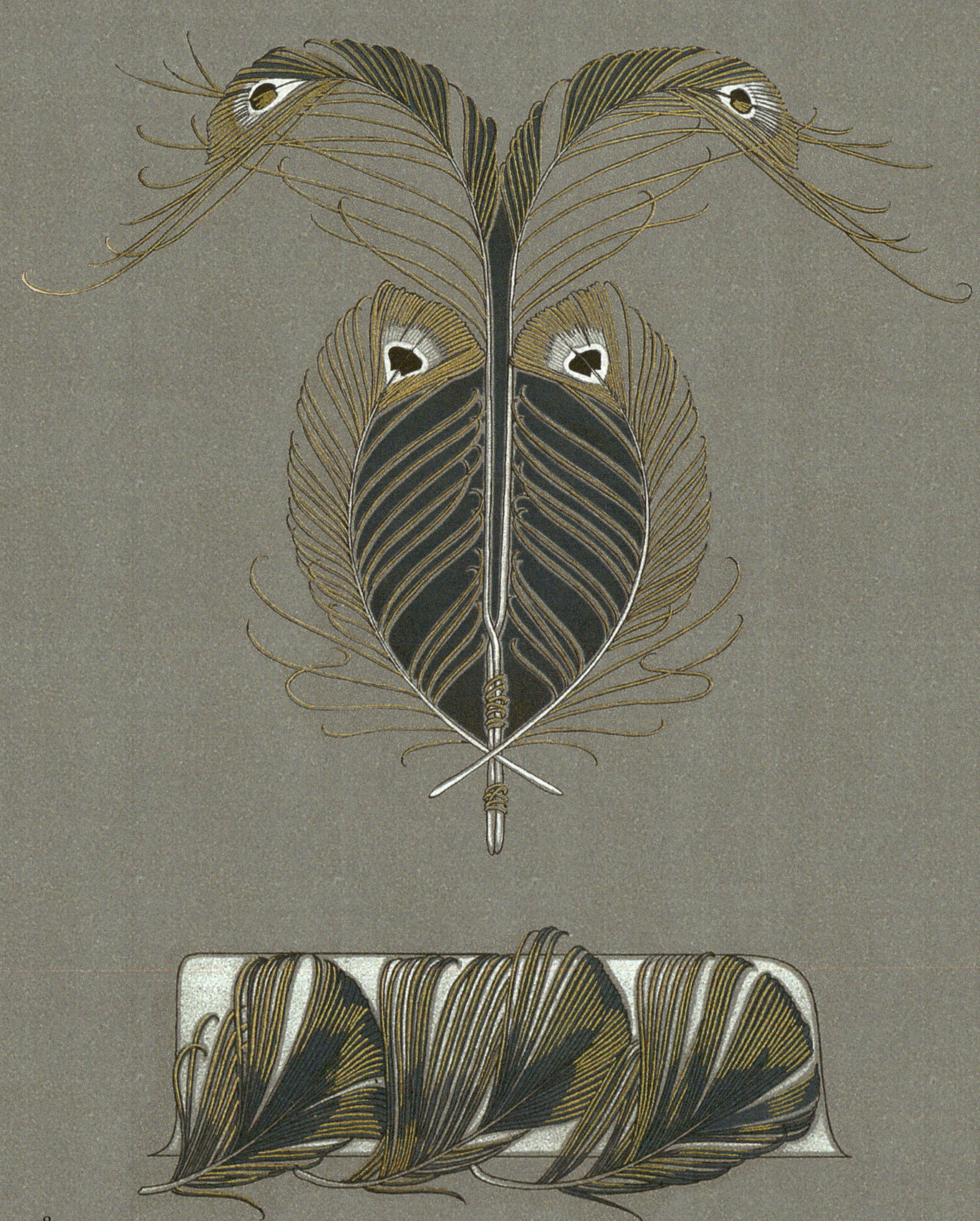

8

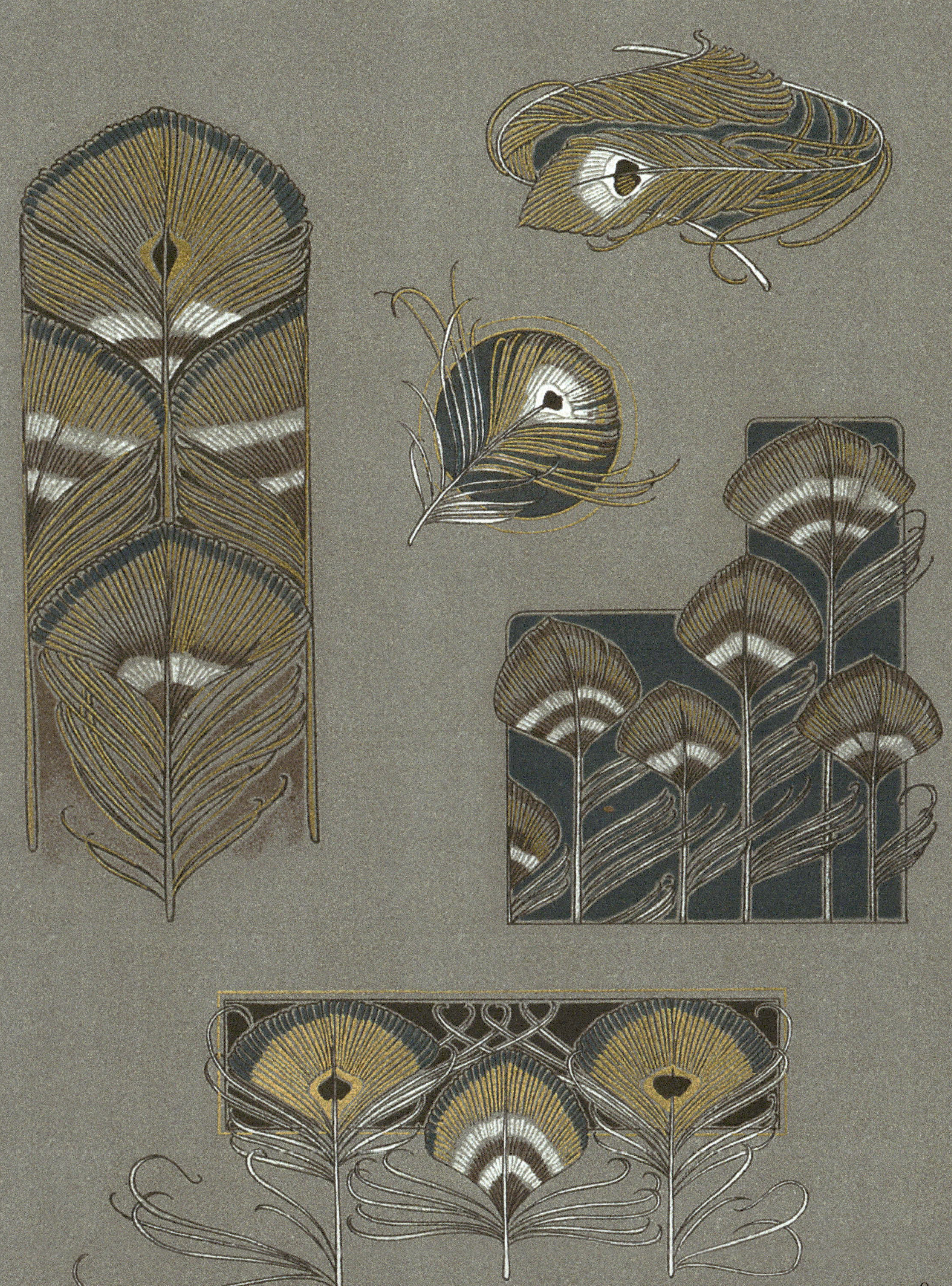

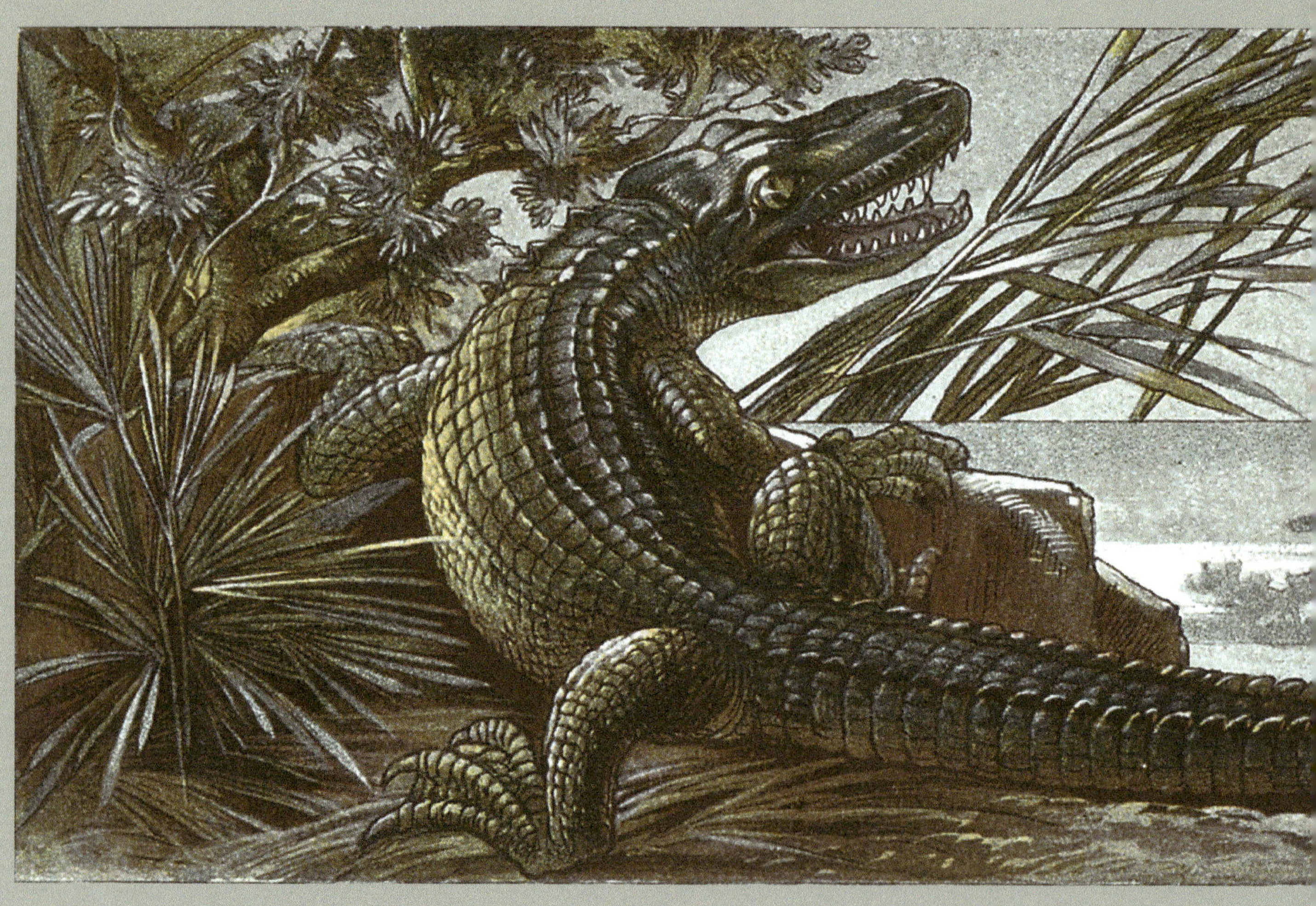

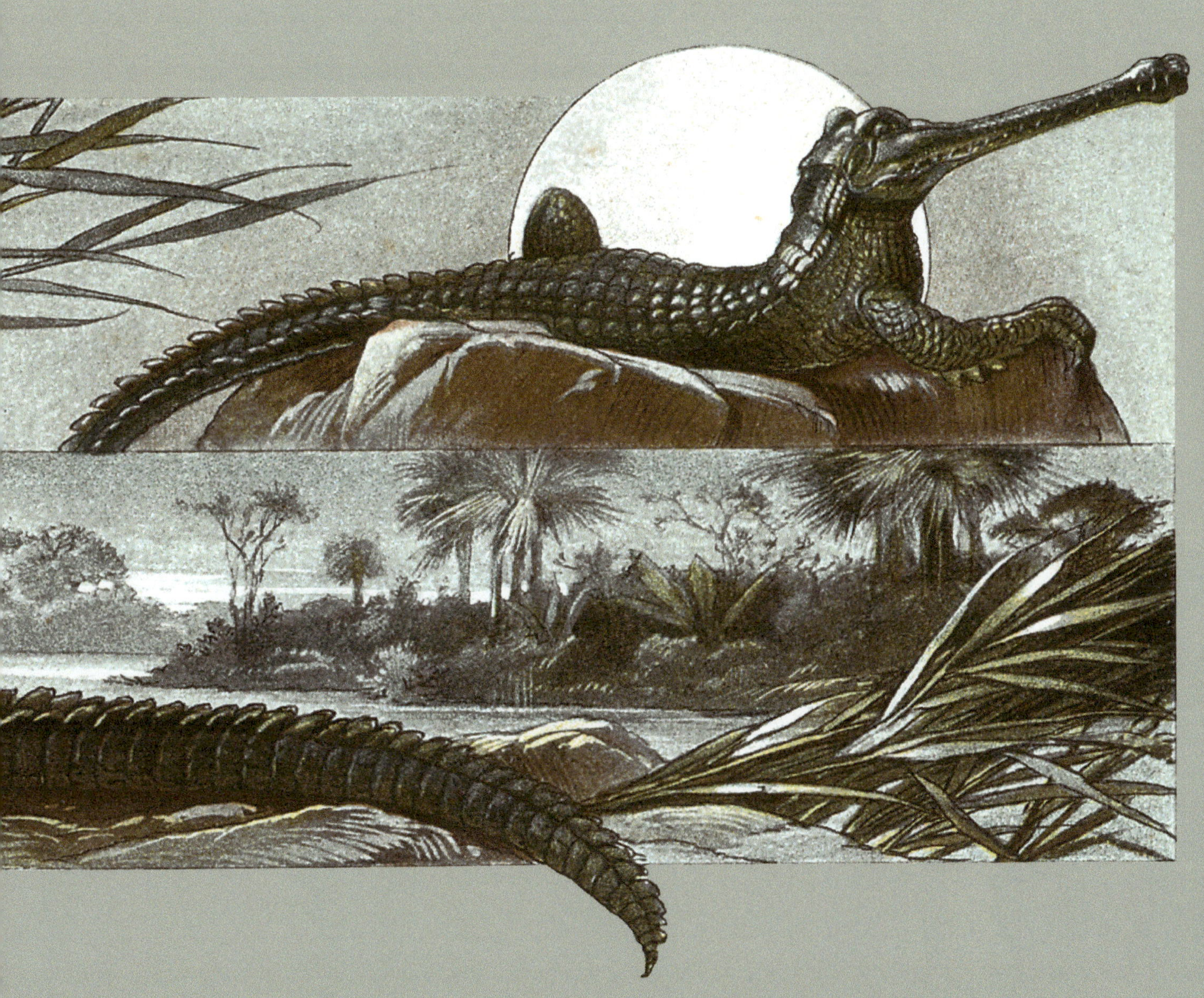

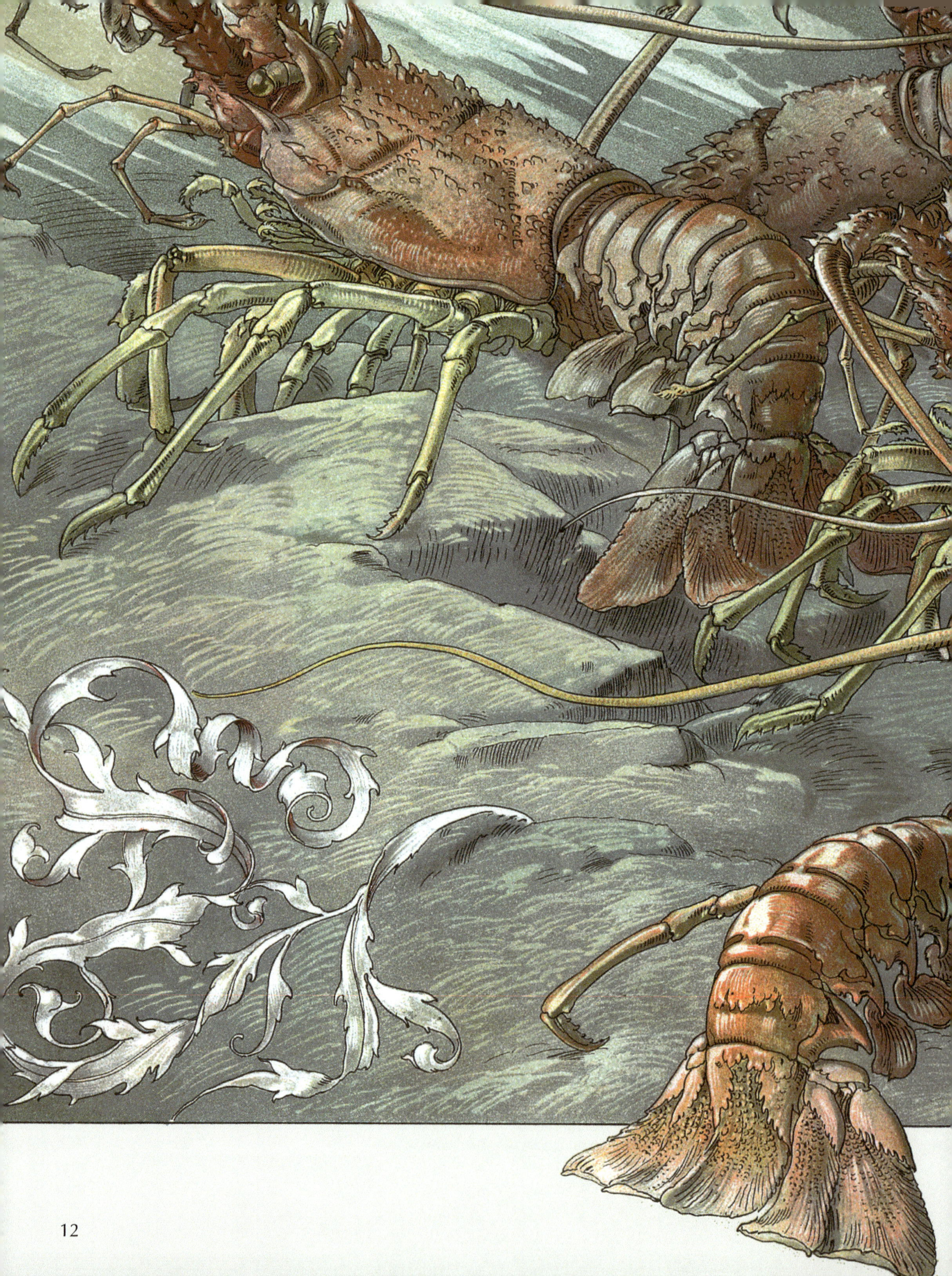

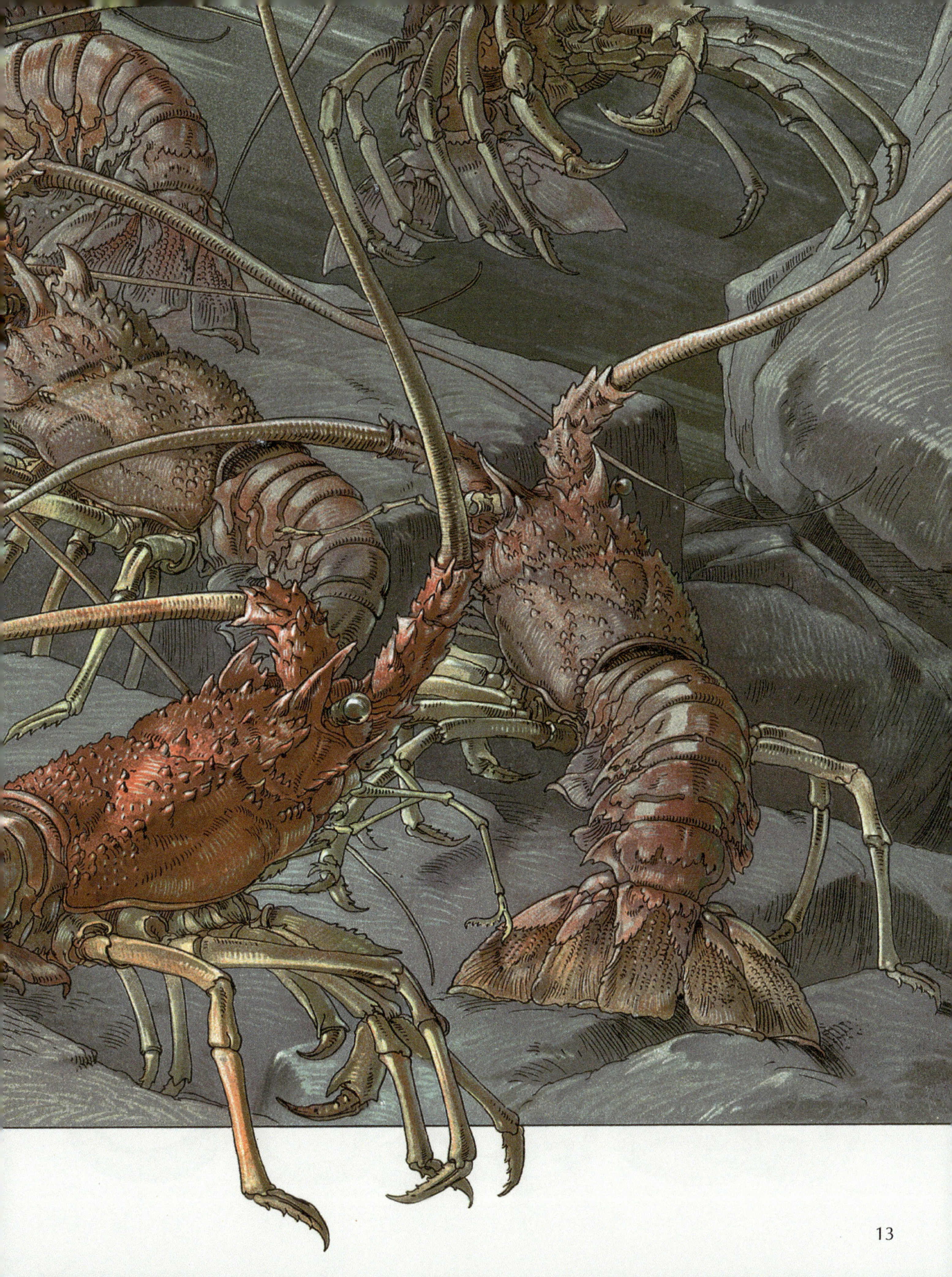

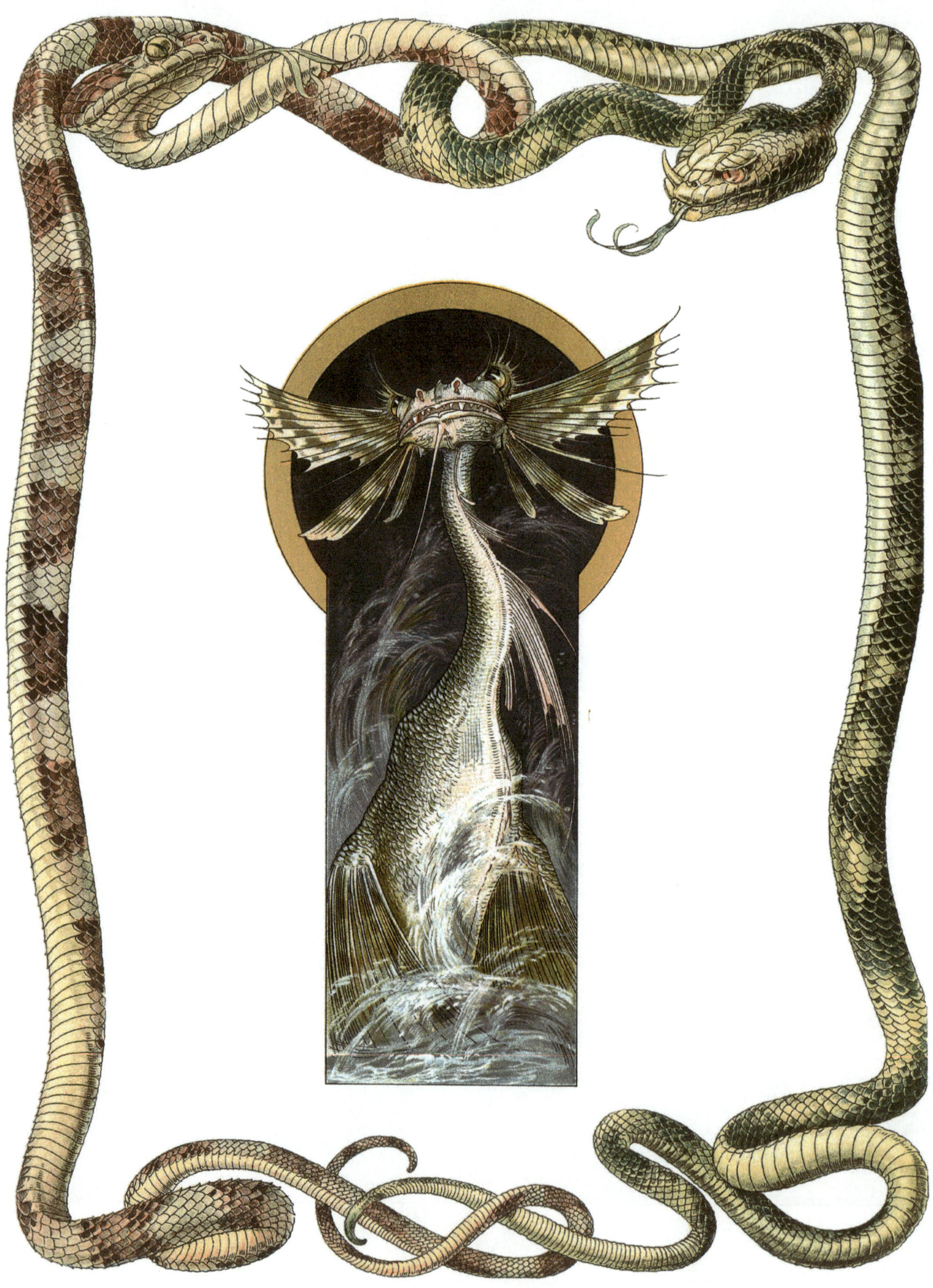

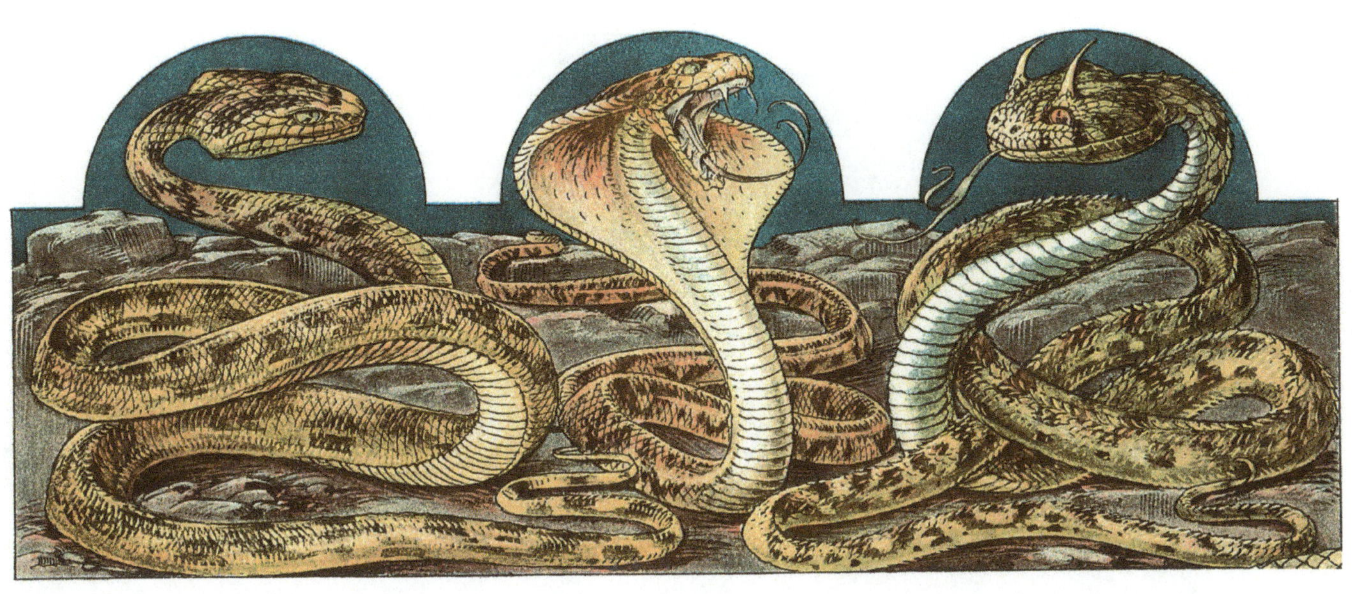

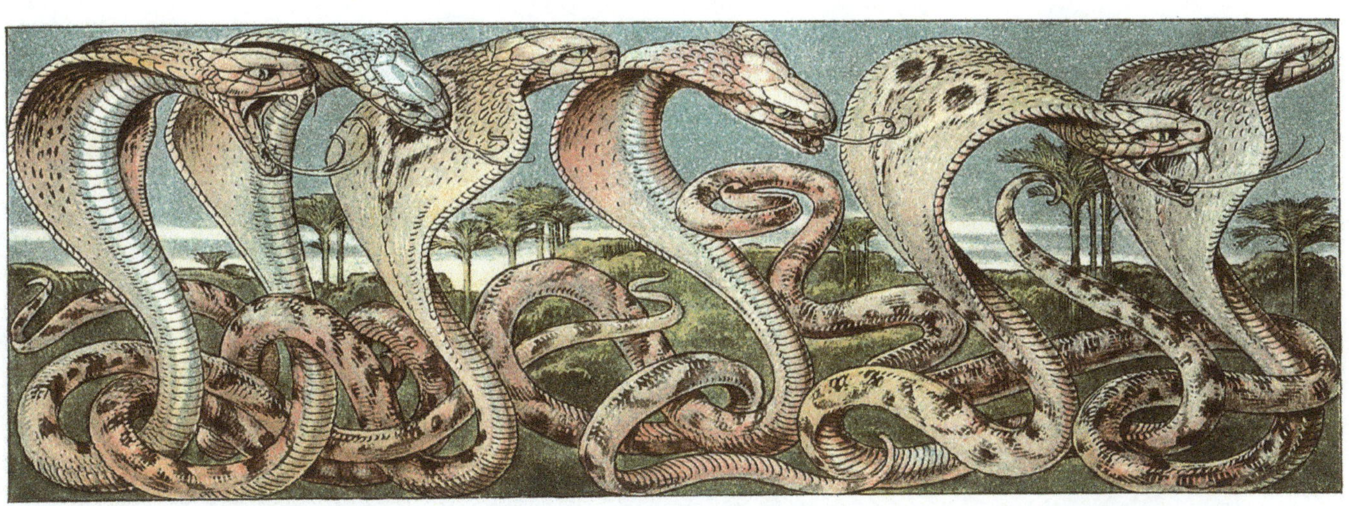

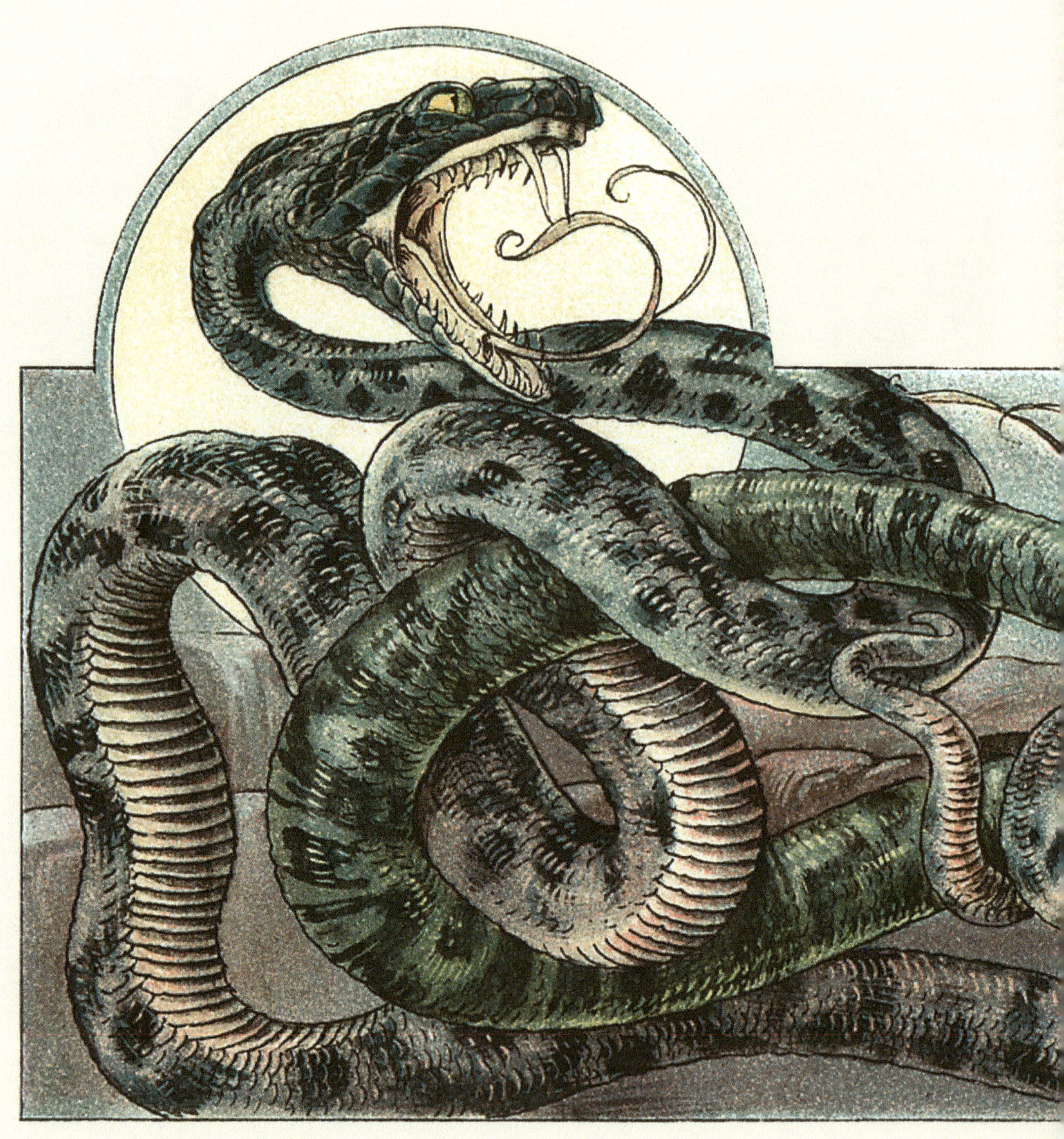

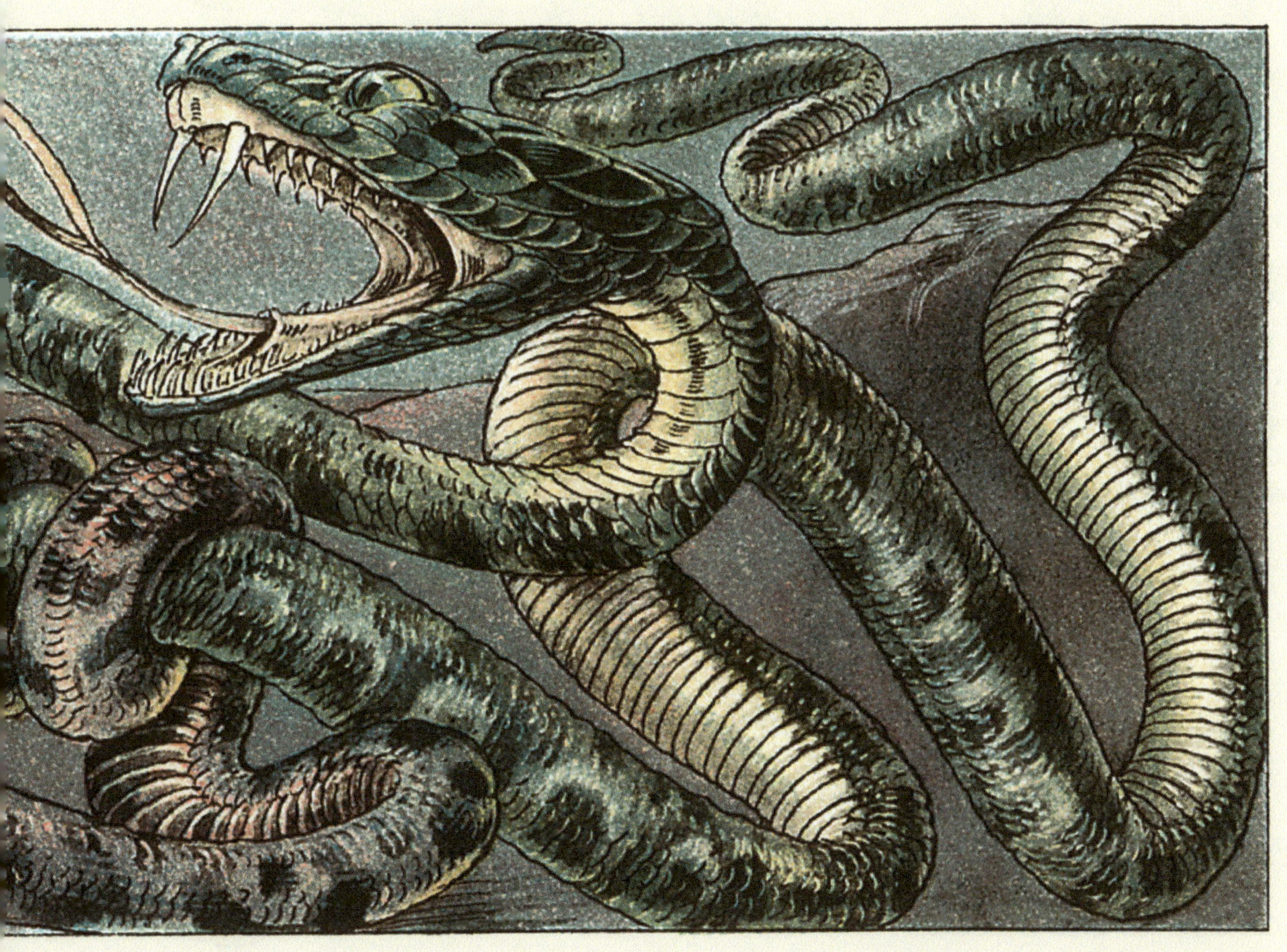

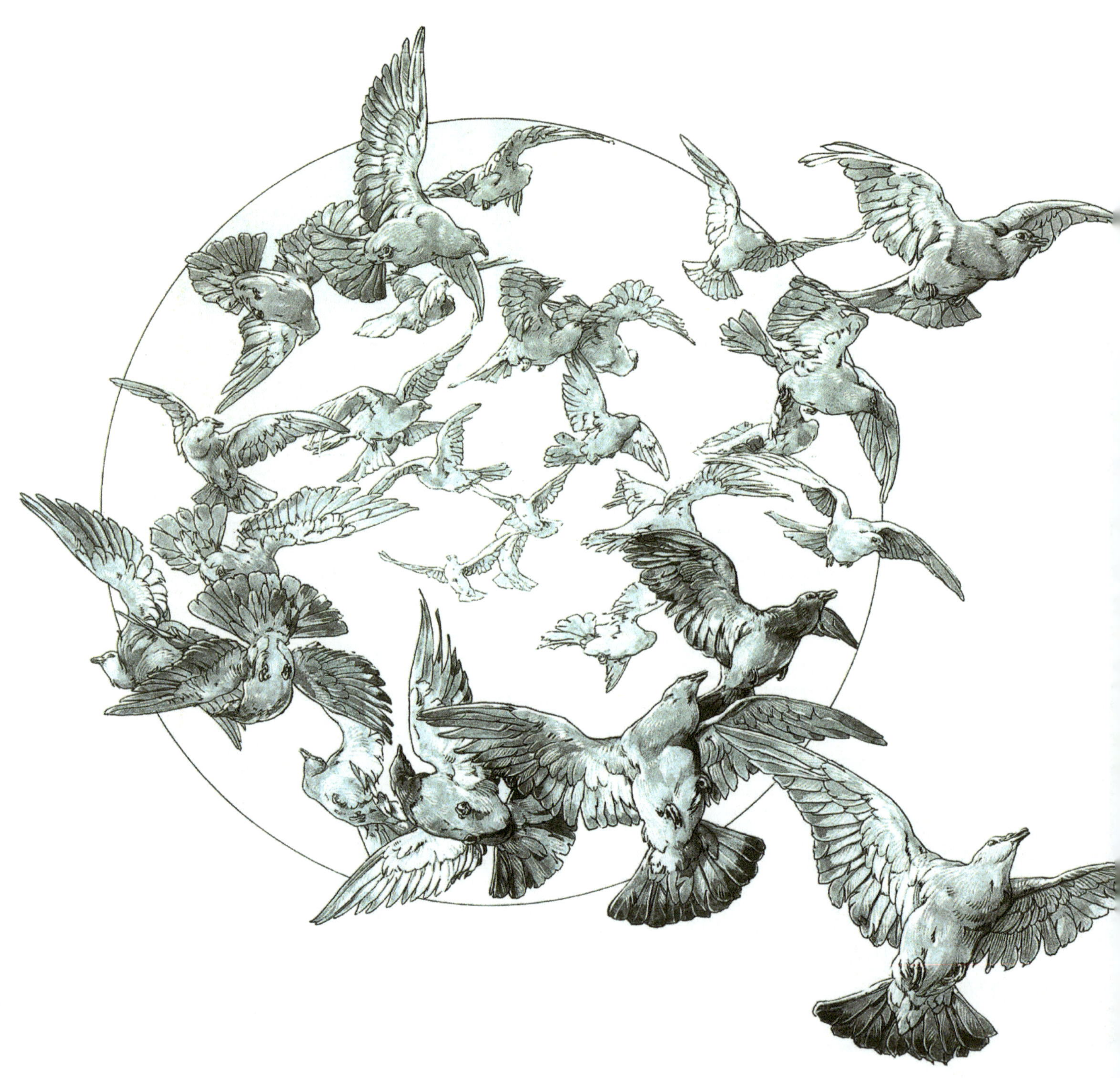

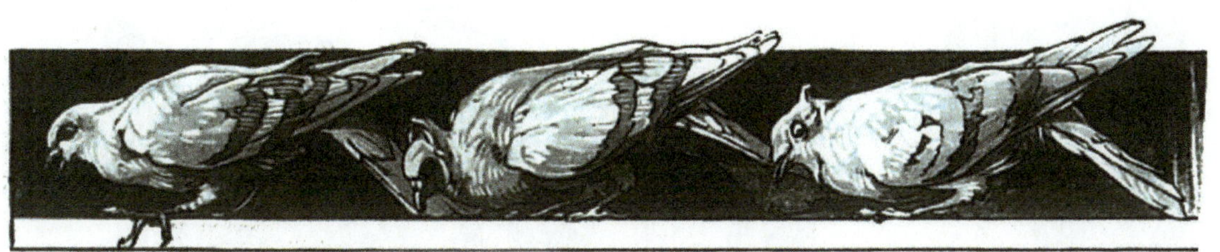

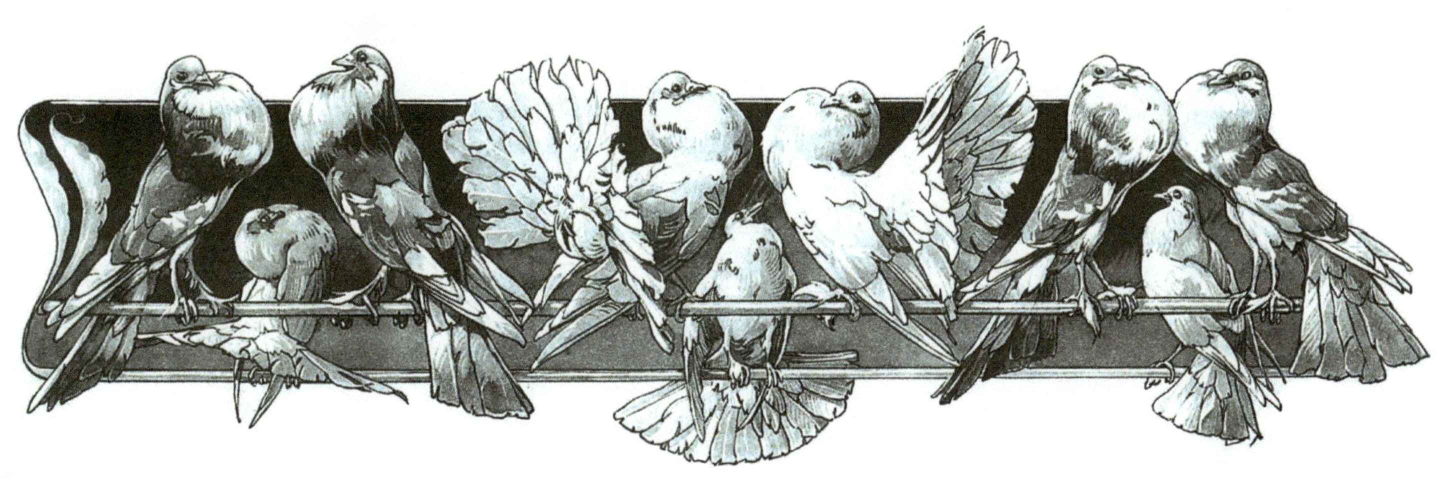

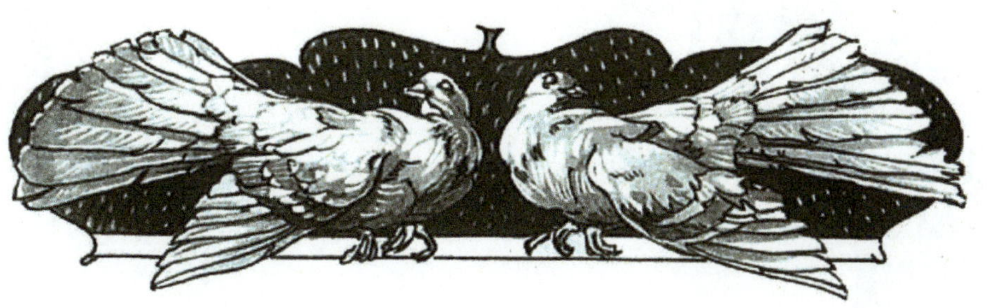

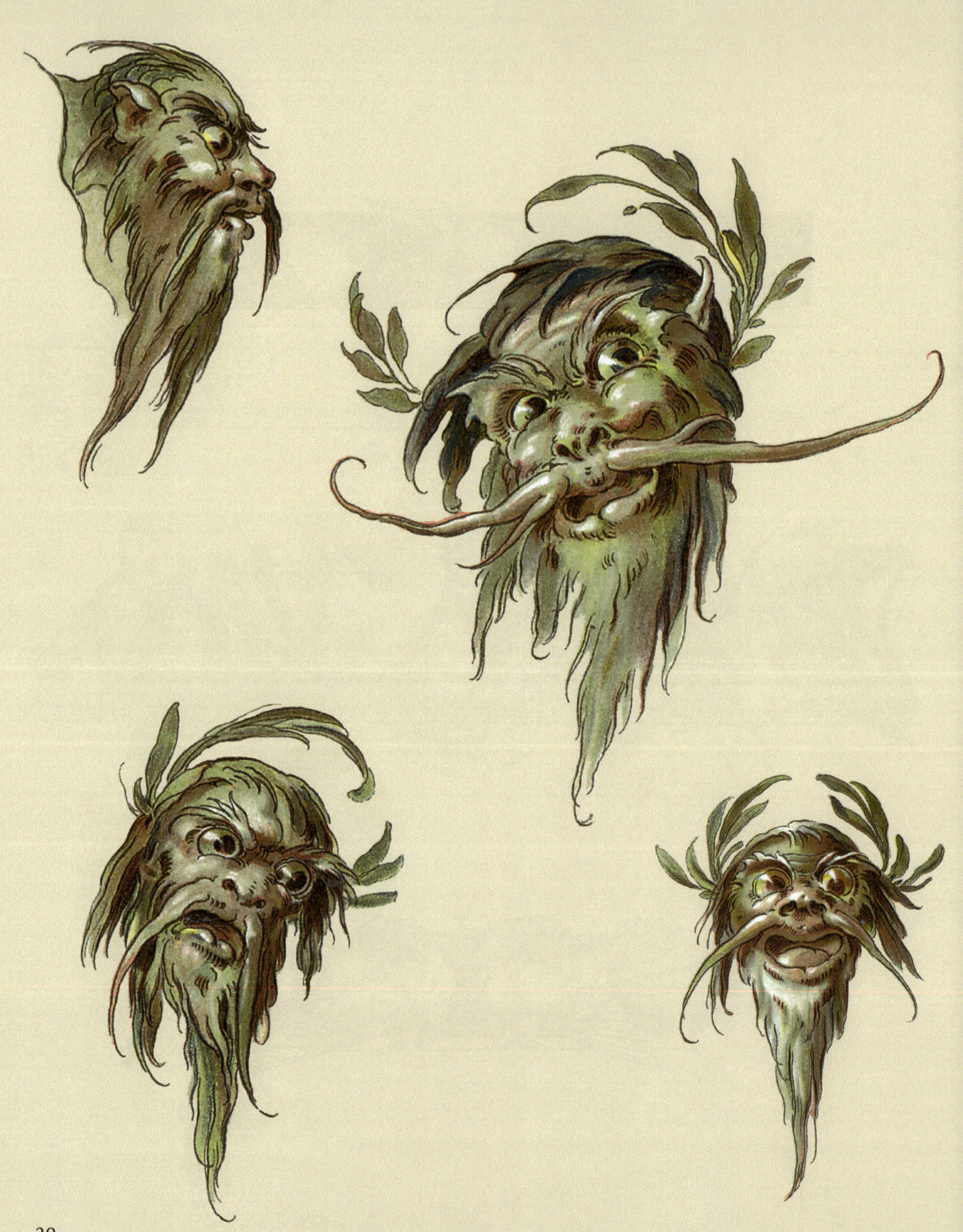

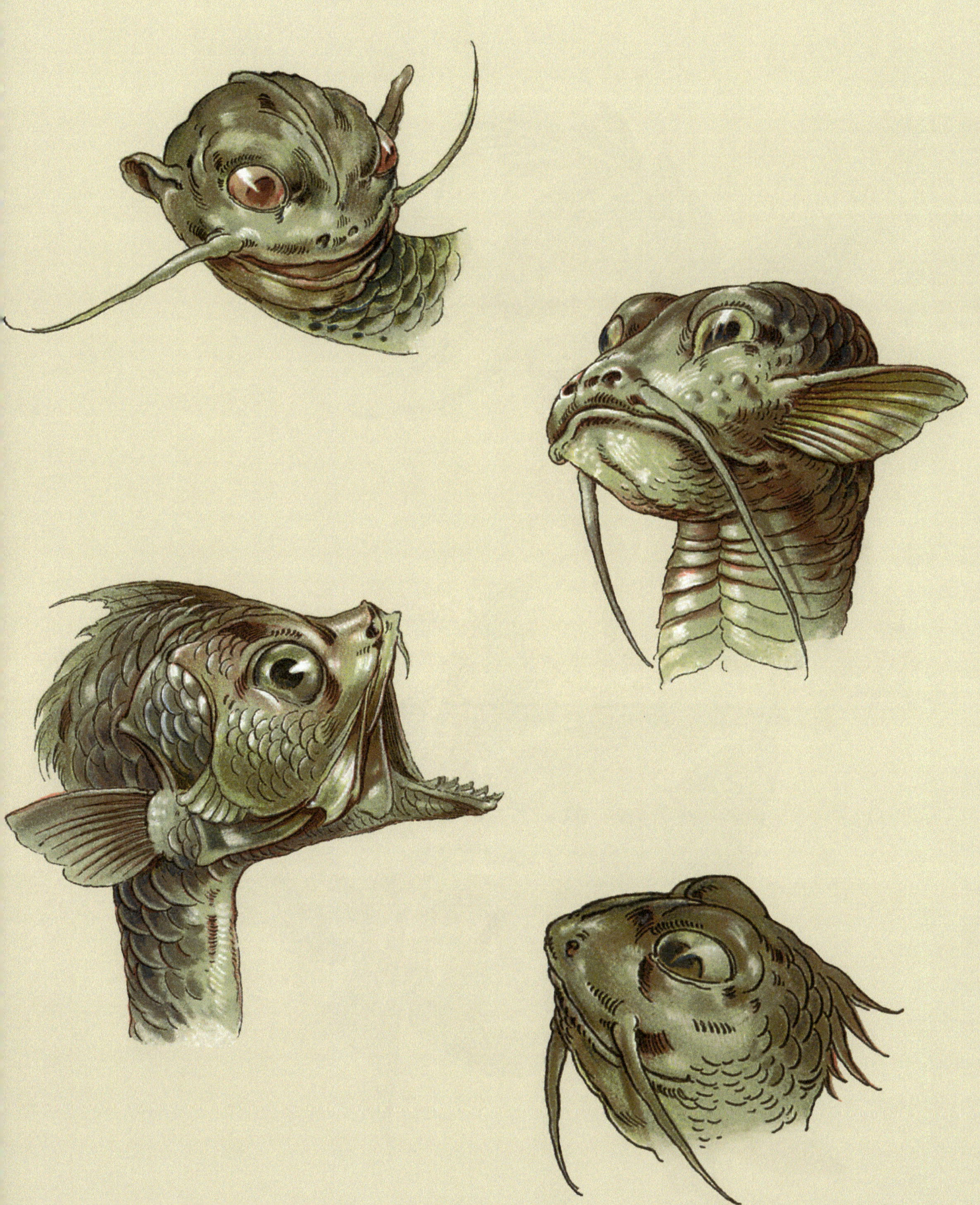

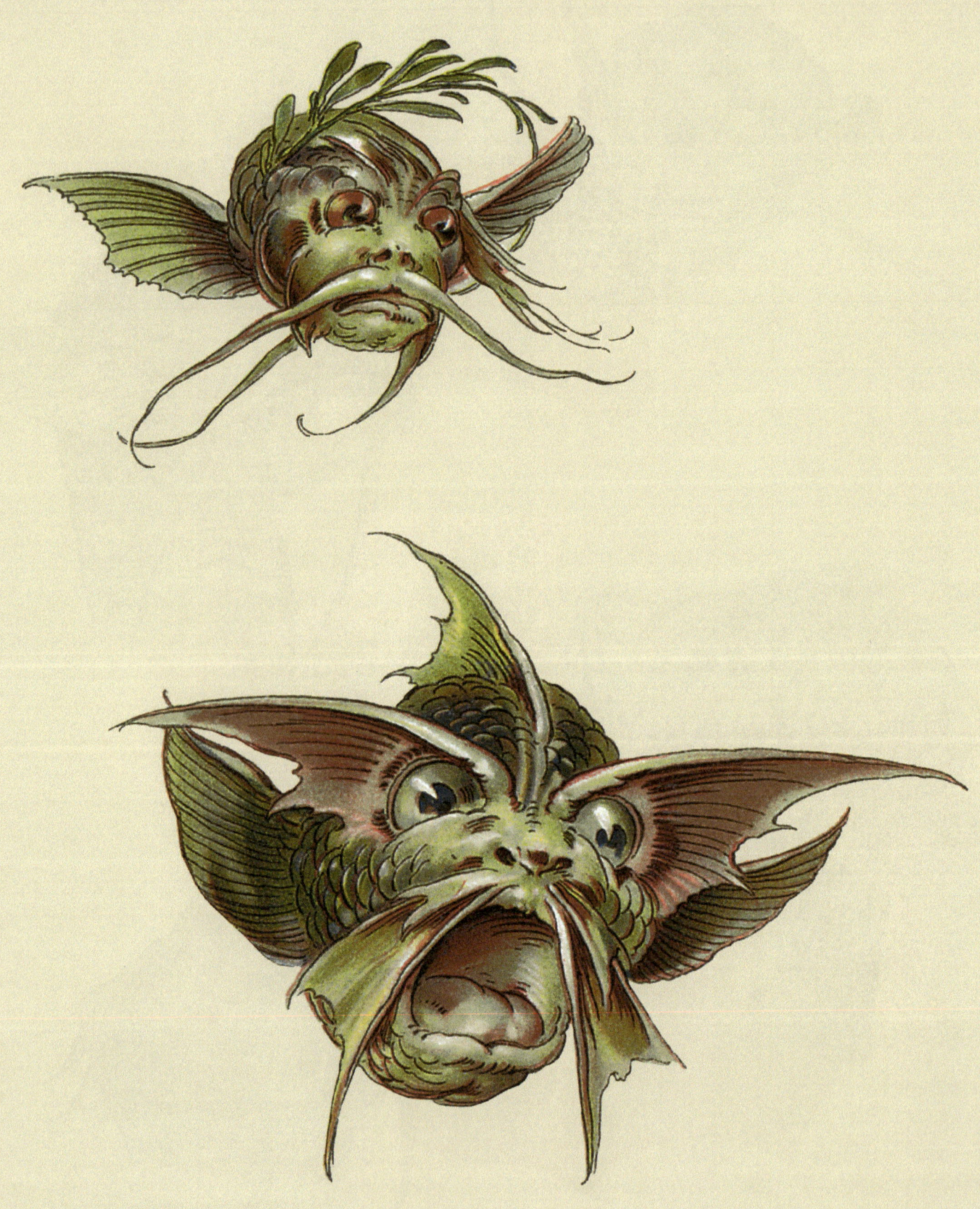

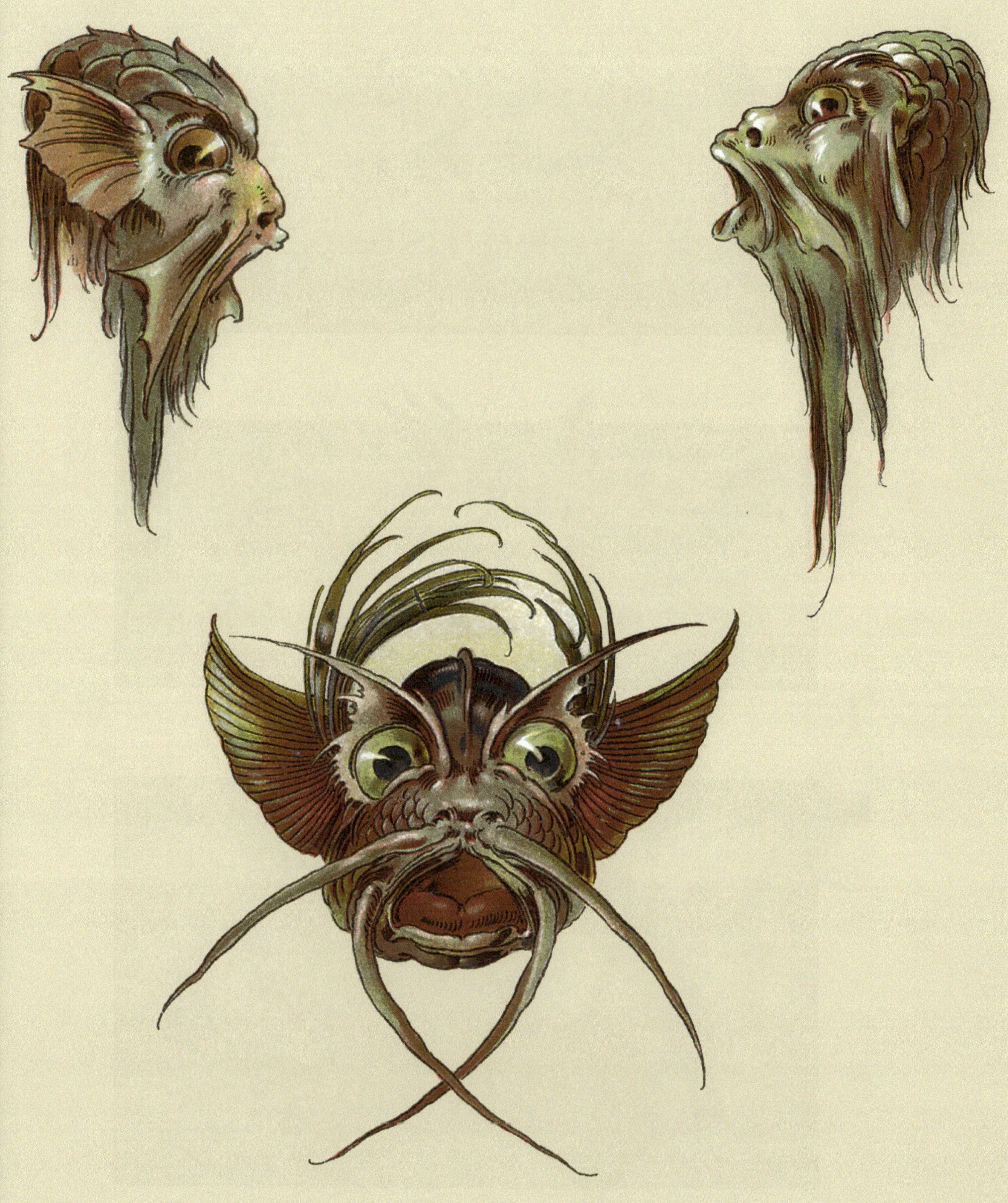

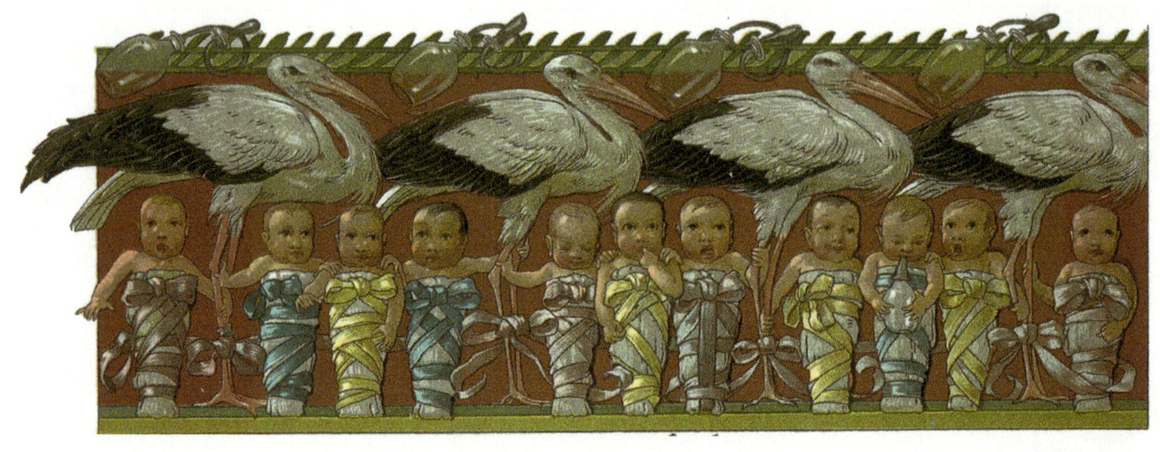

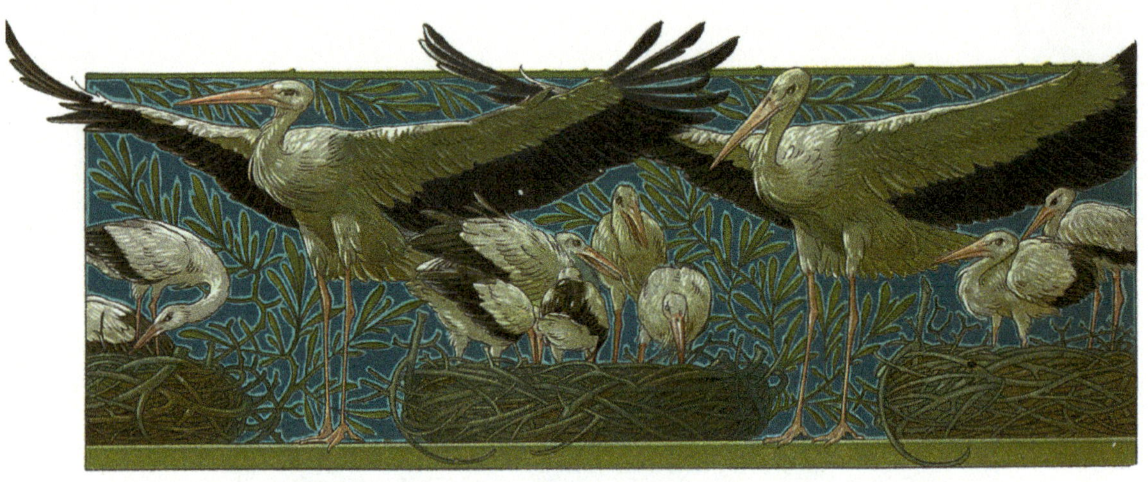

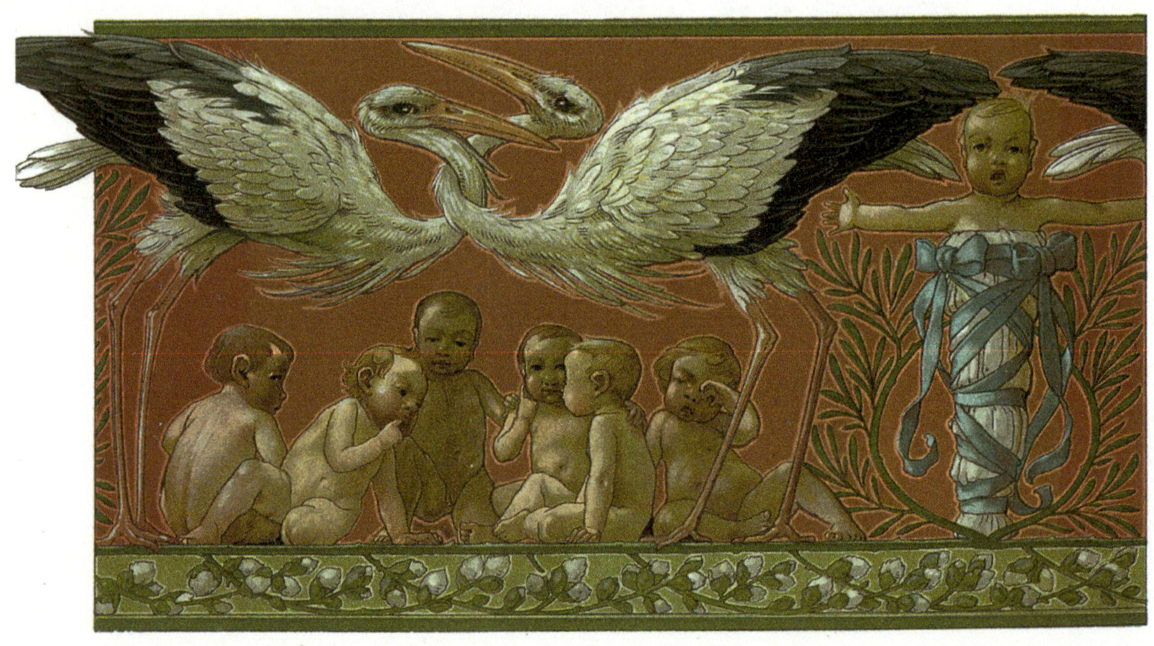

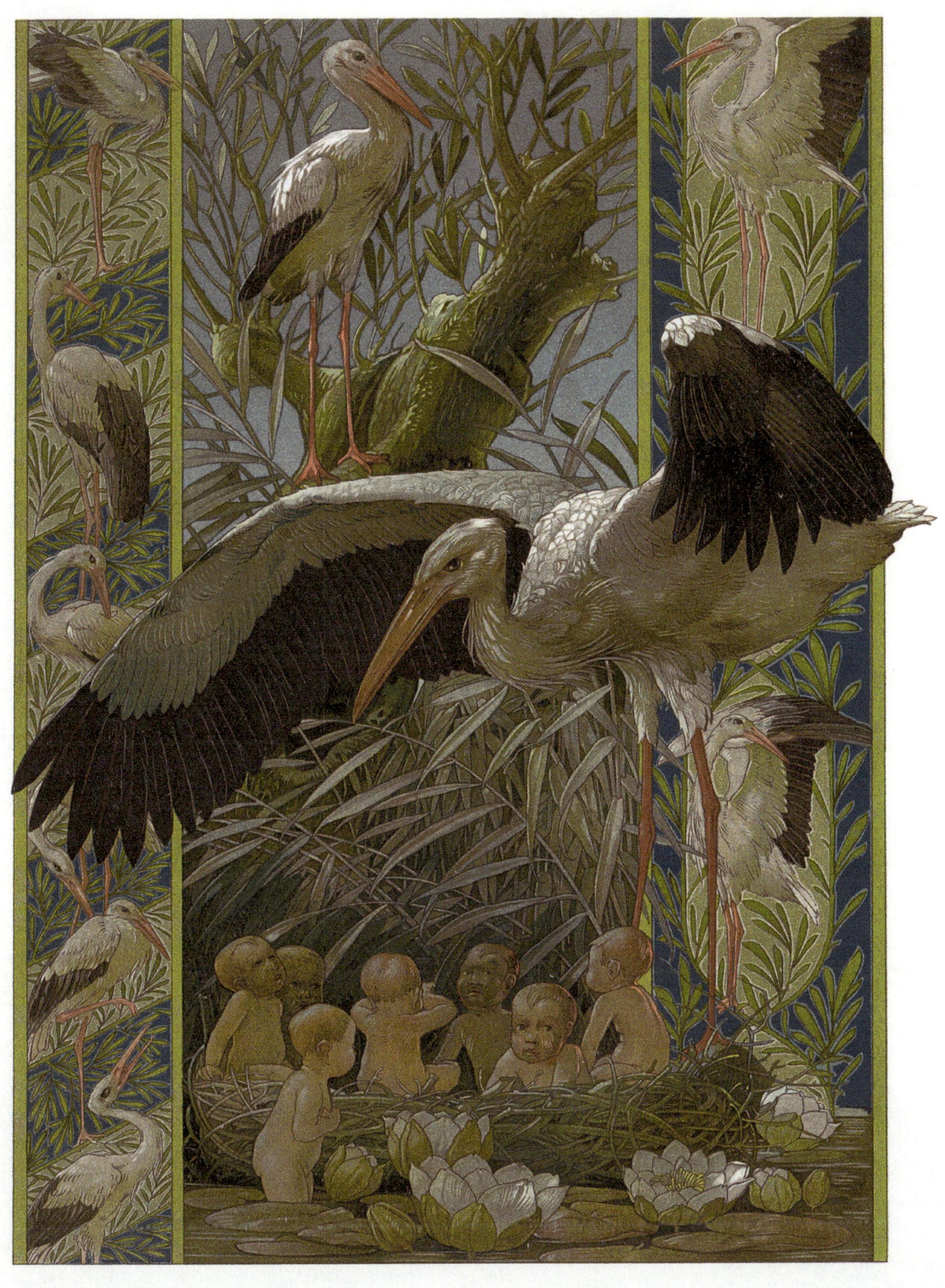

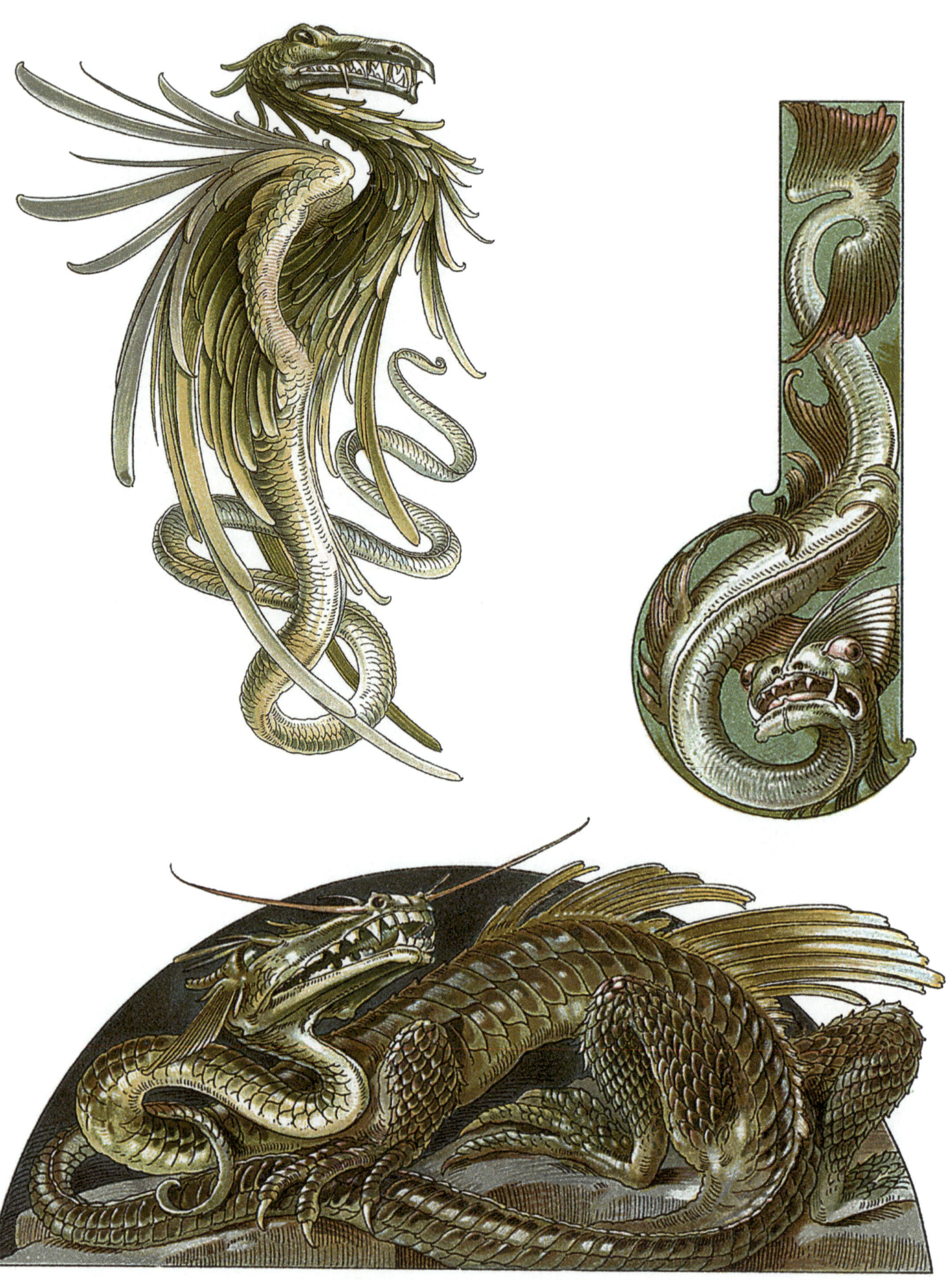

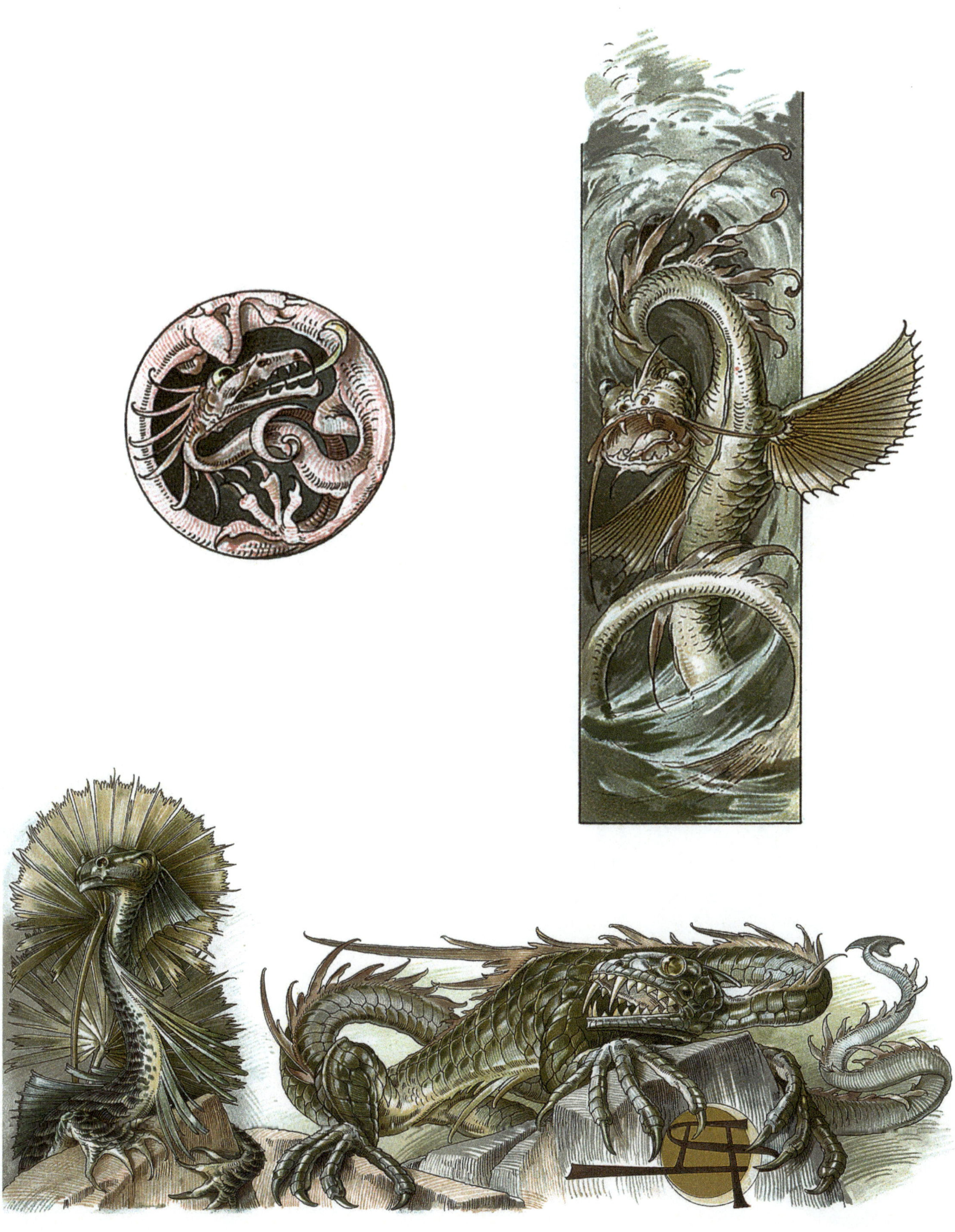

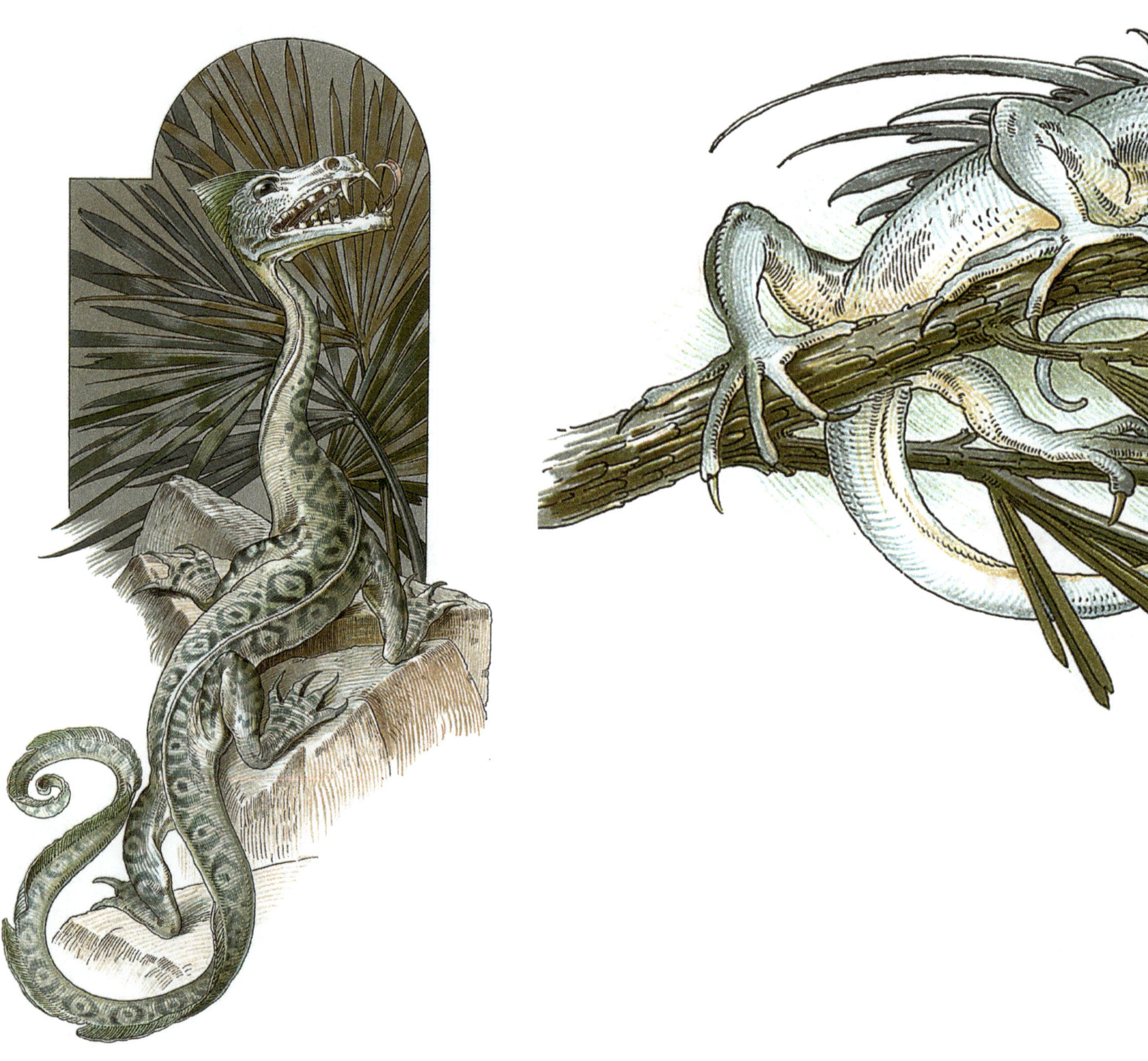

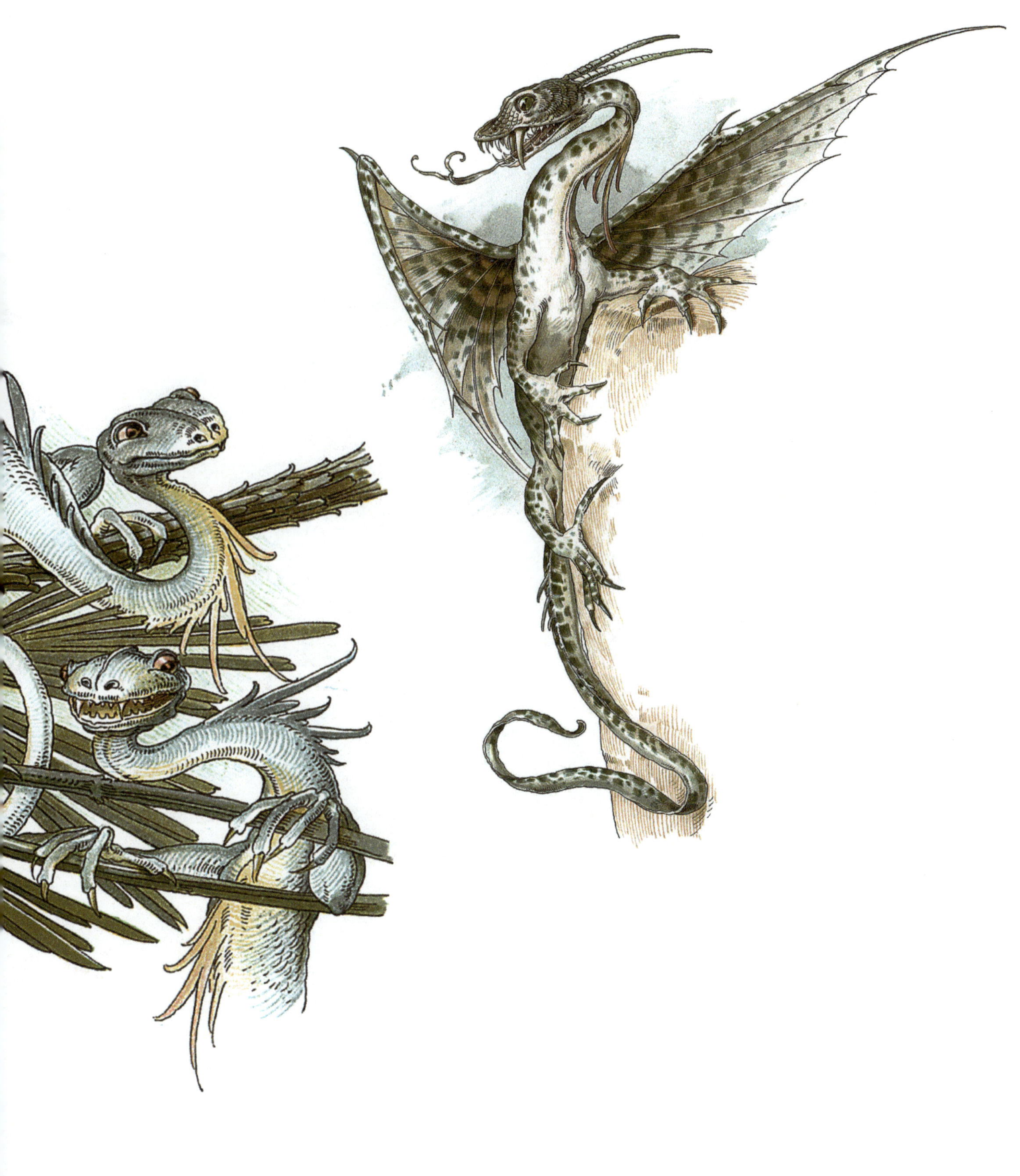

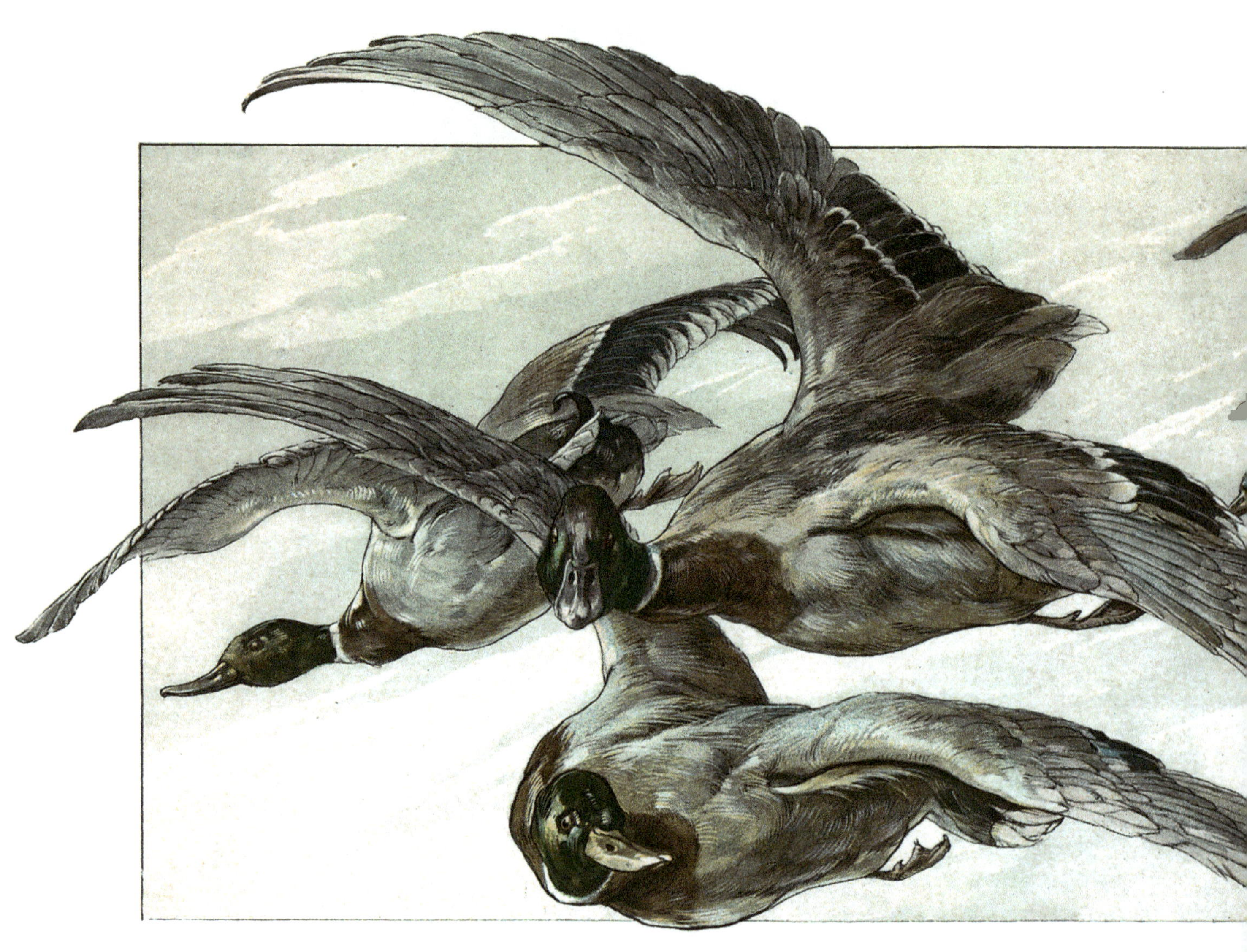

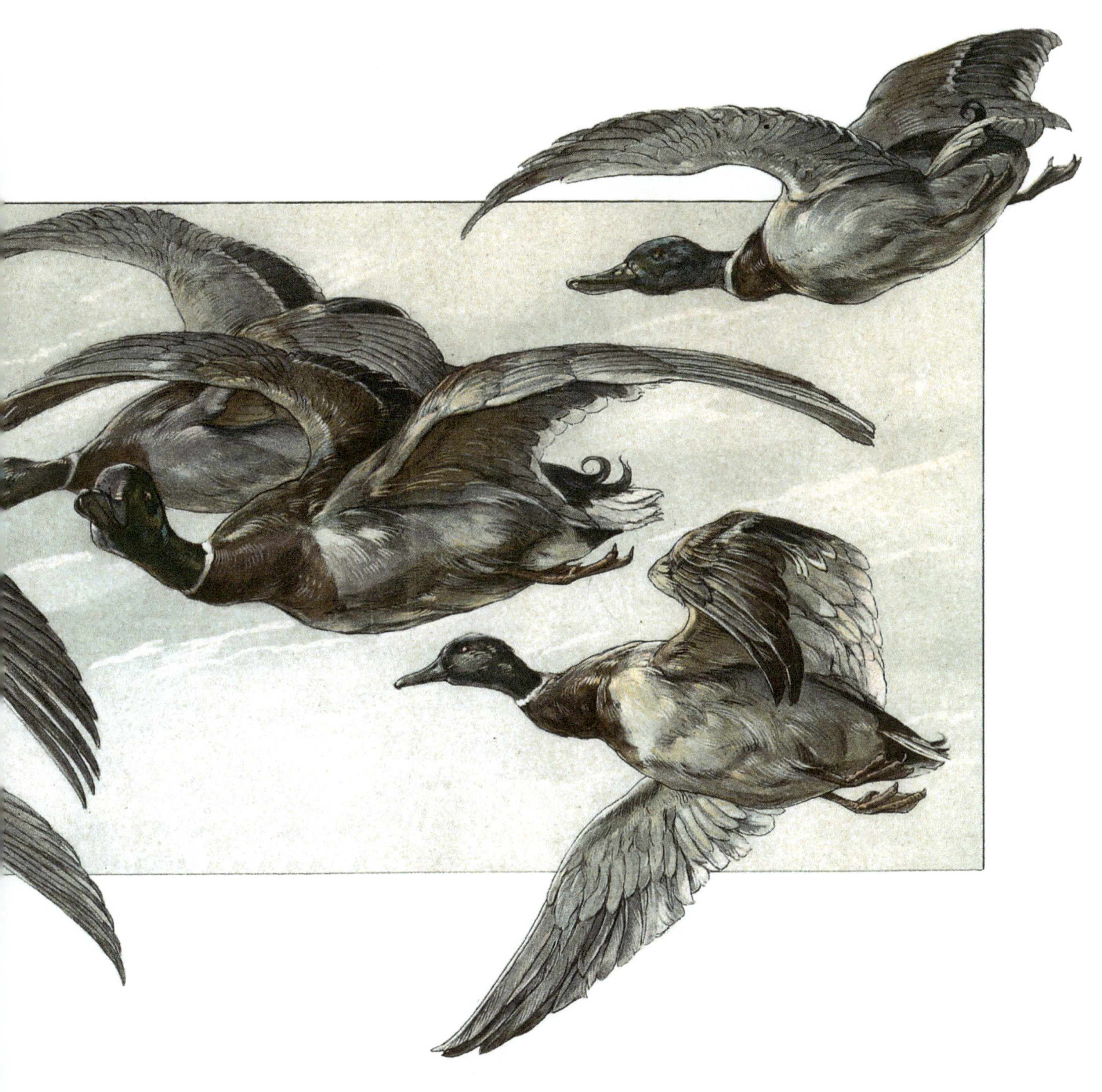

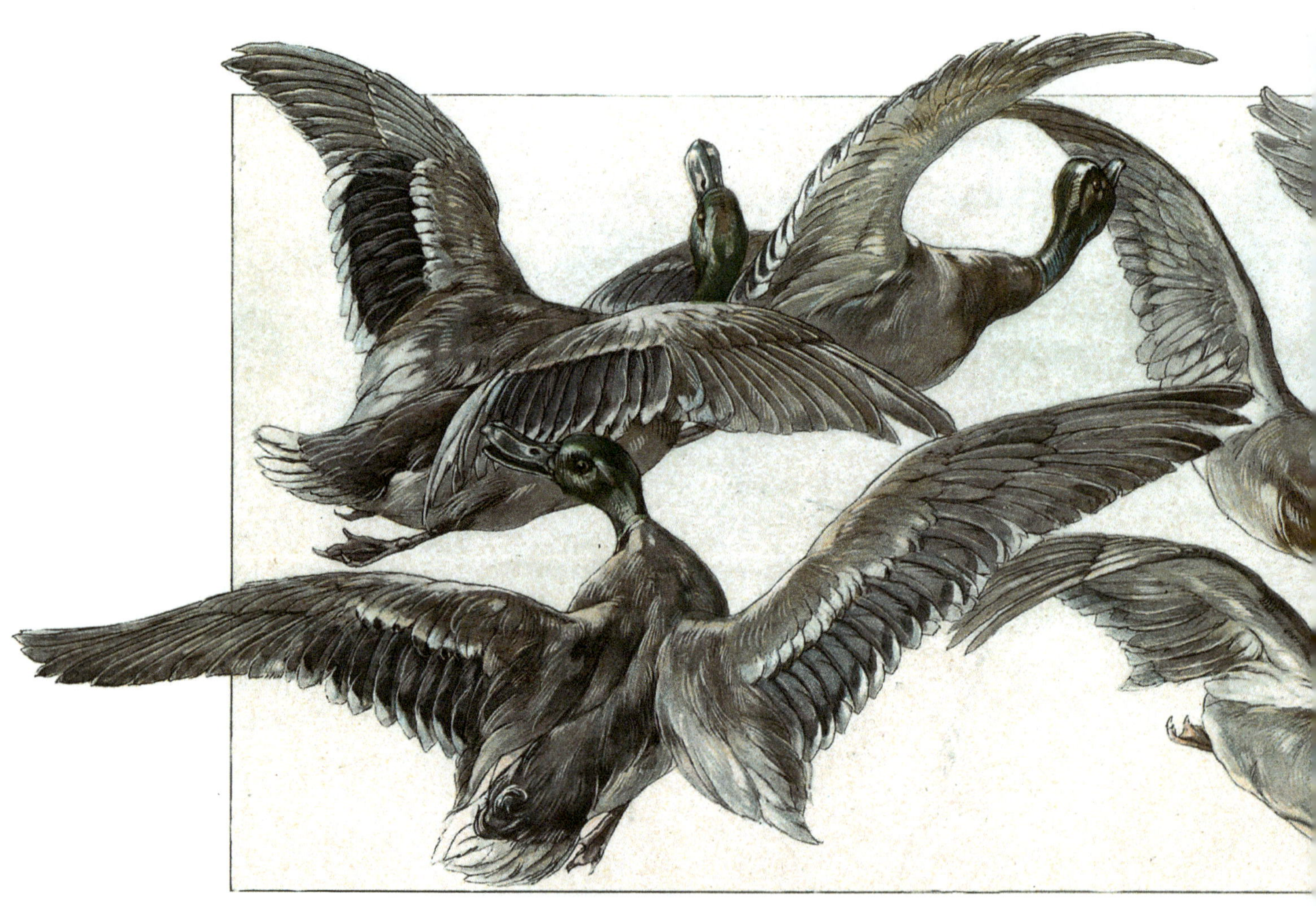

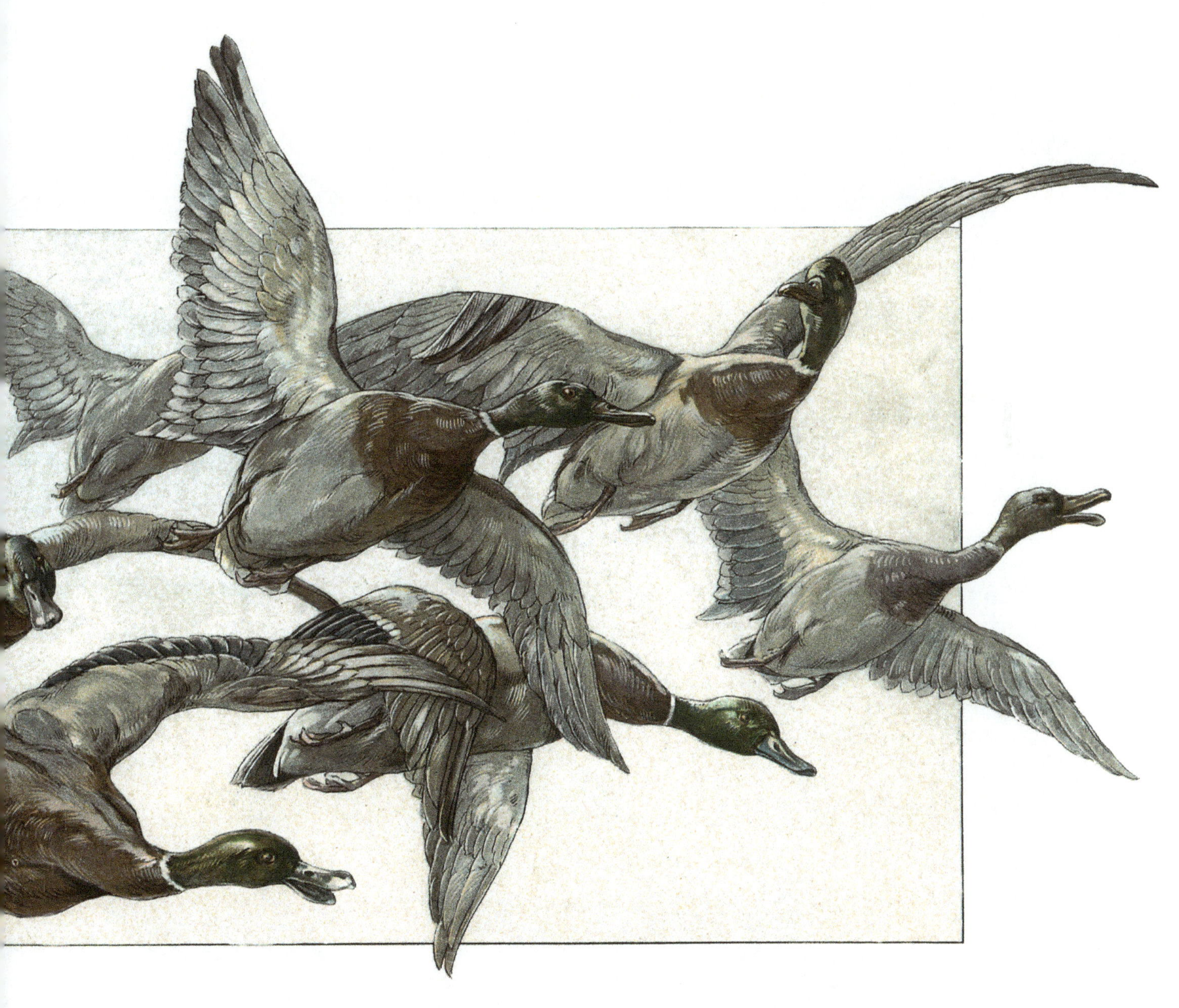

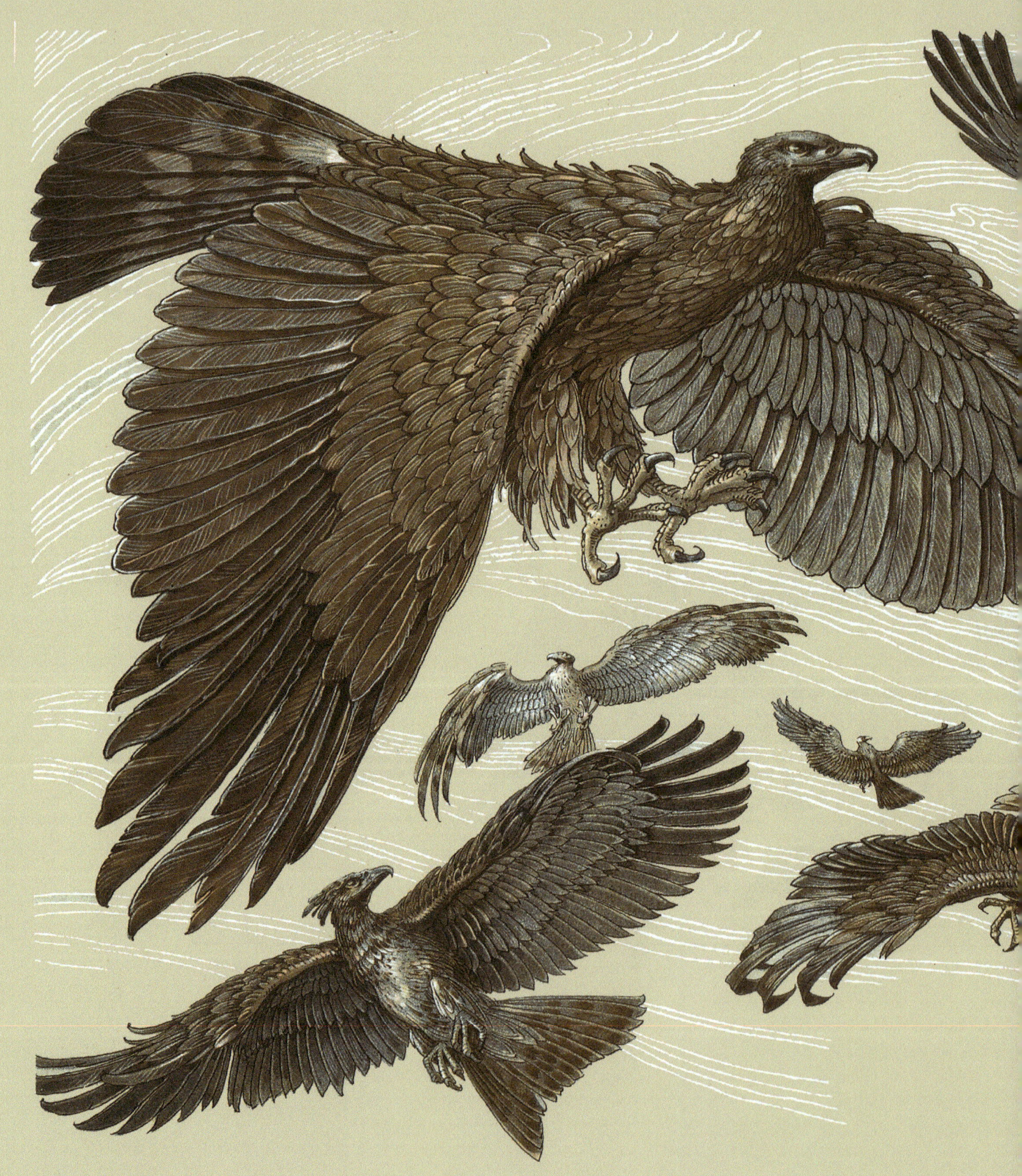

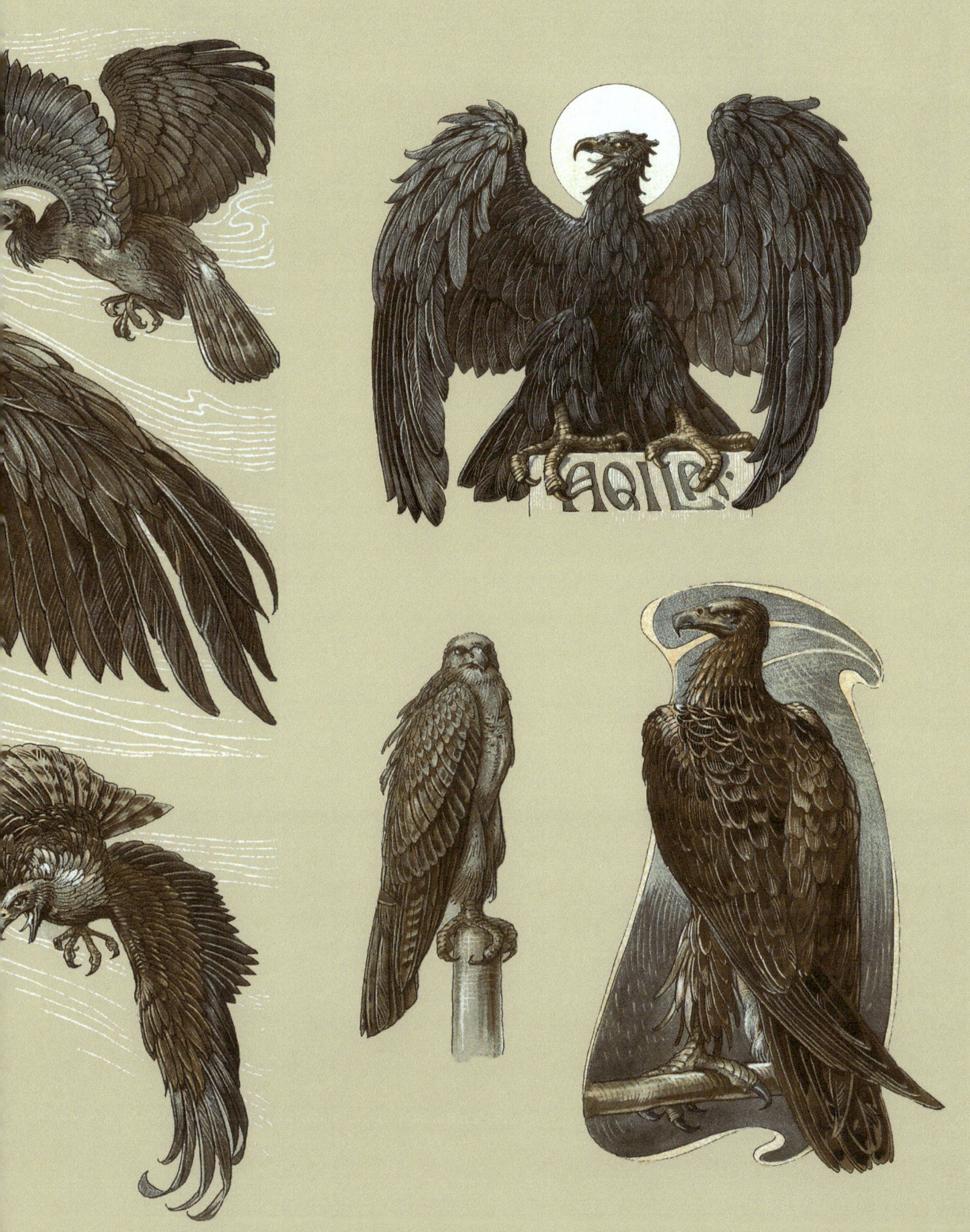

AQVILE

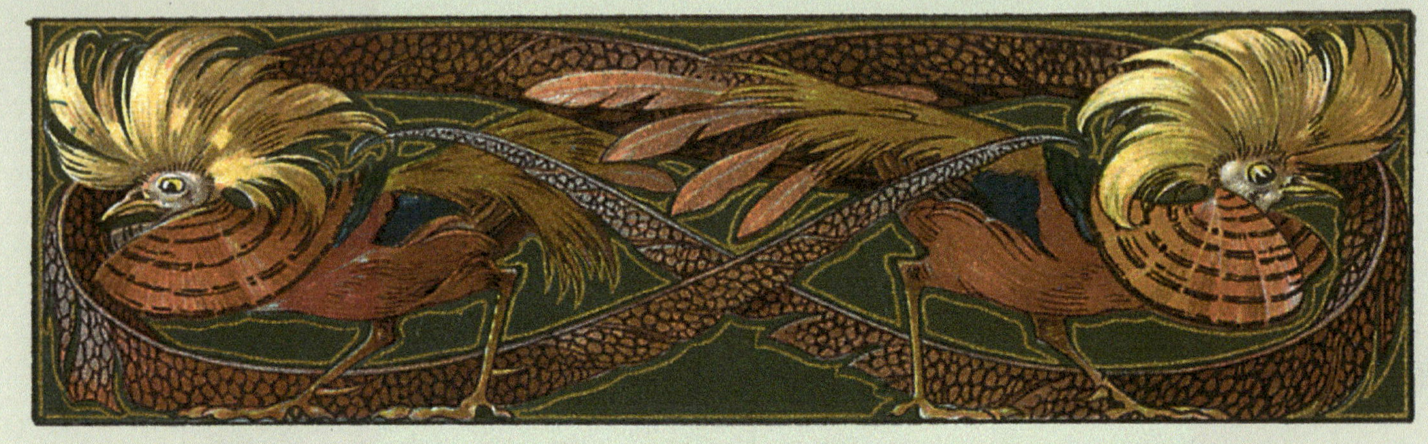

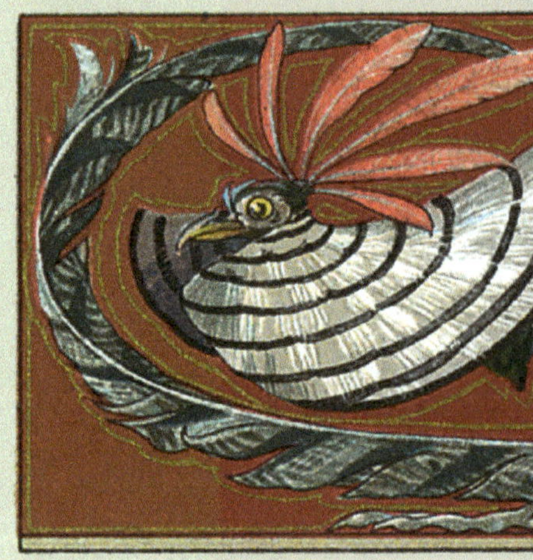

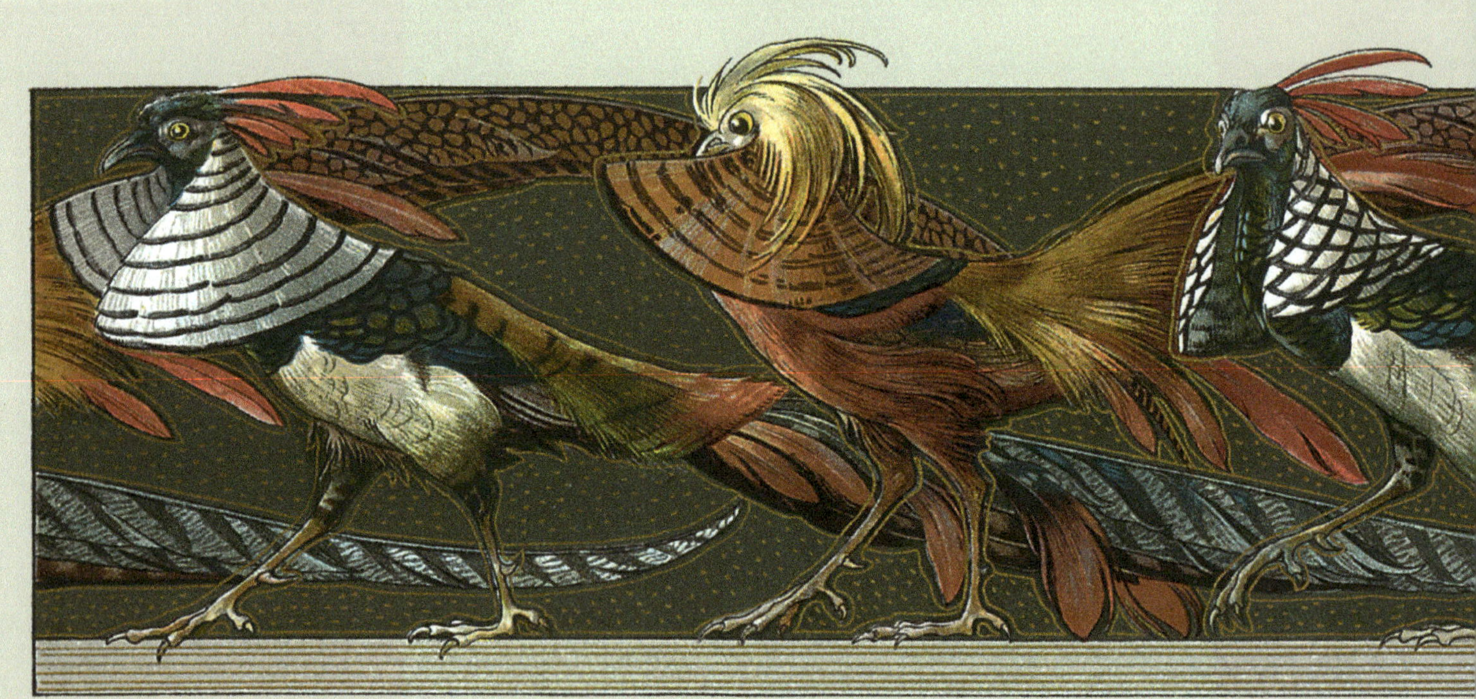

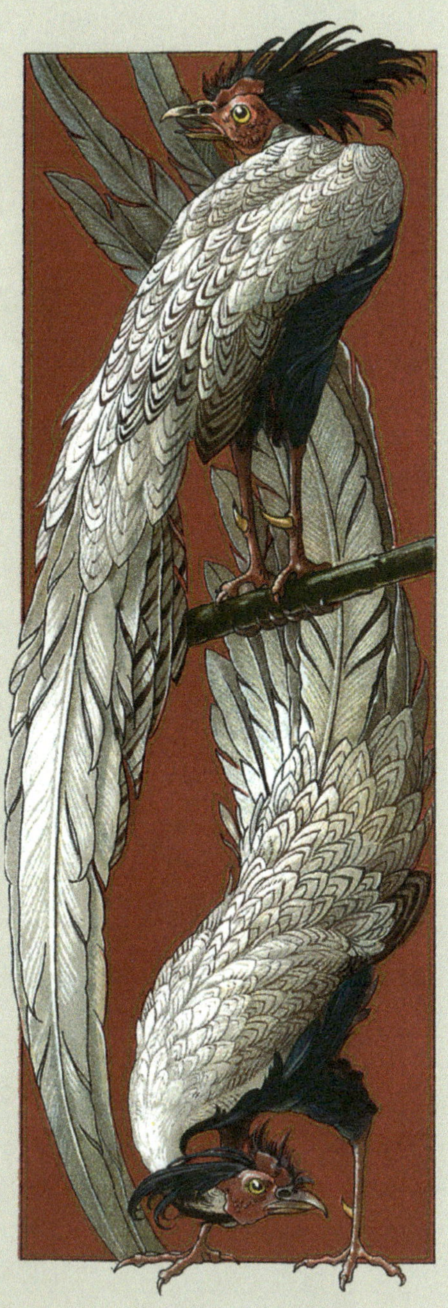

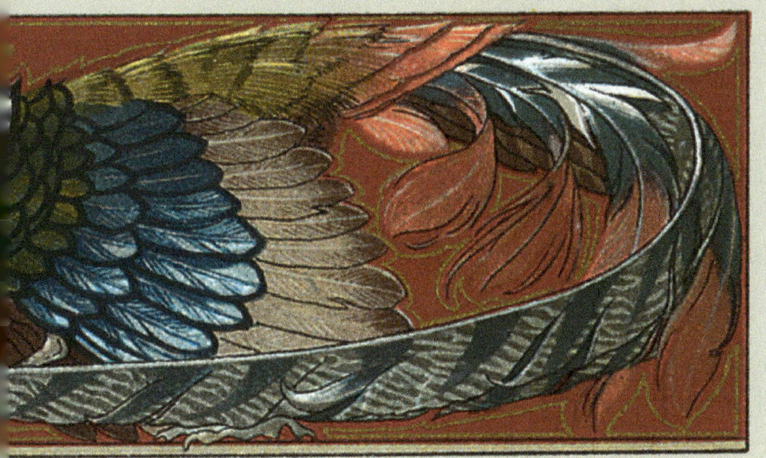

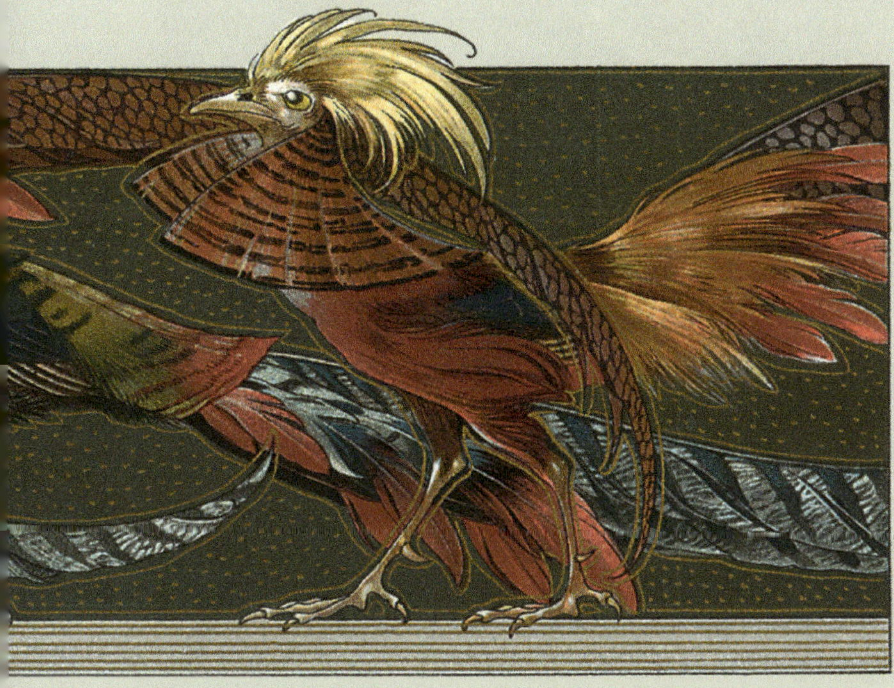

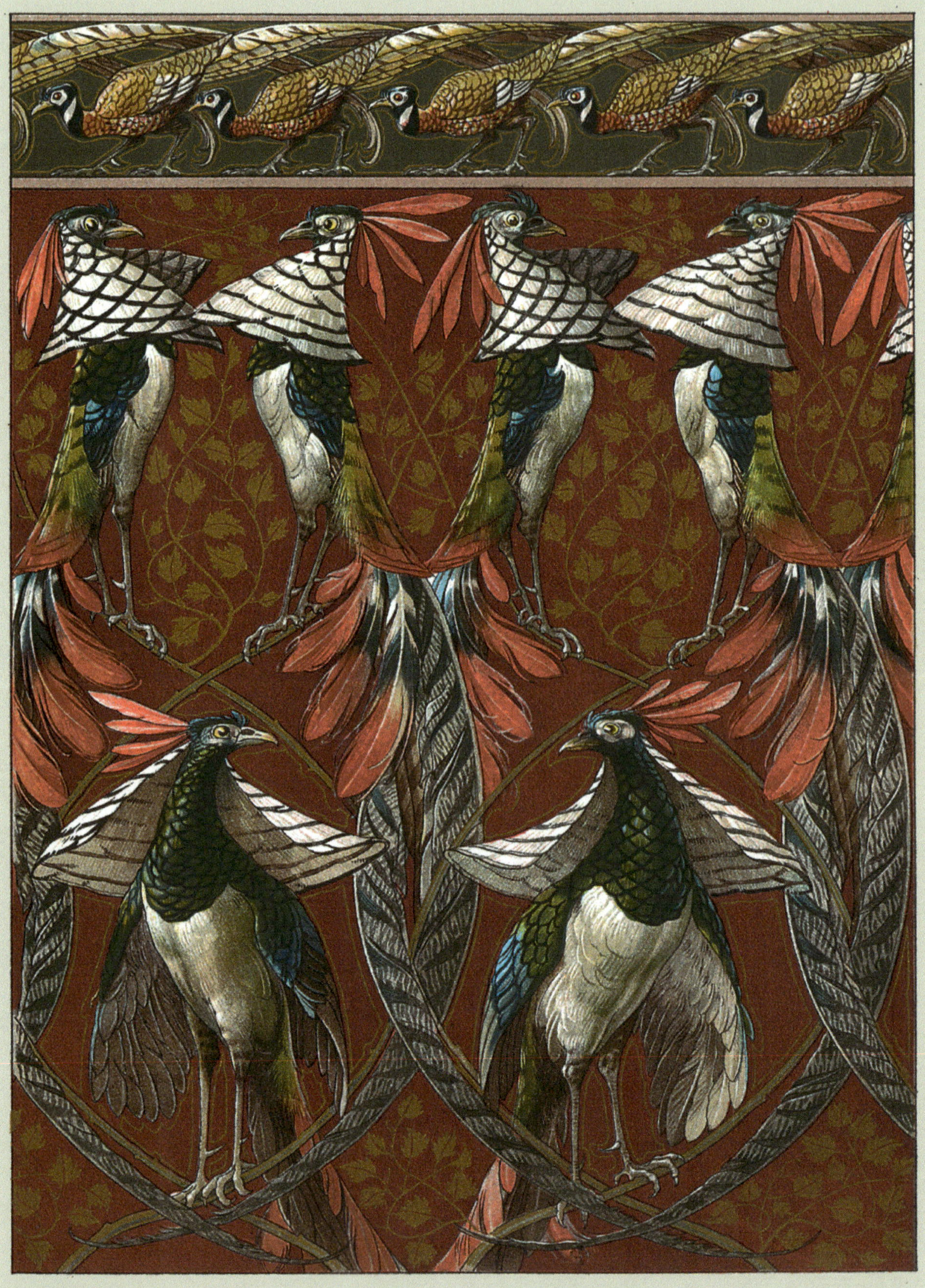

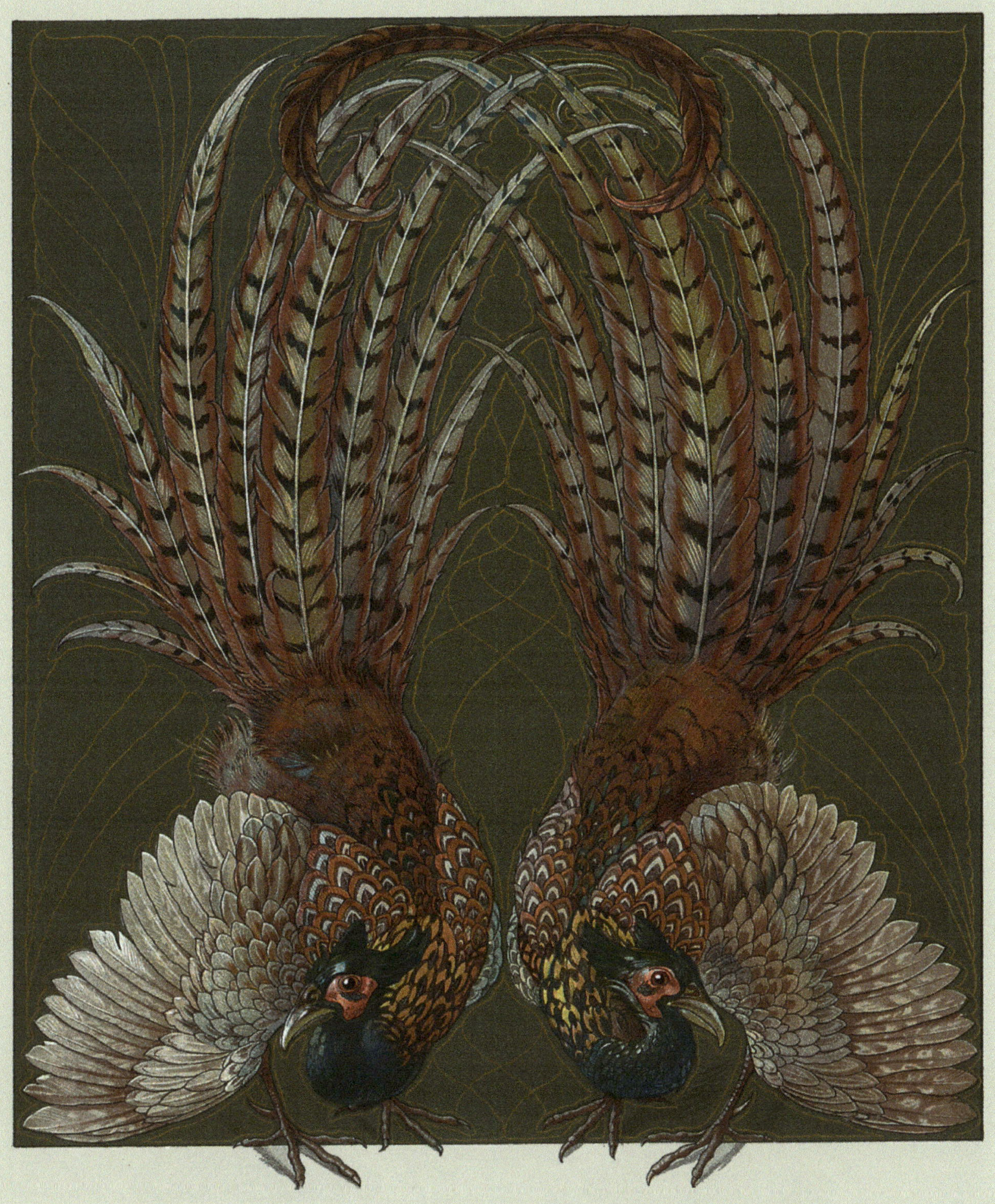

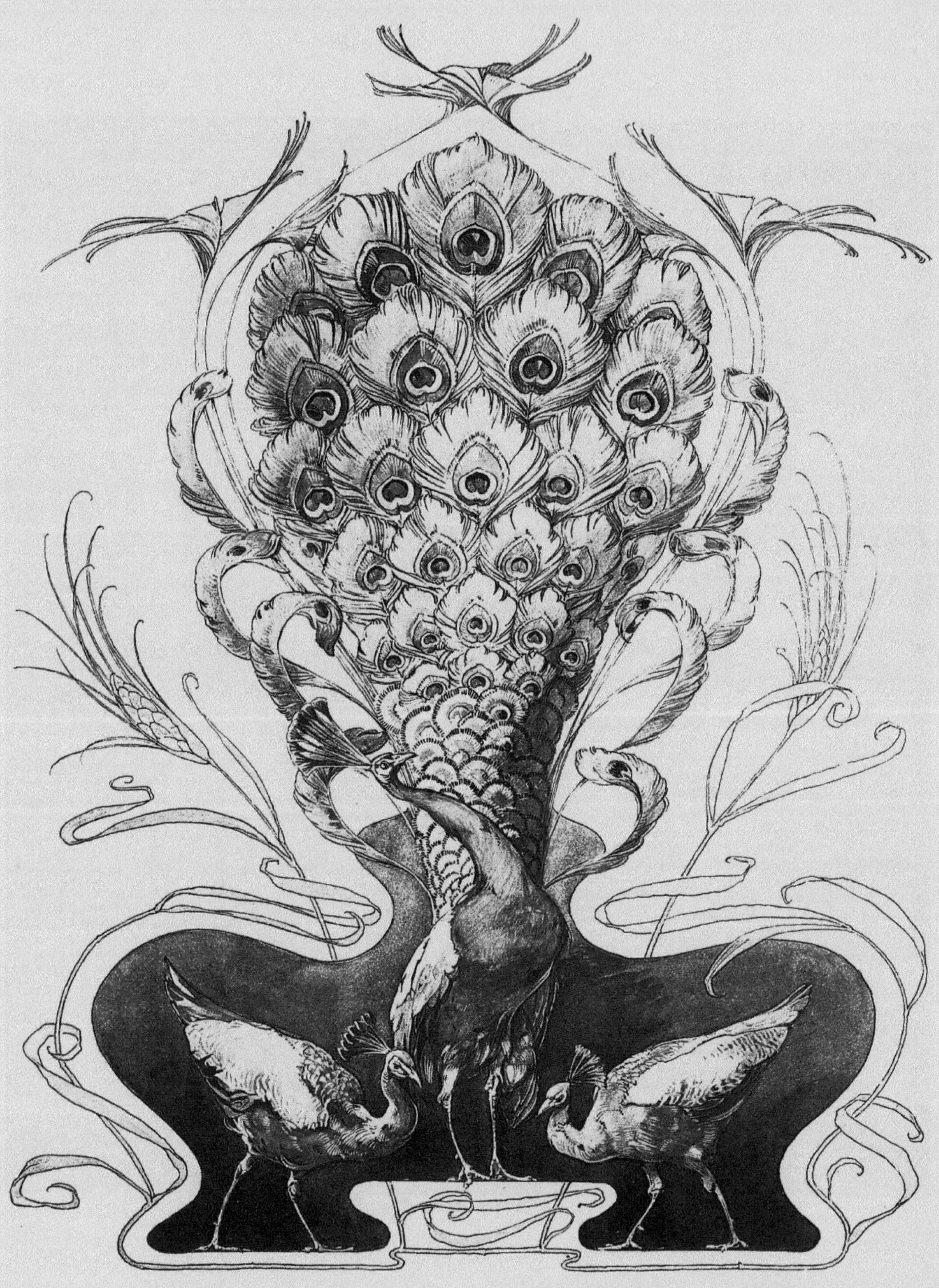

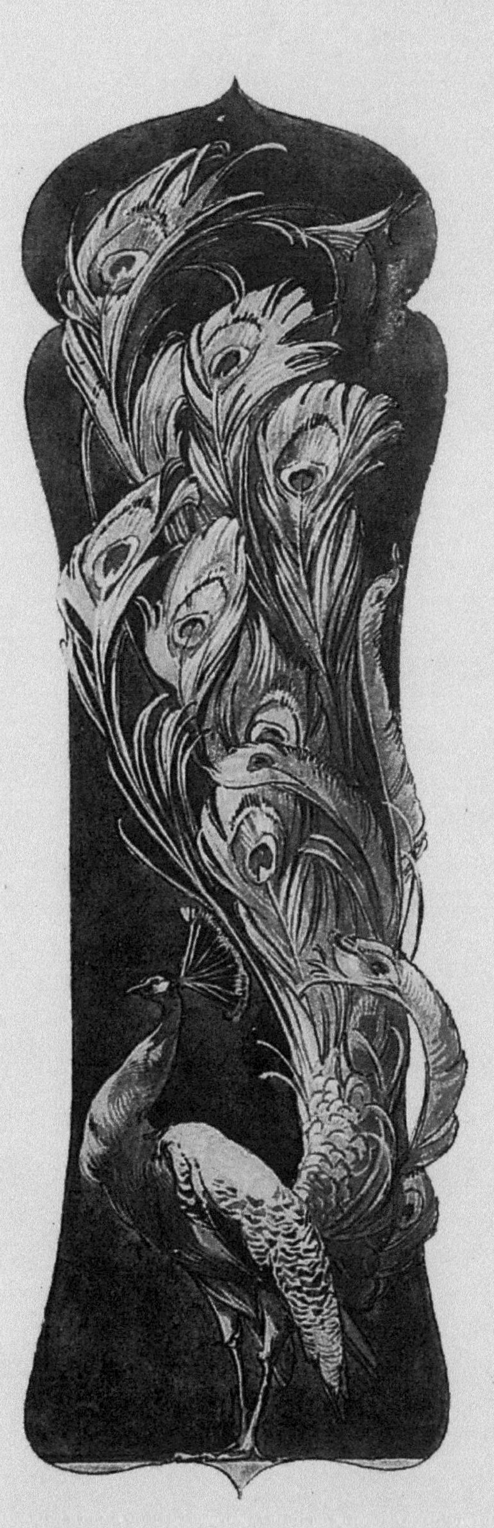

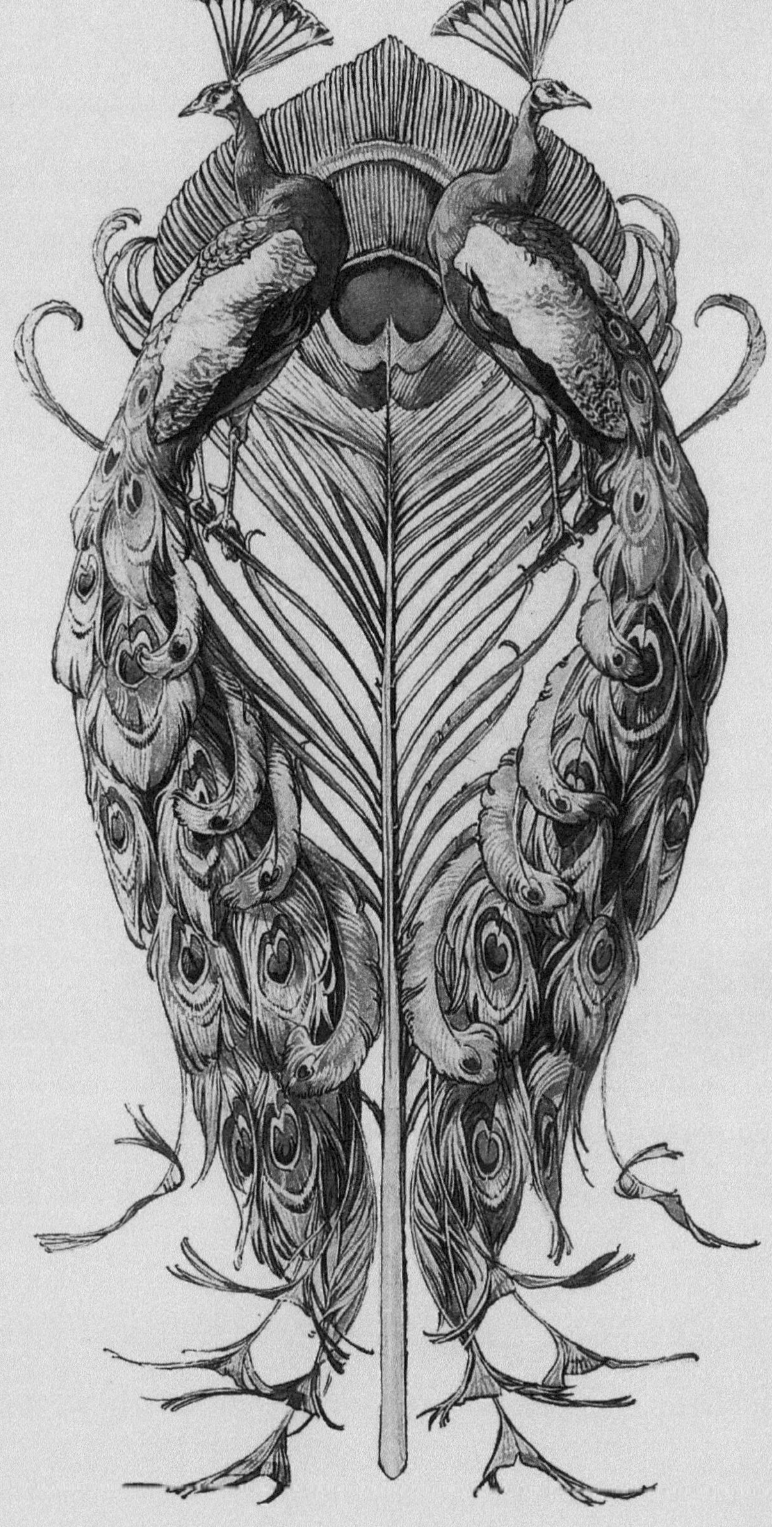

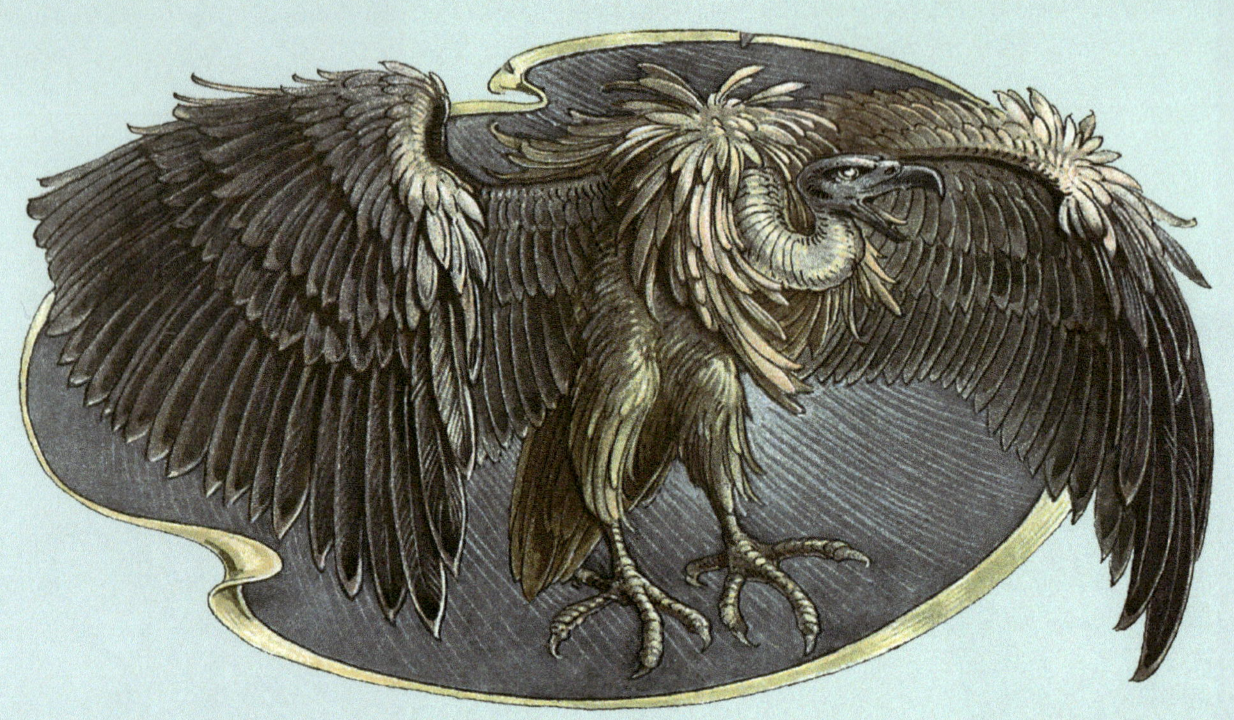

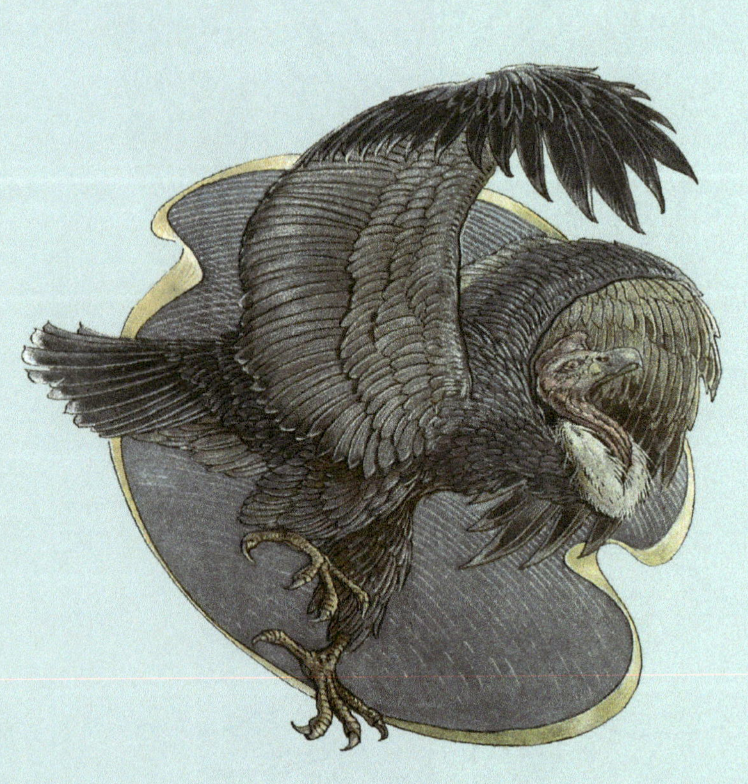

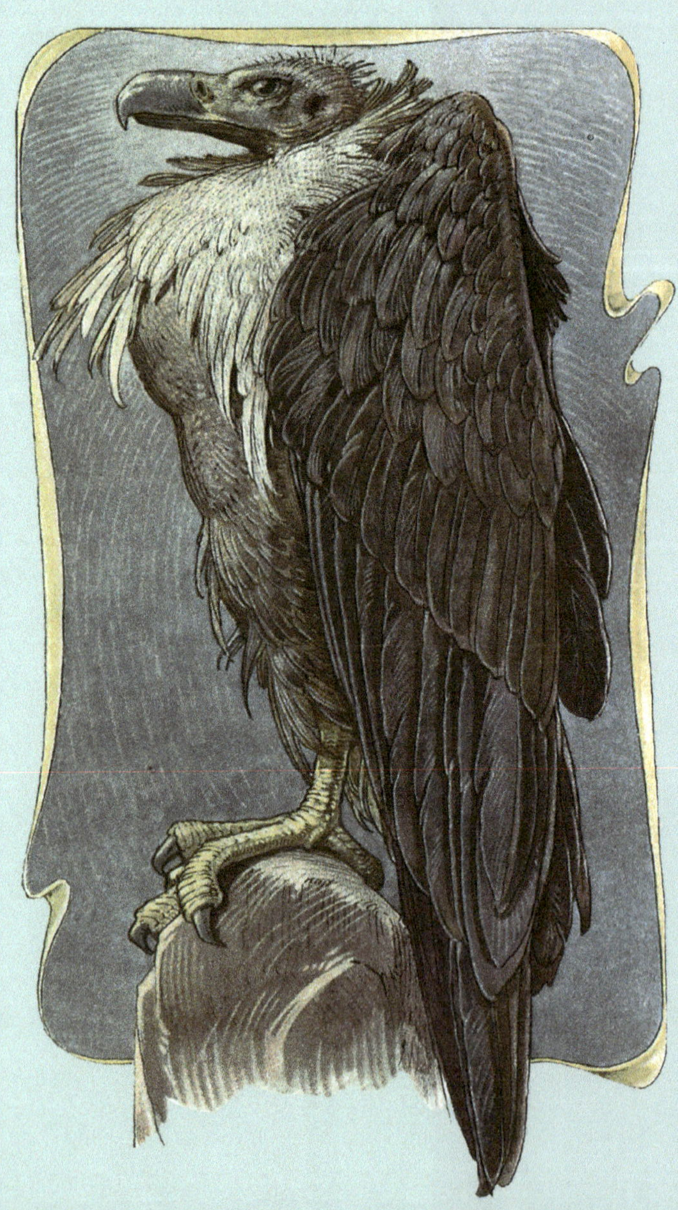

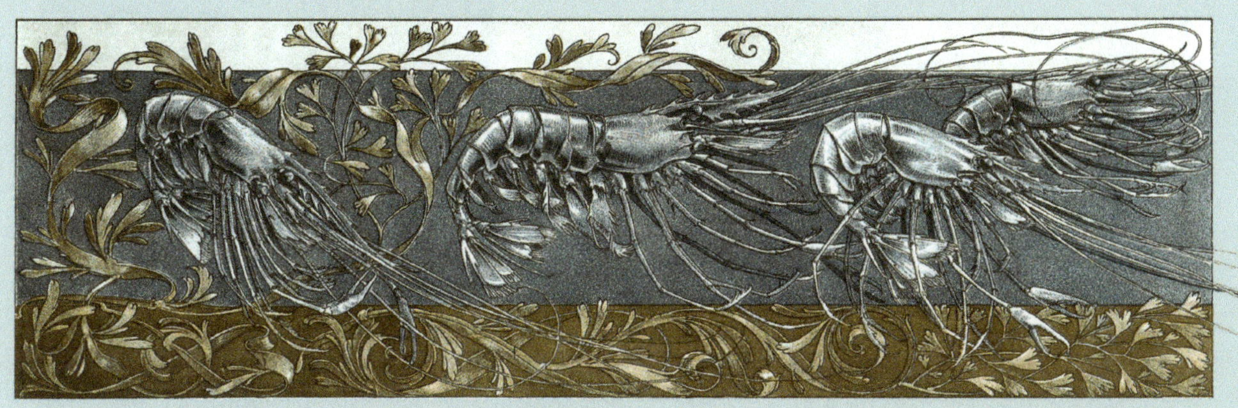

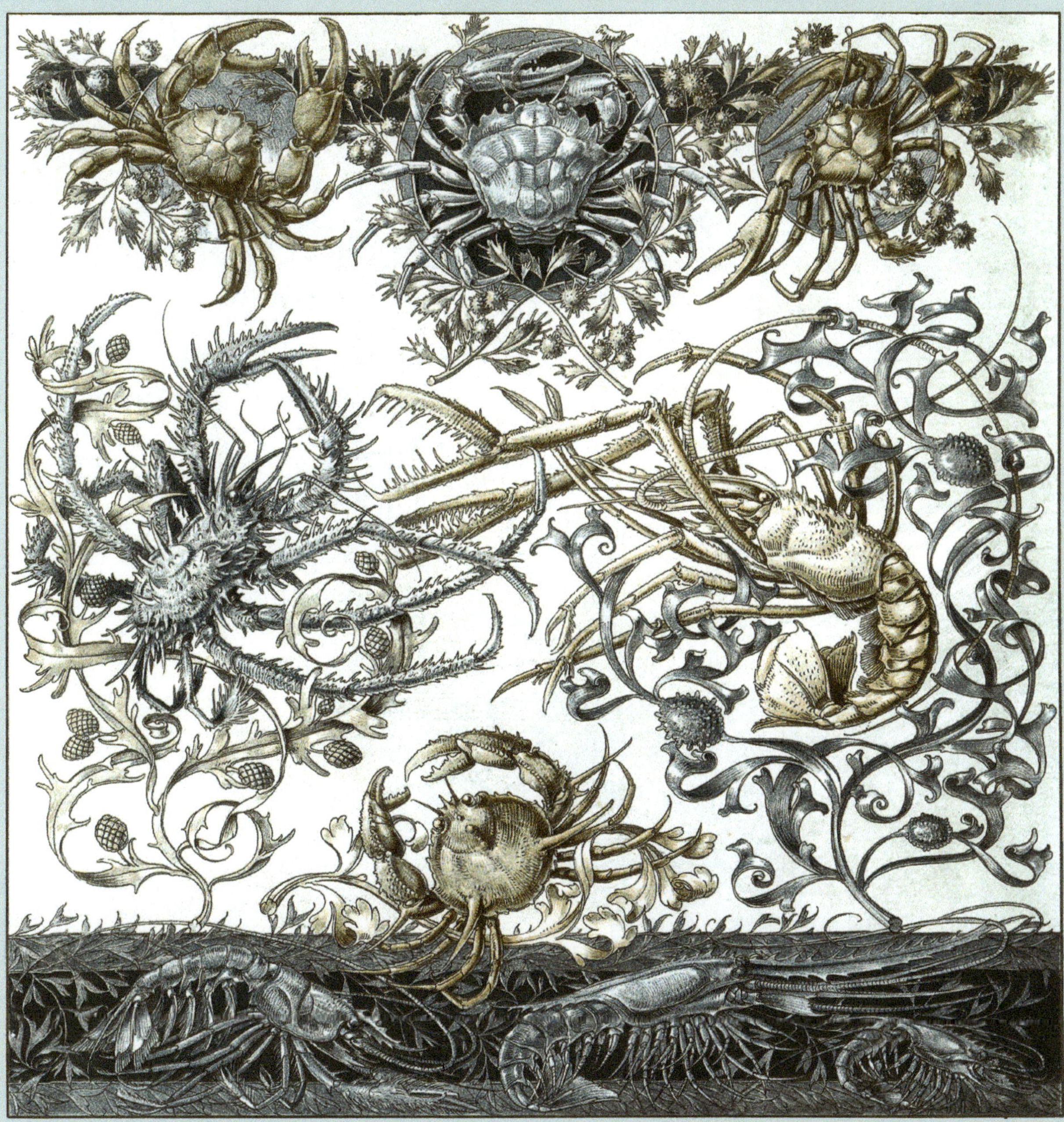

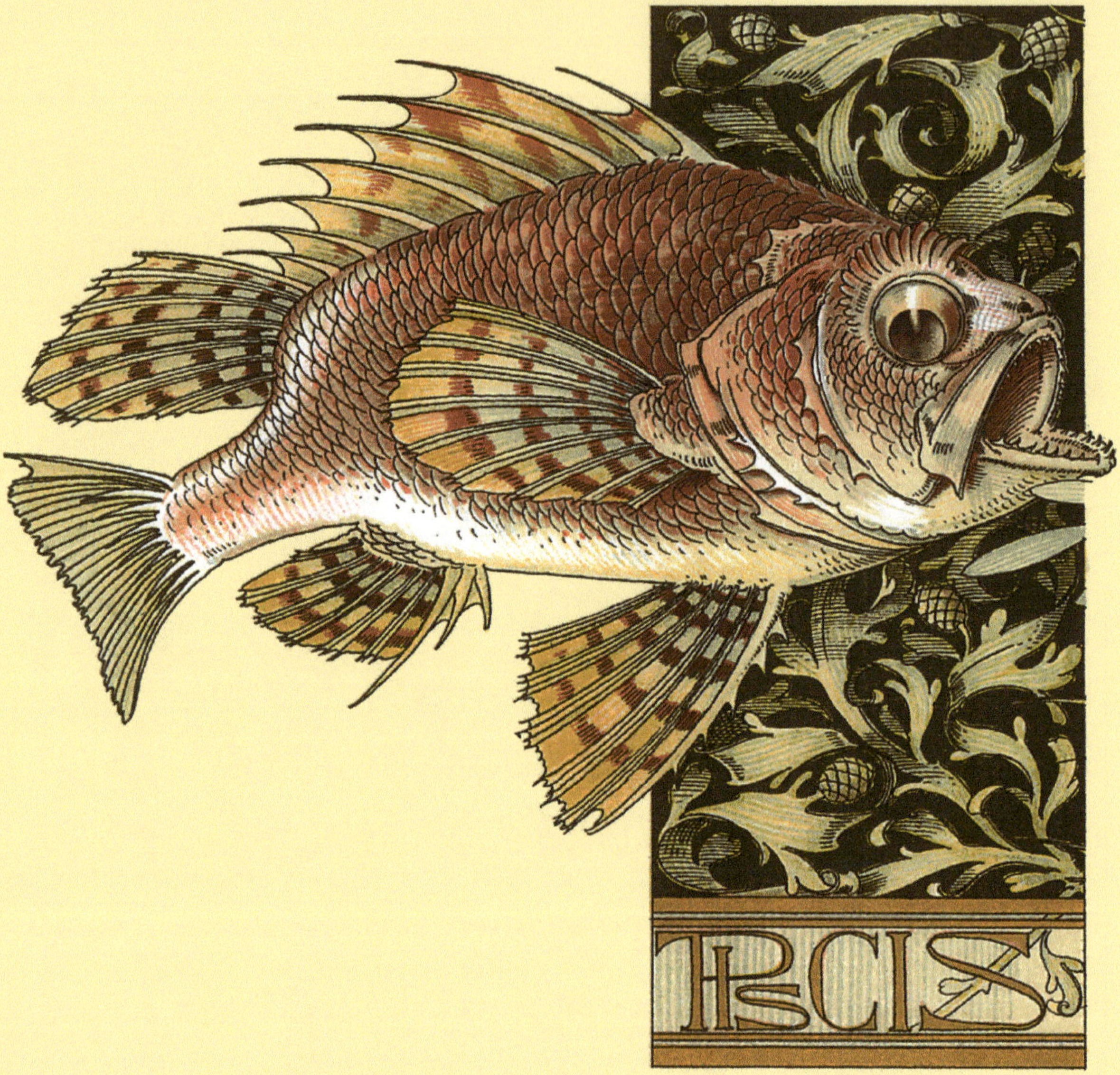

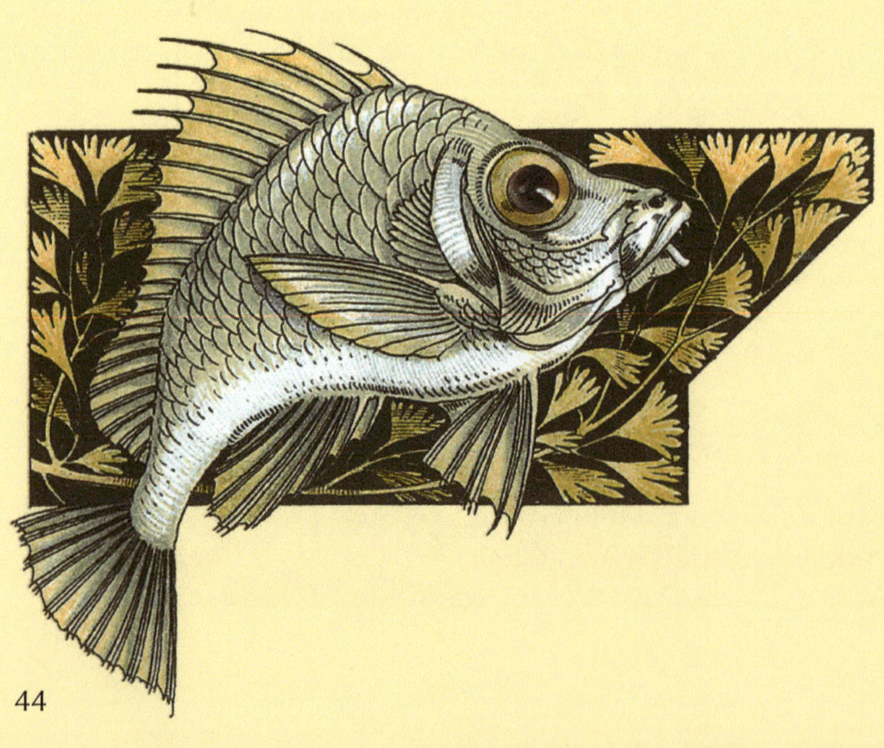

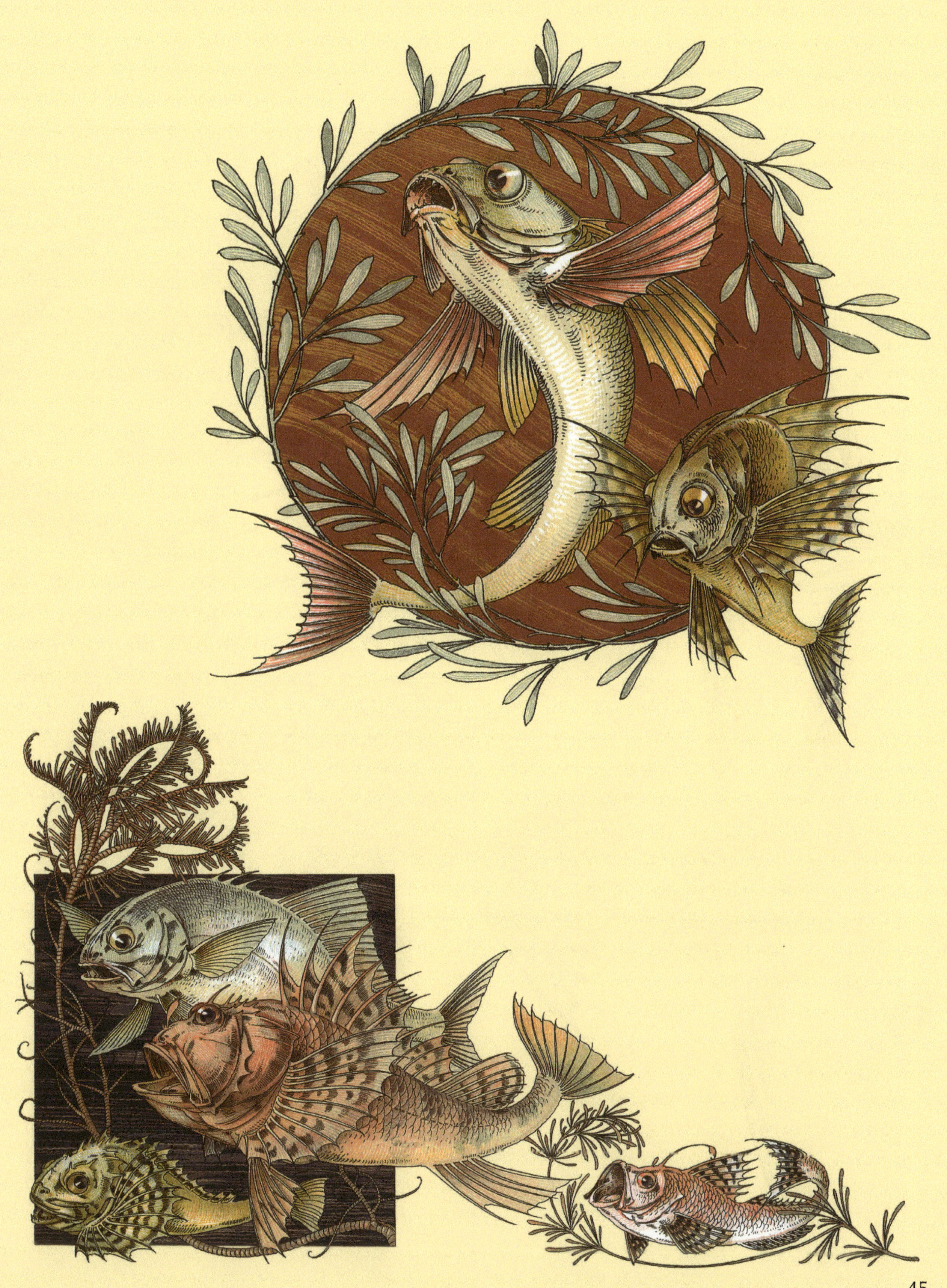

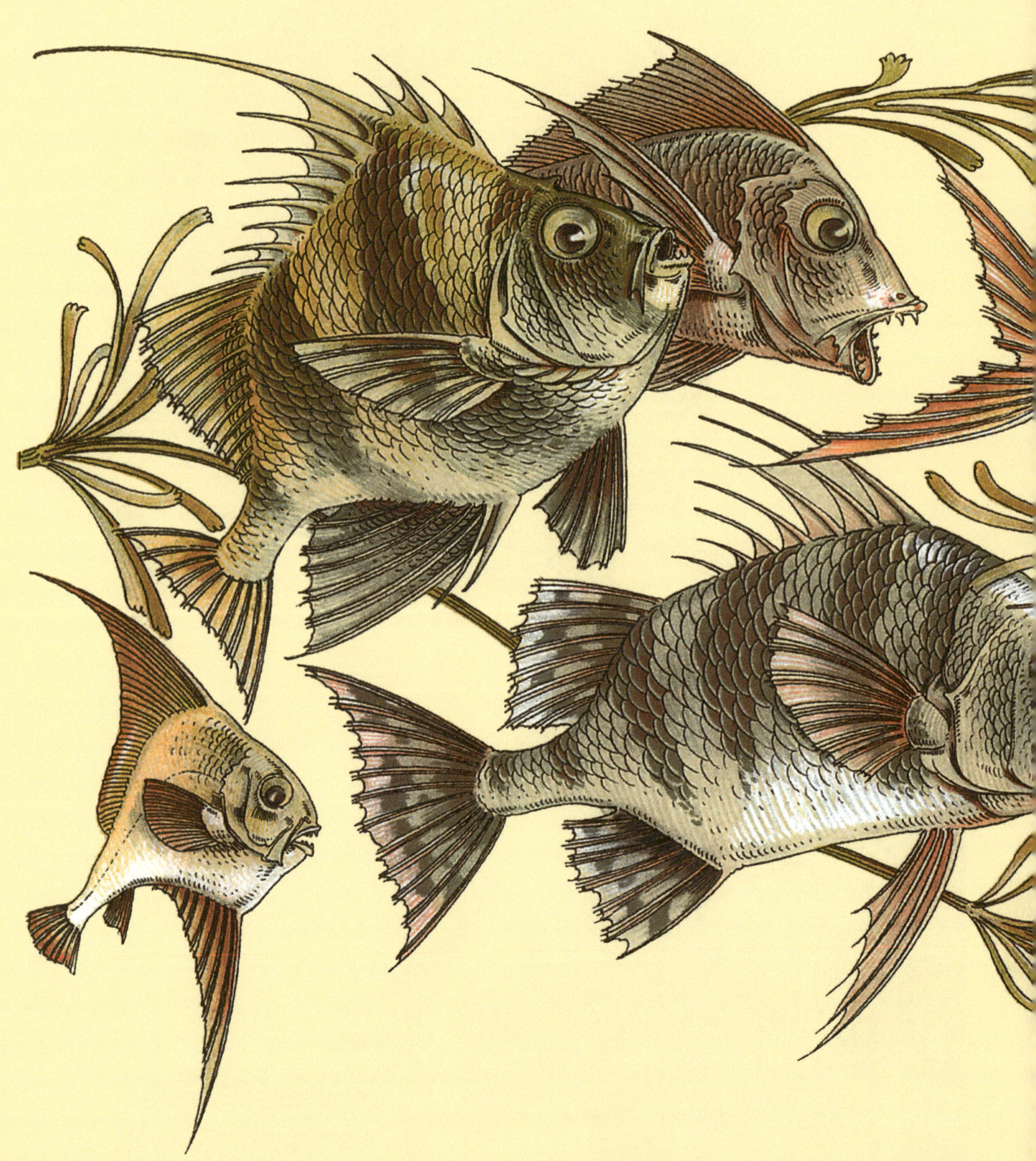

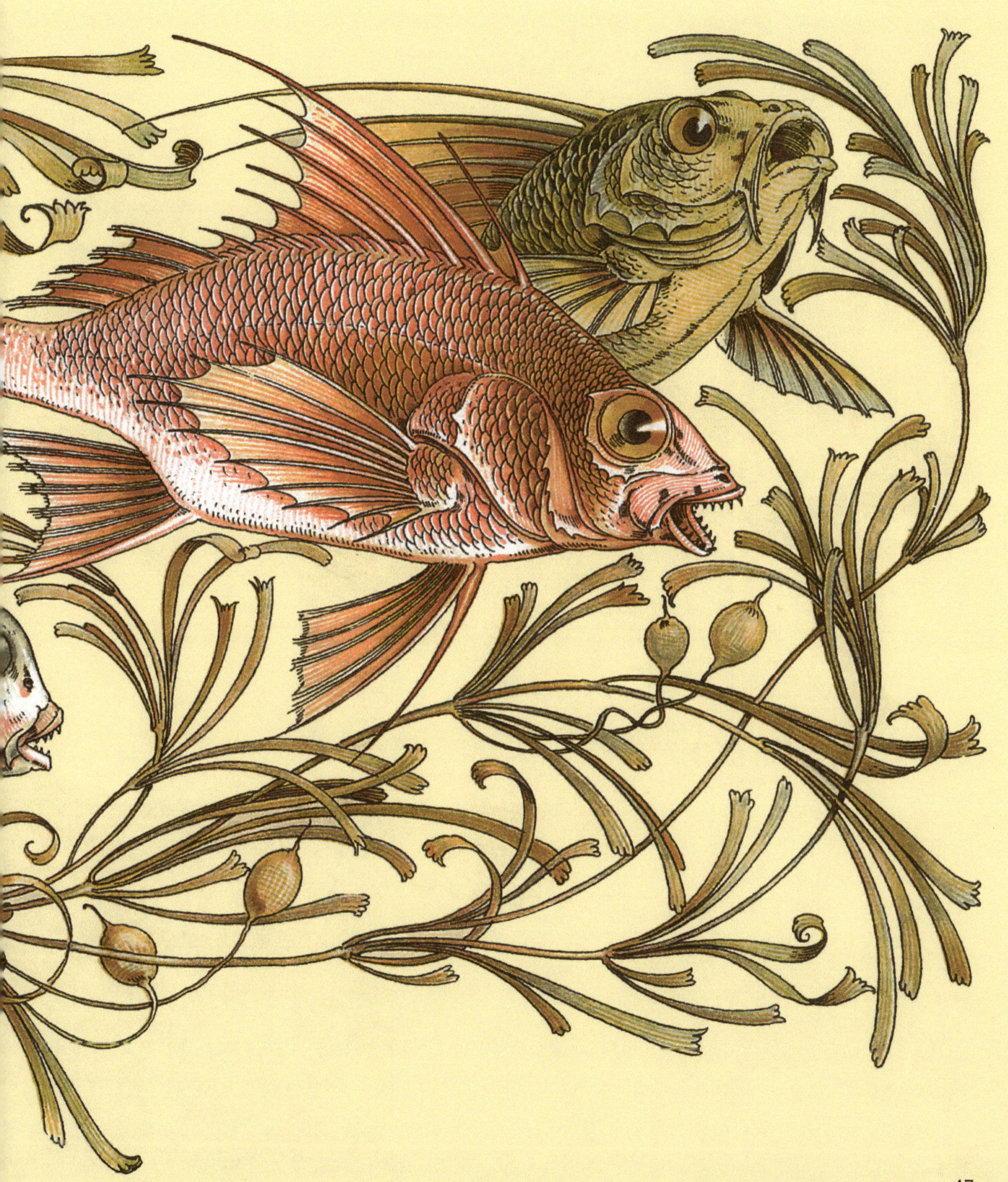

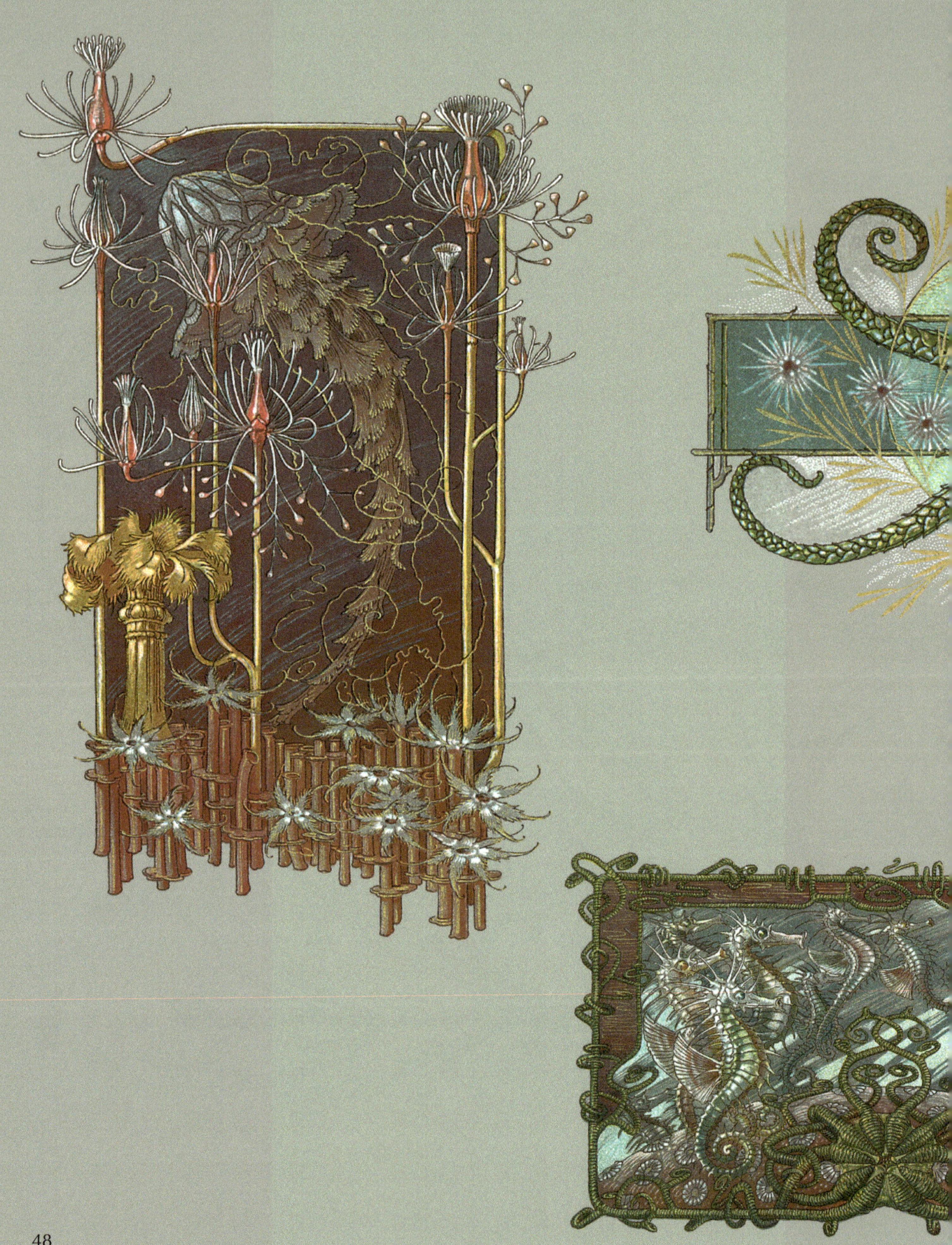

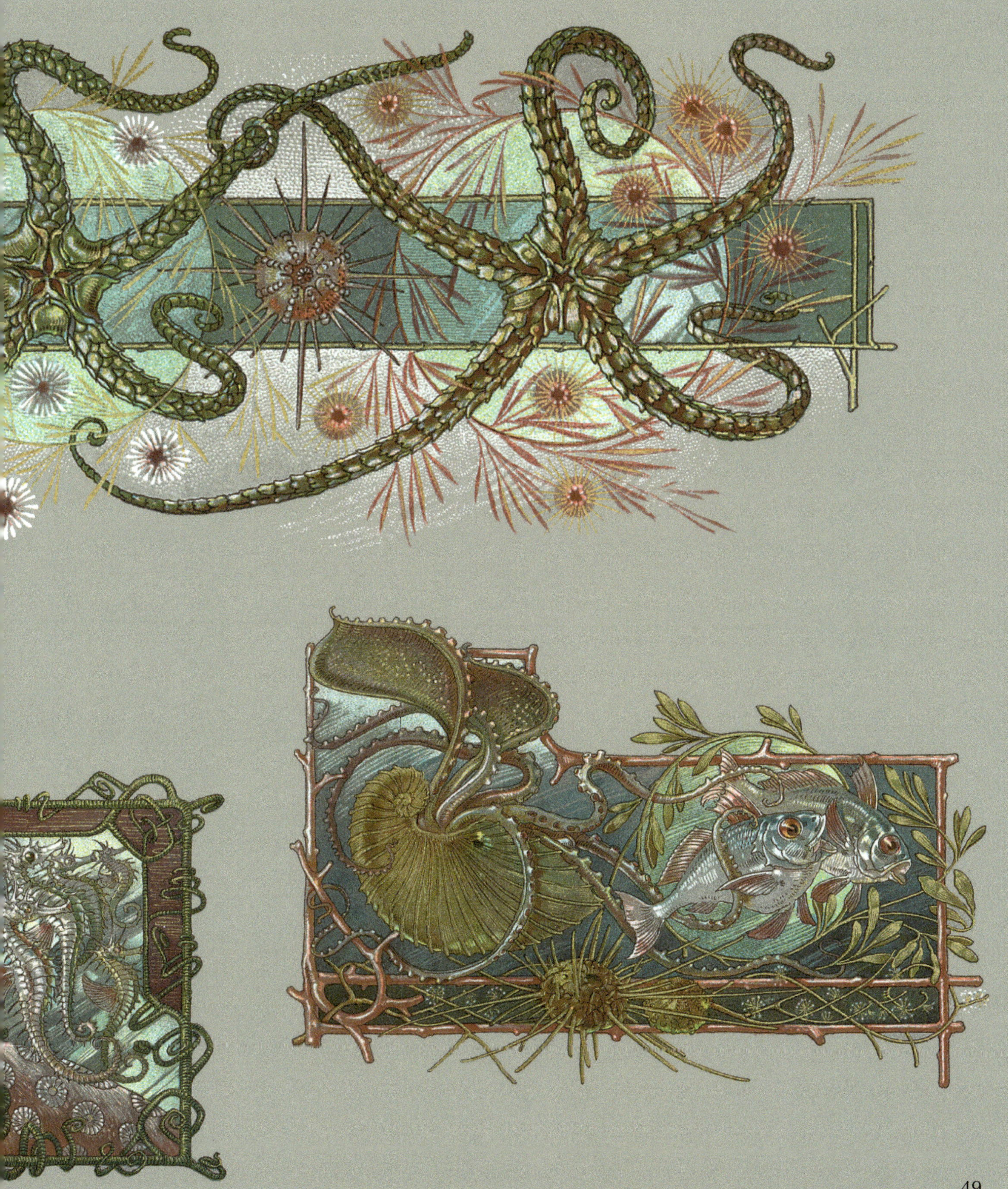

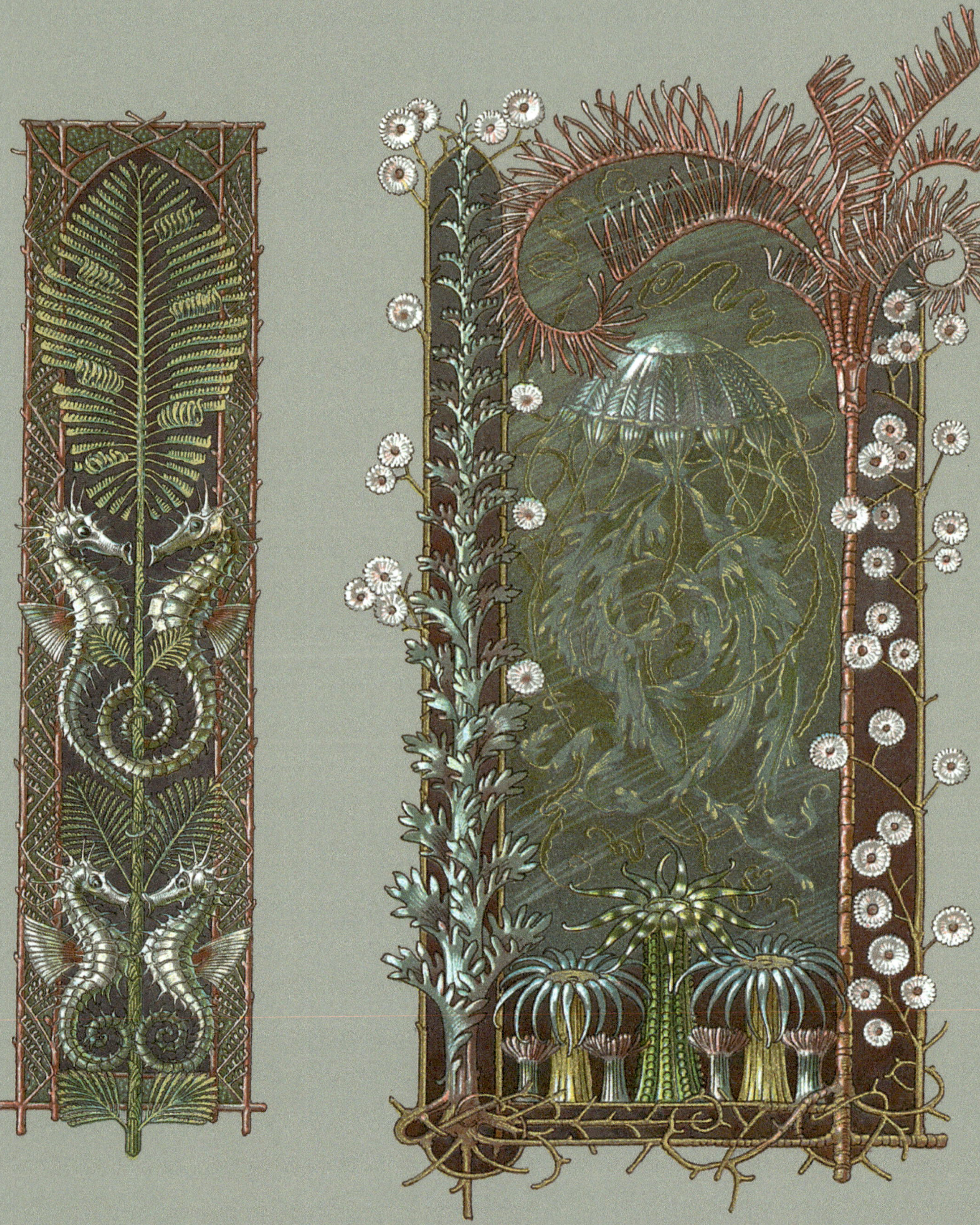

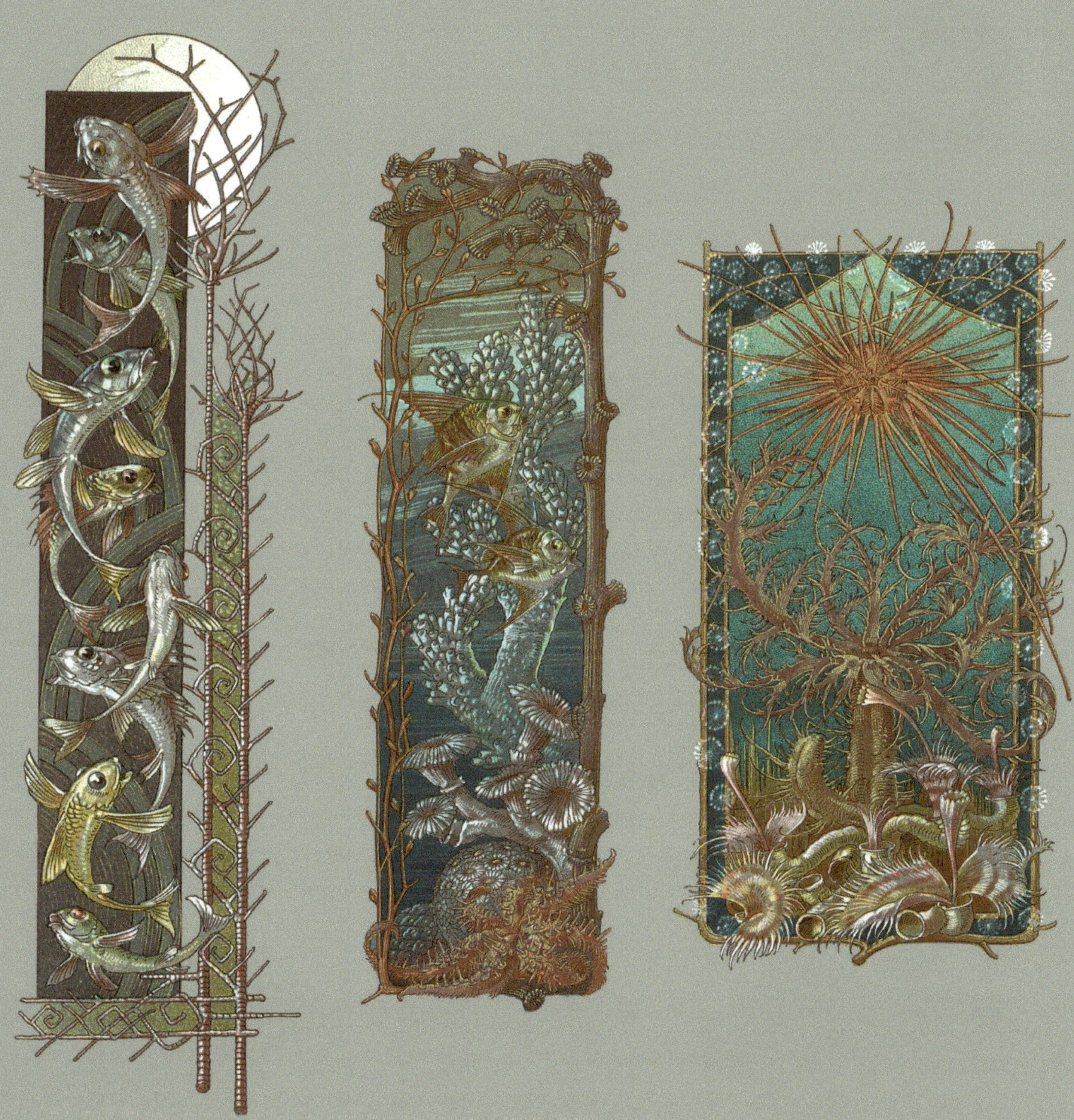

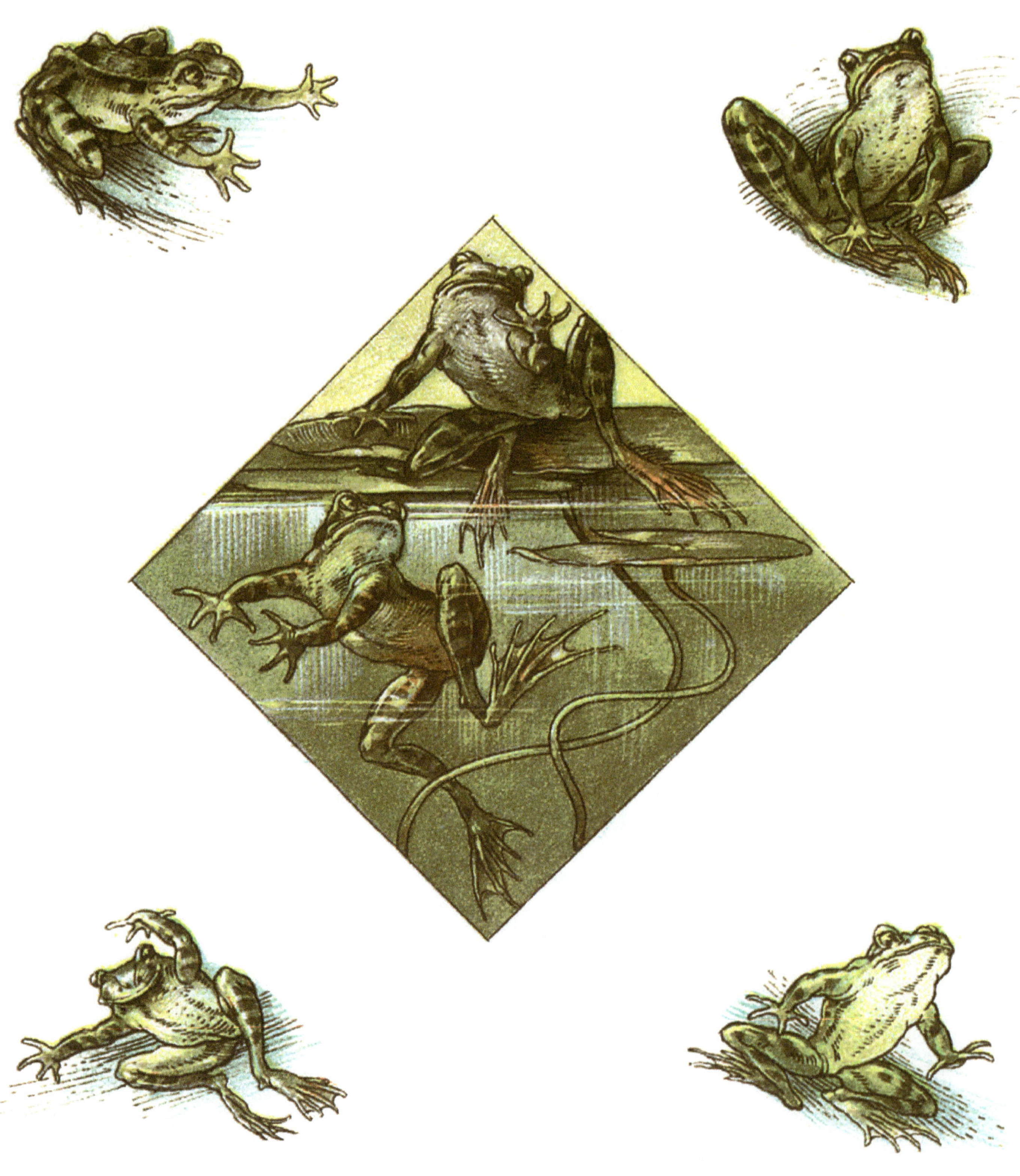

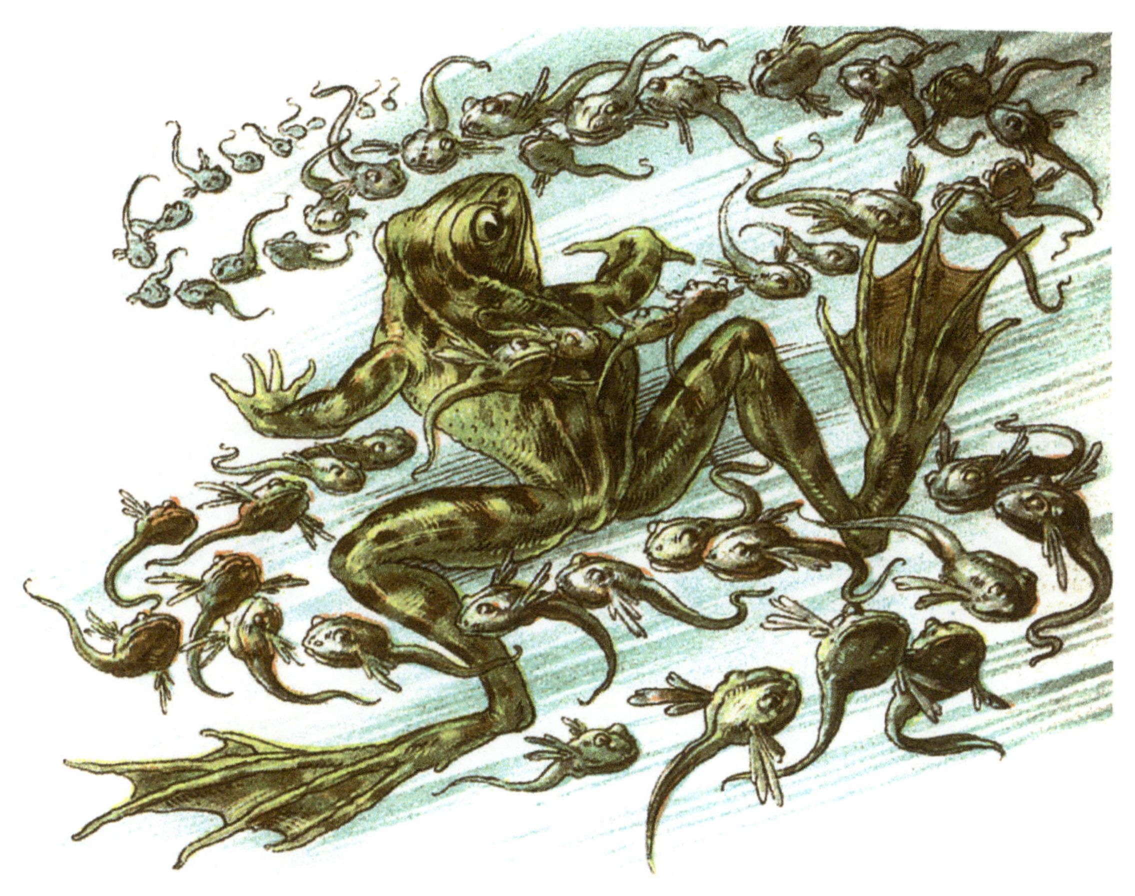

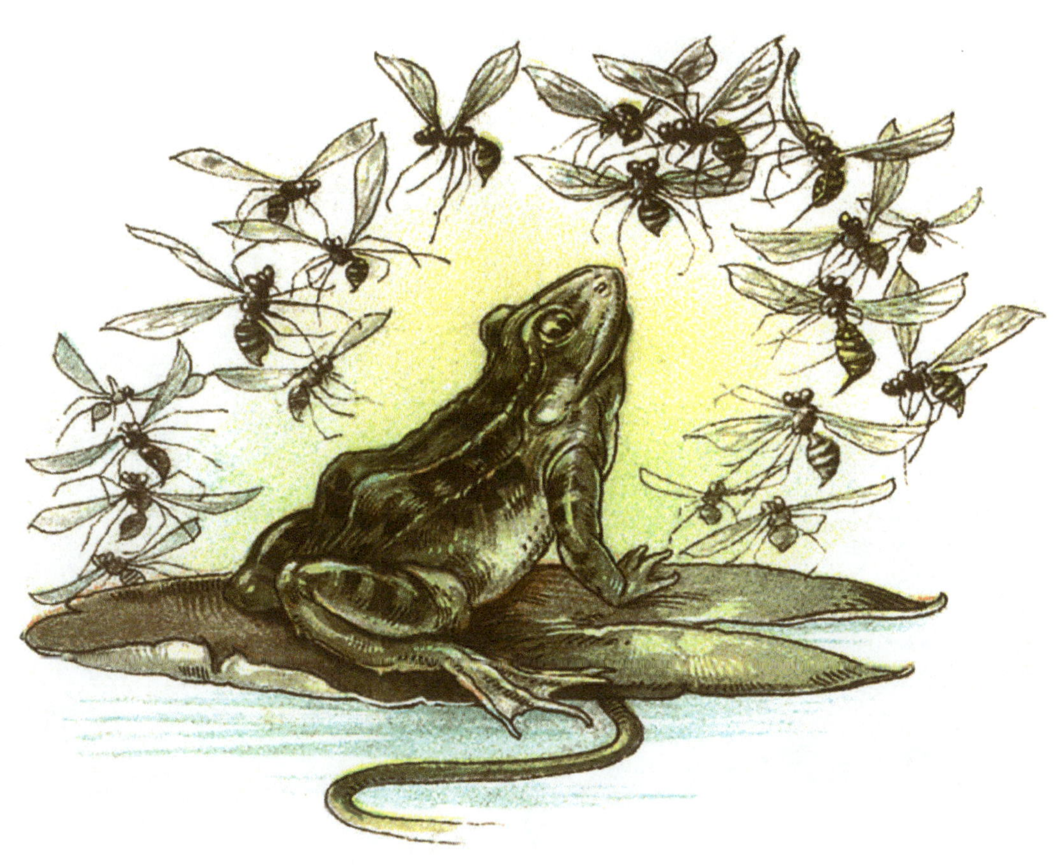

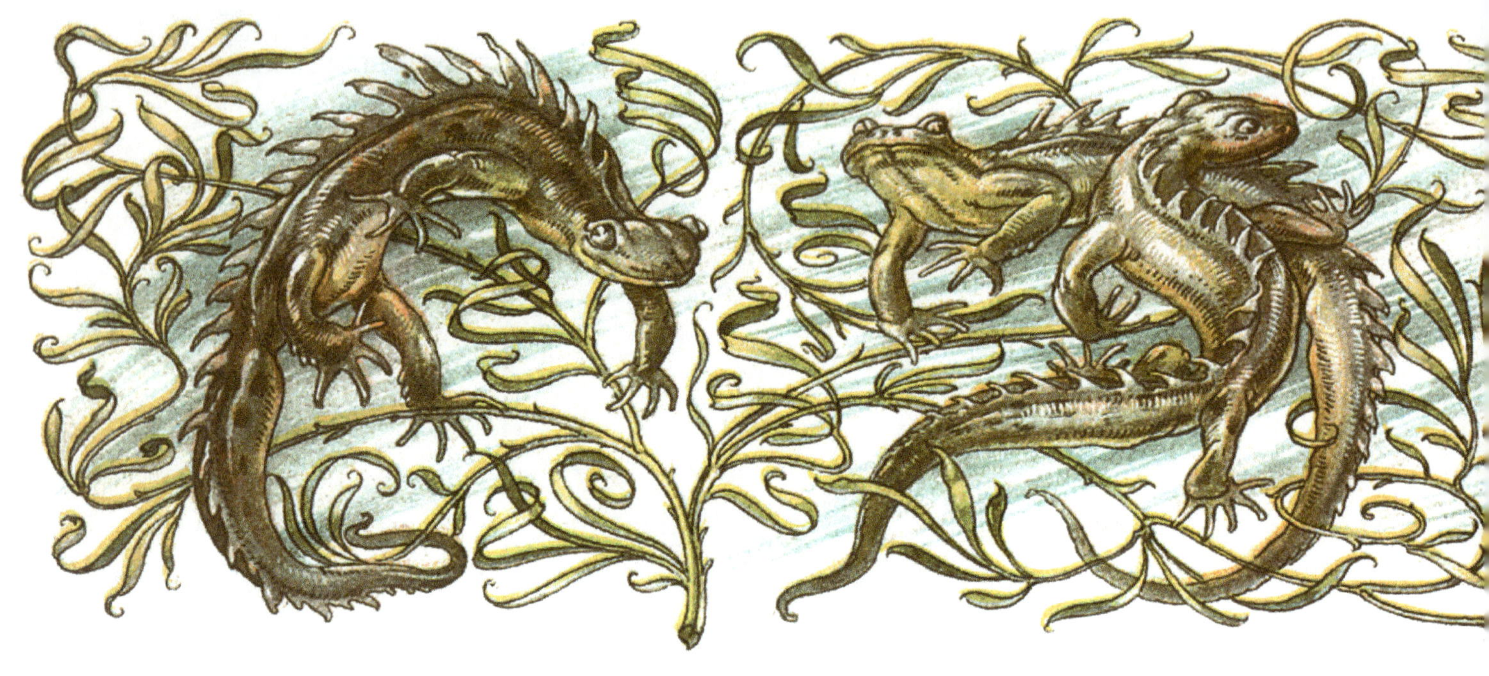

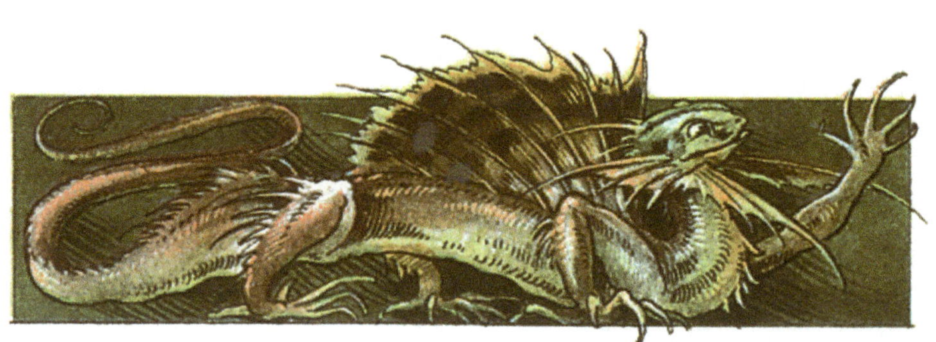

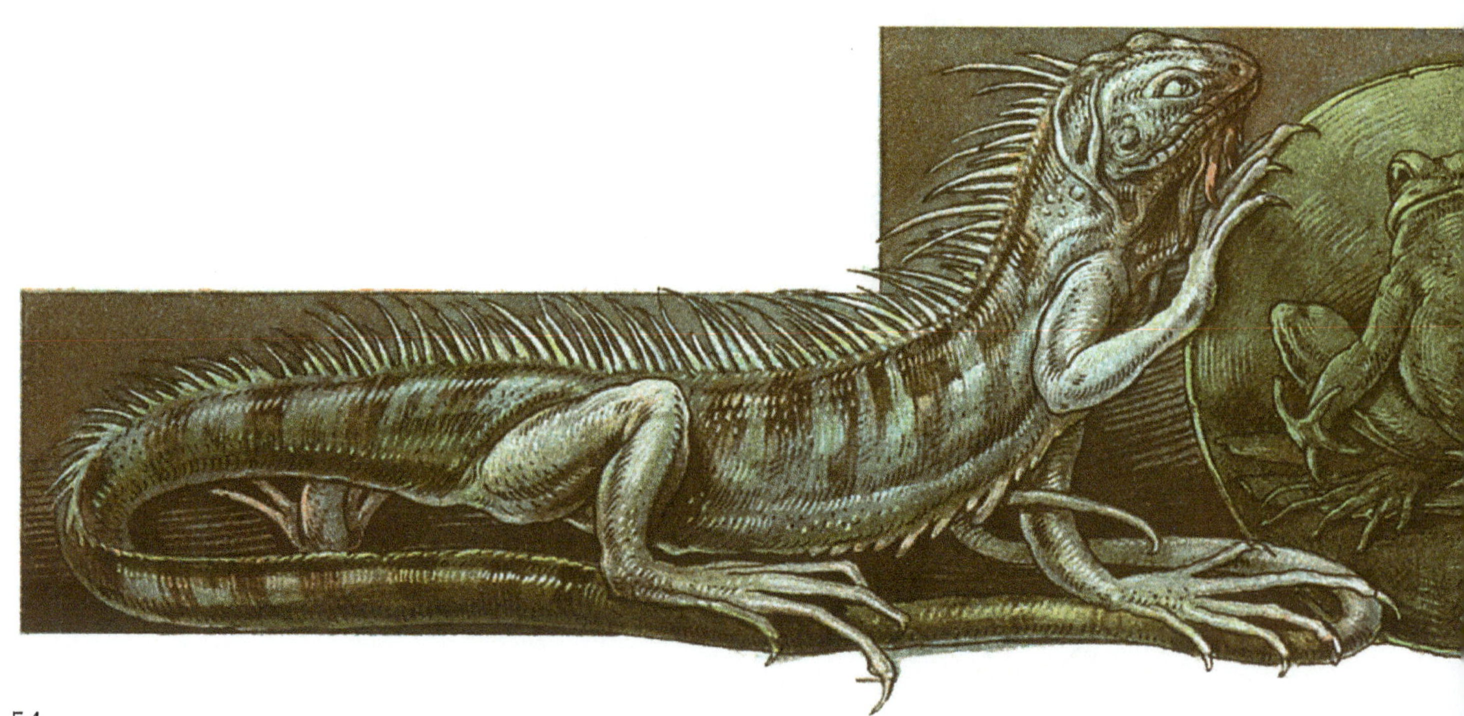

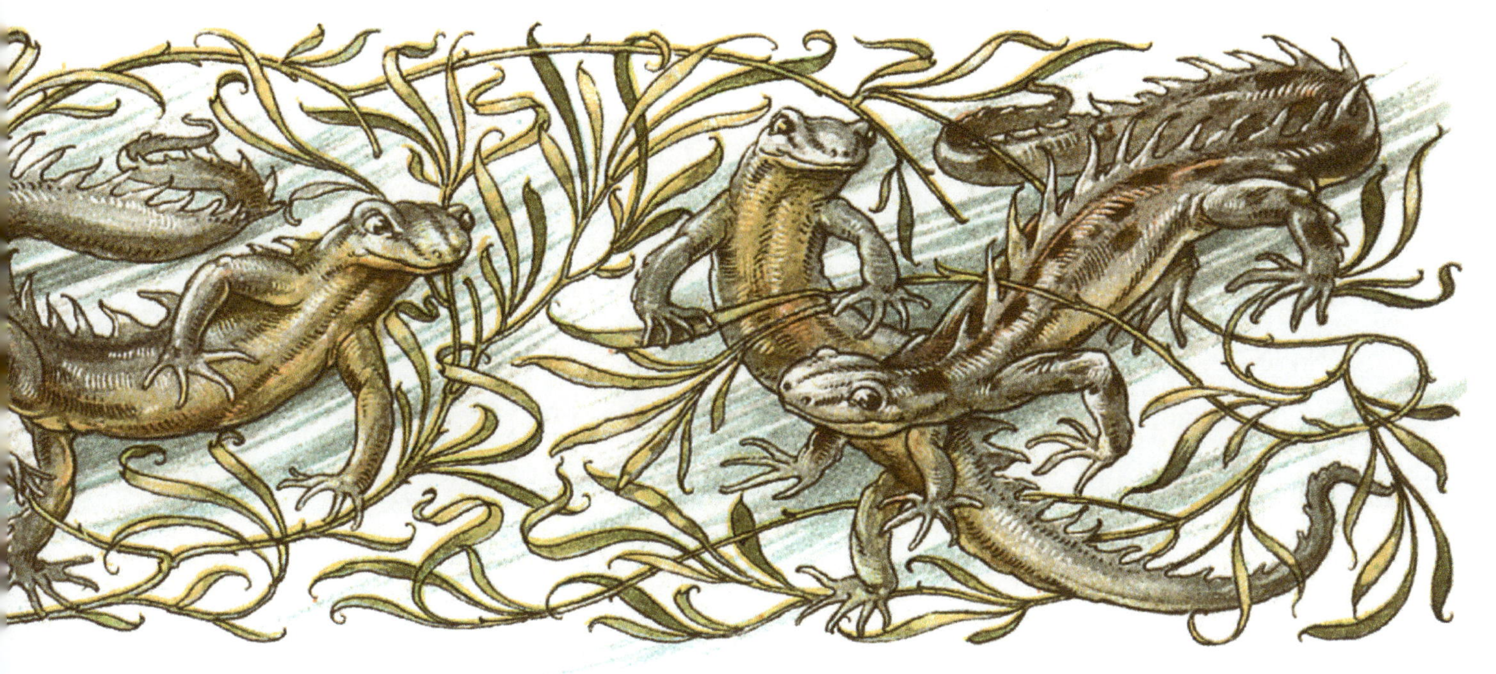

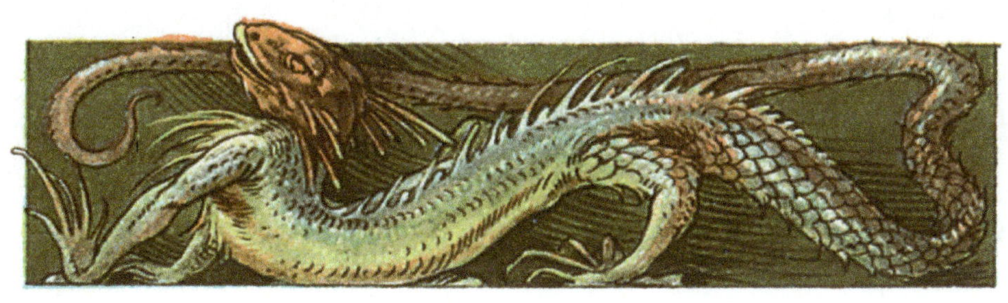

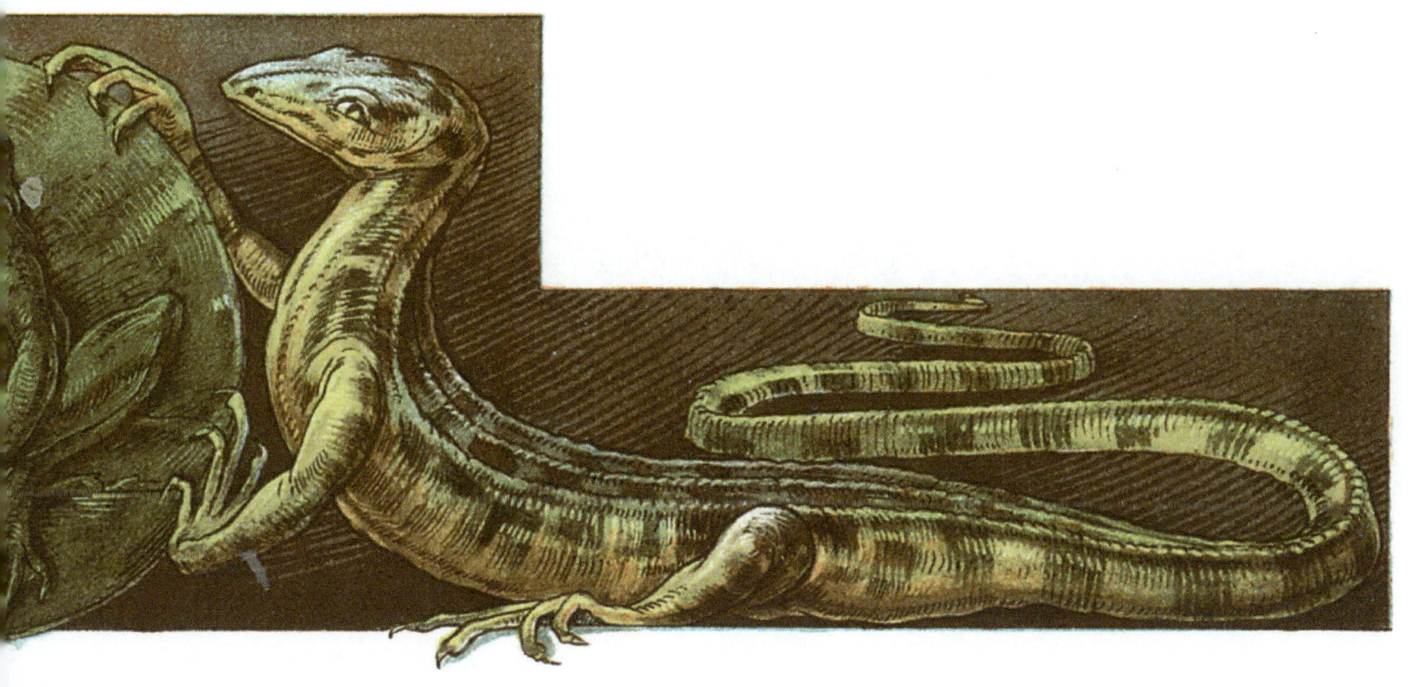

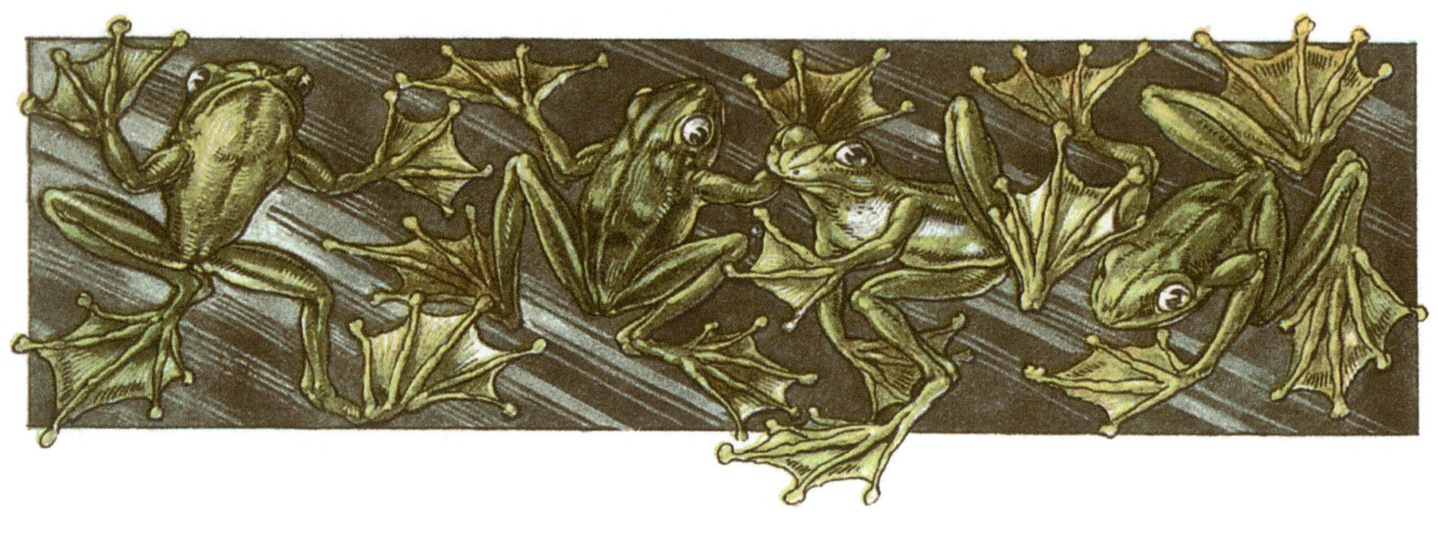

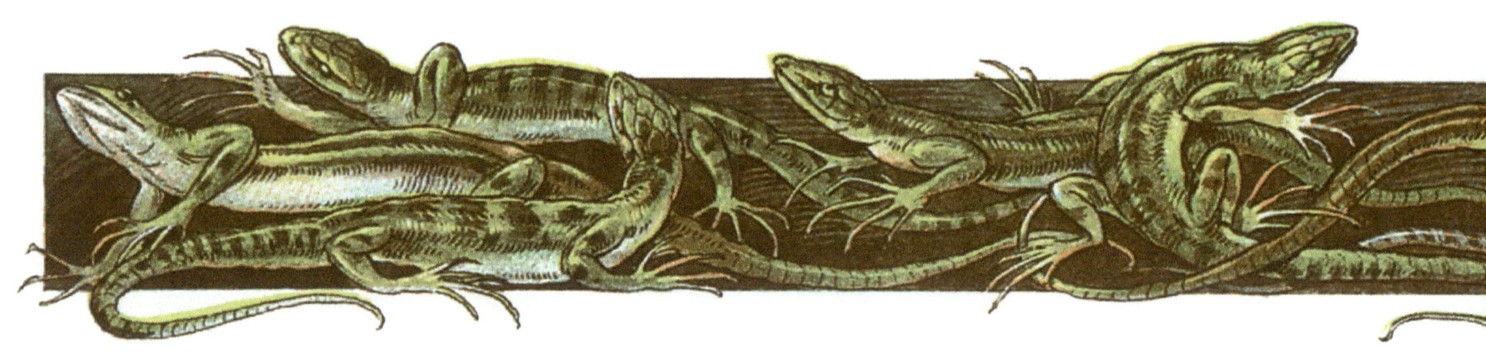

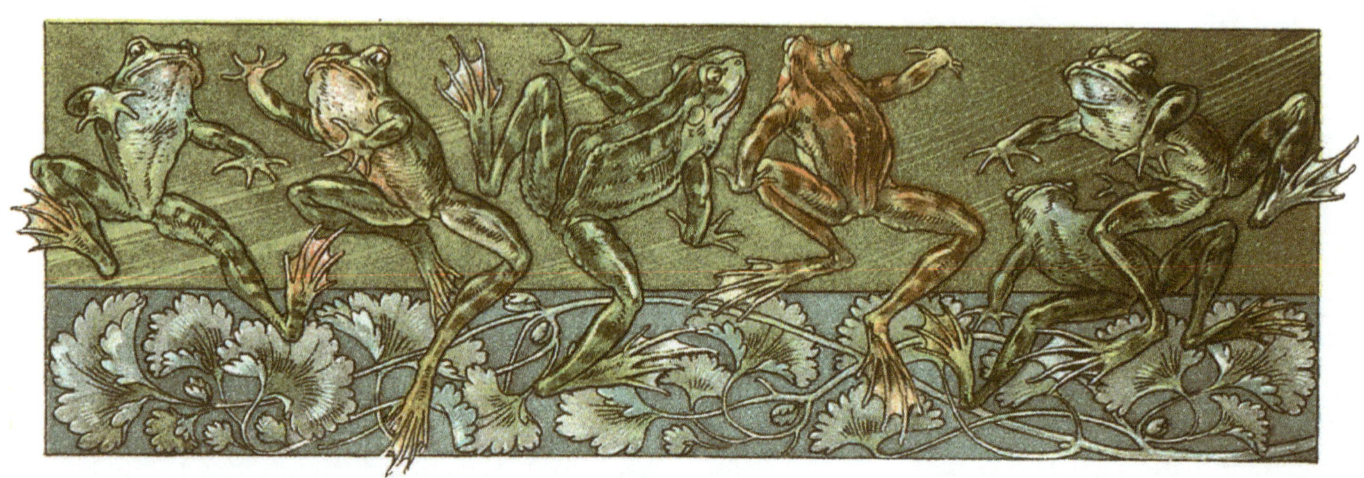

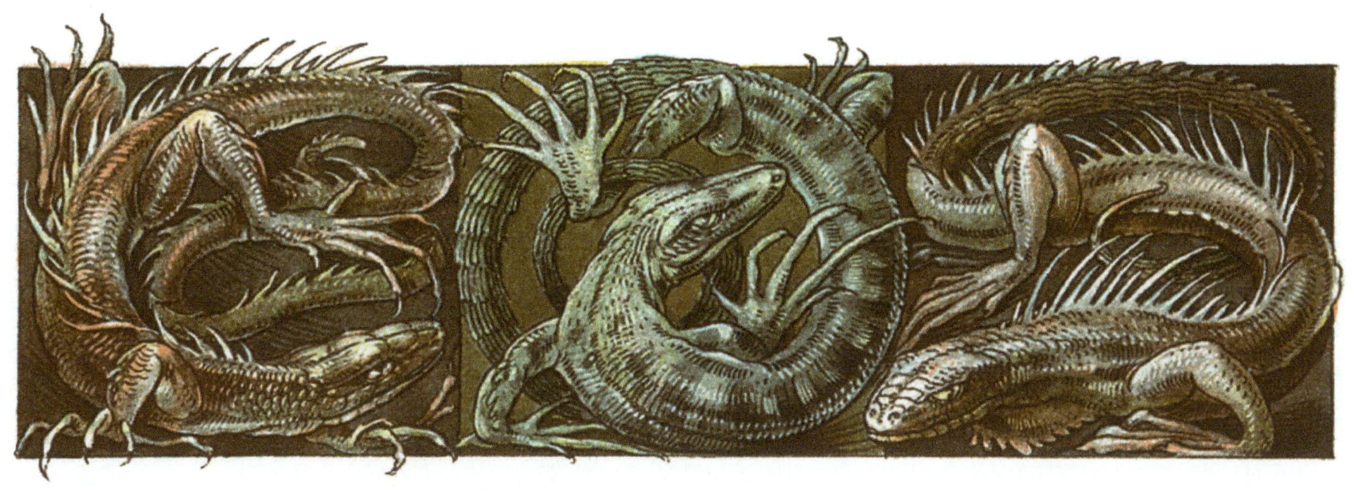

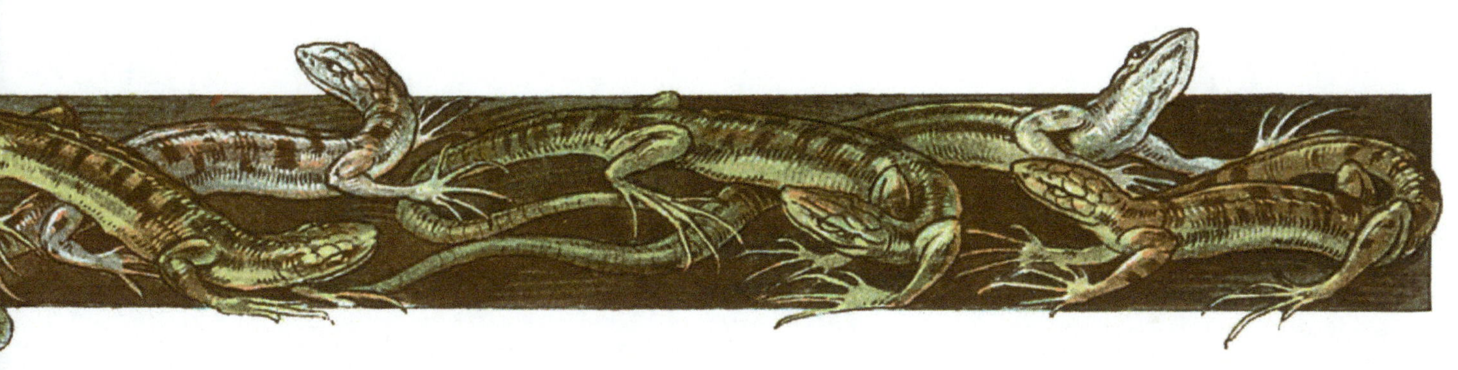

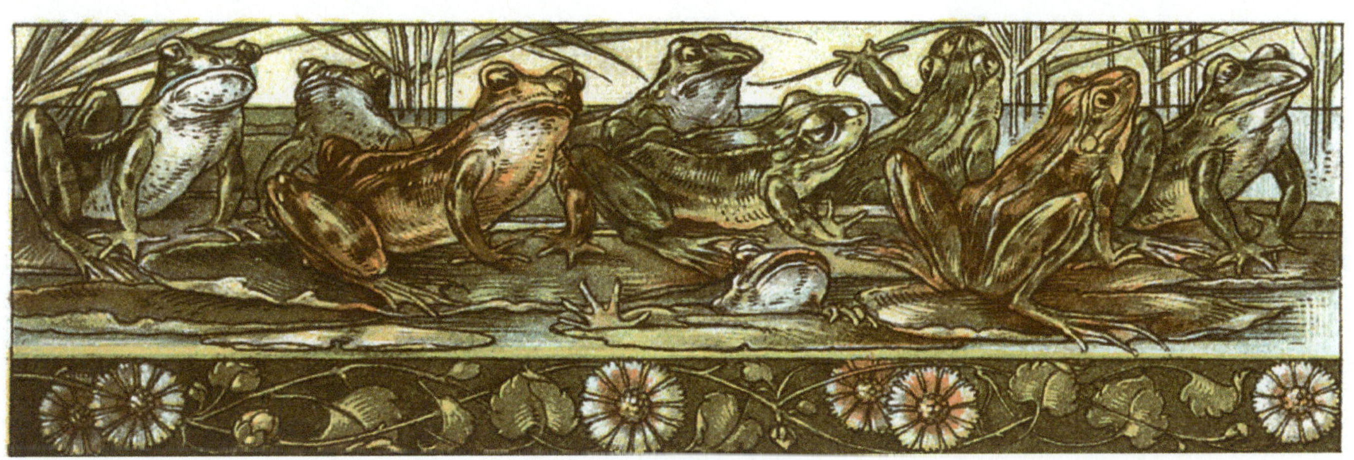

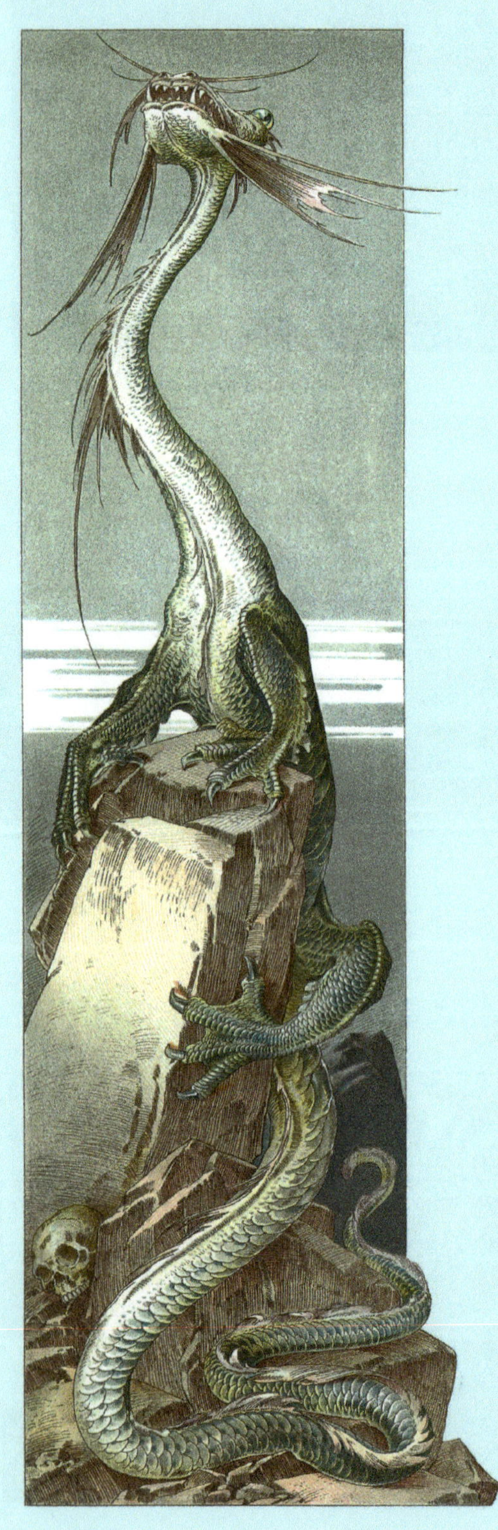

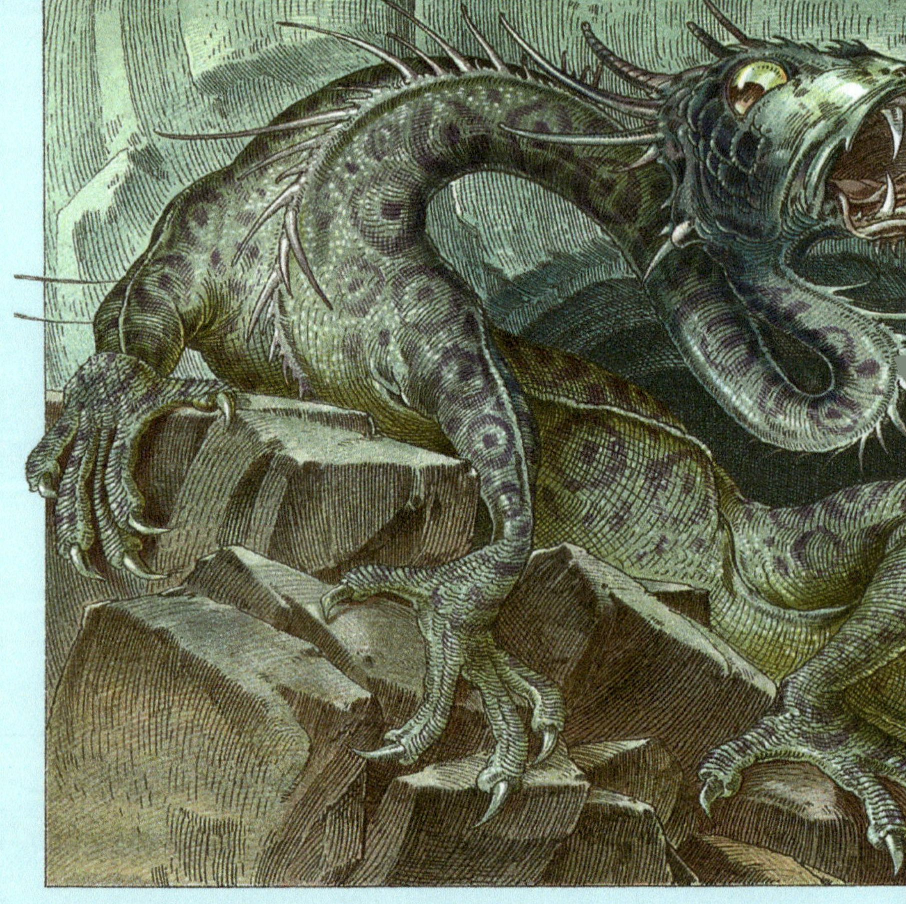

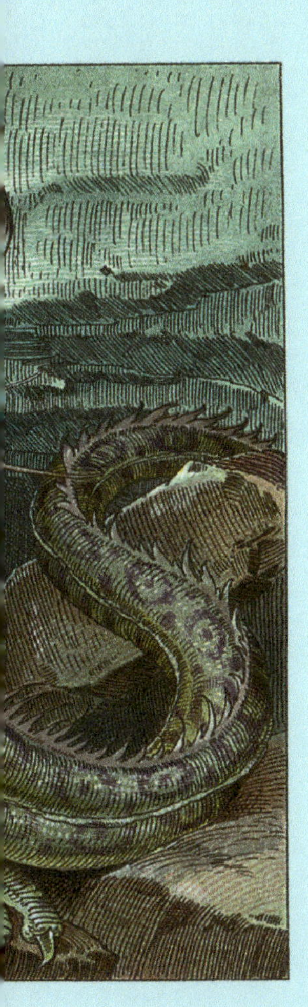

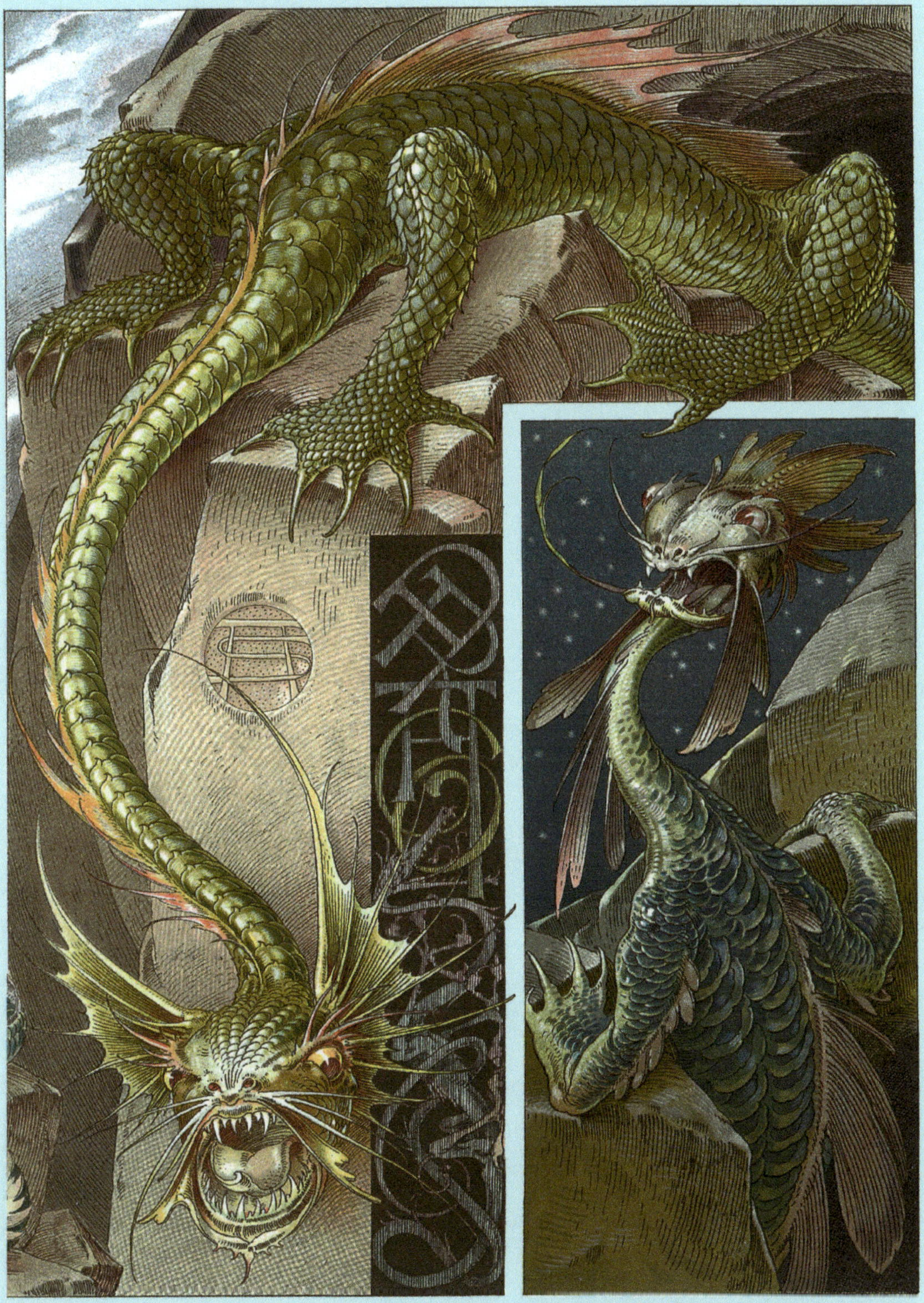

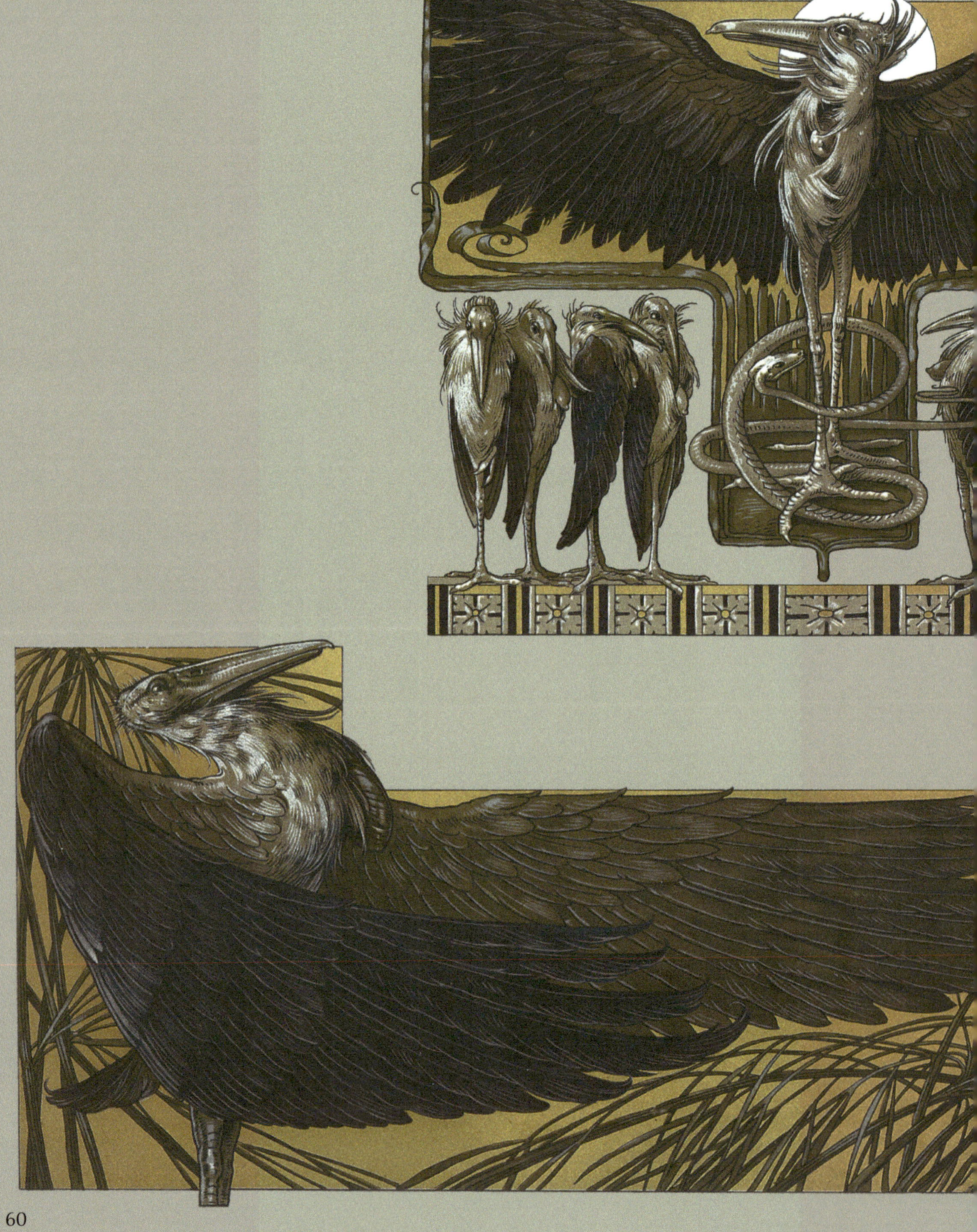

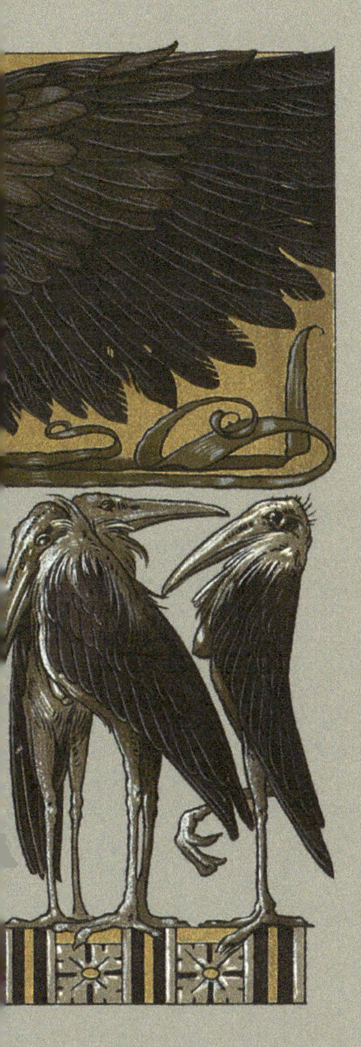

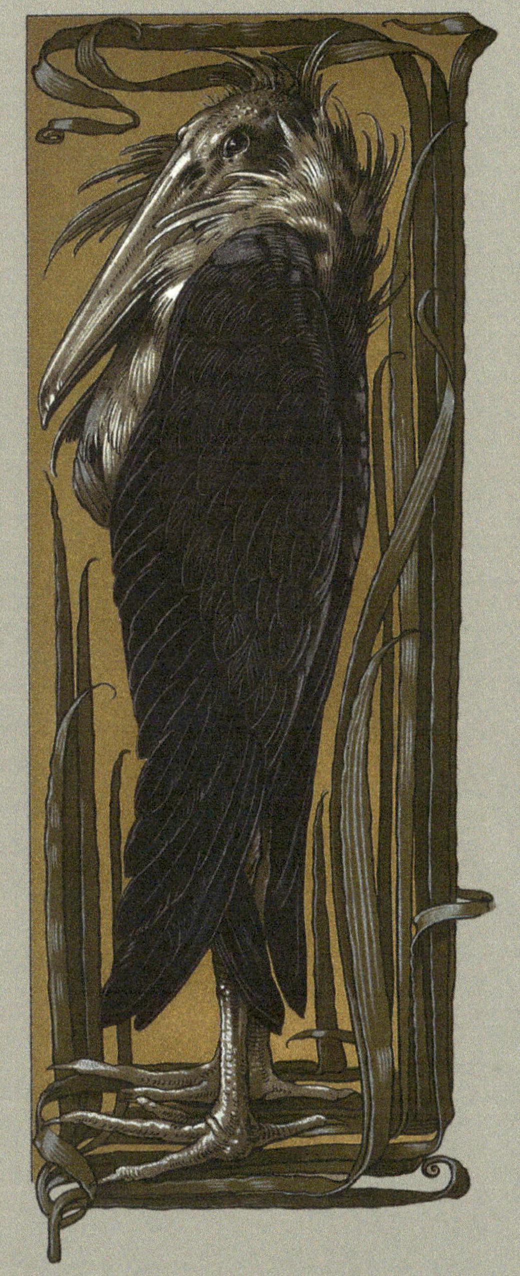

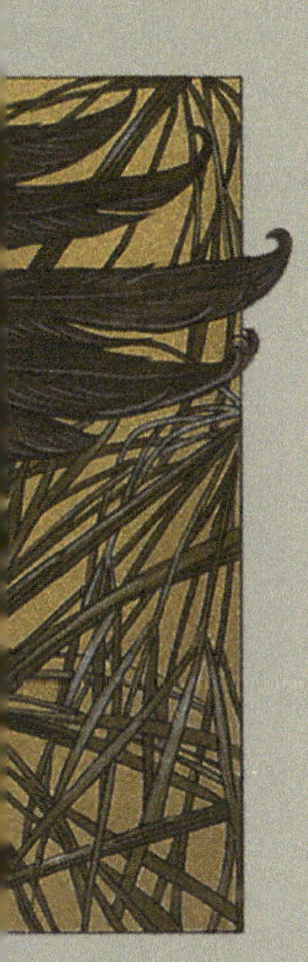

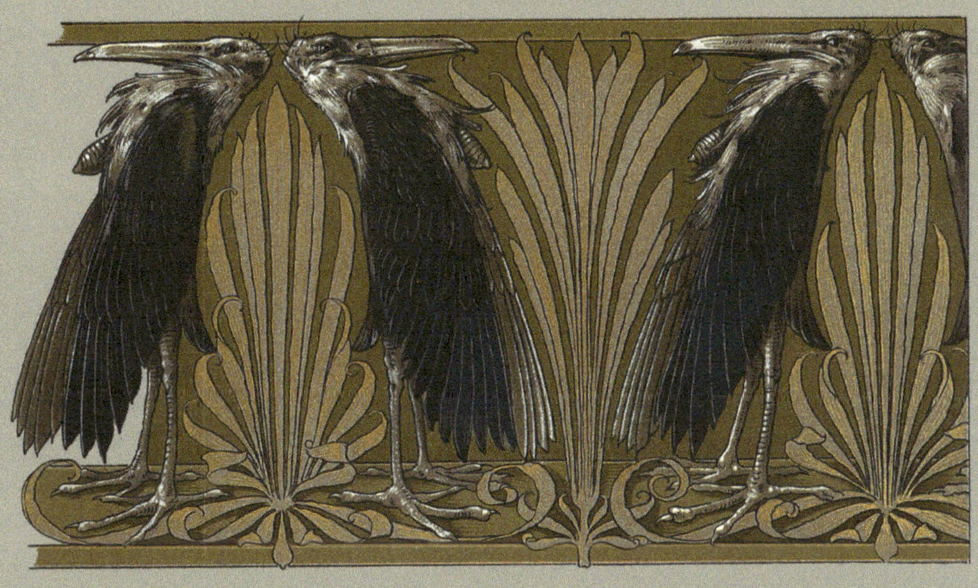

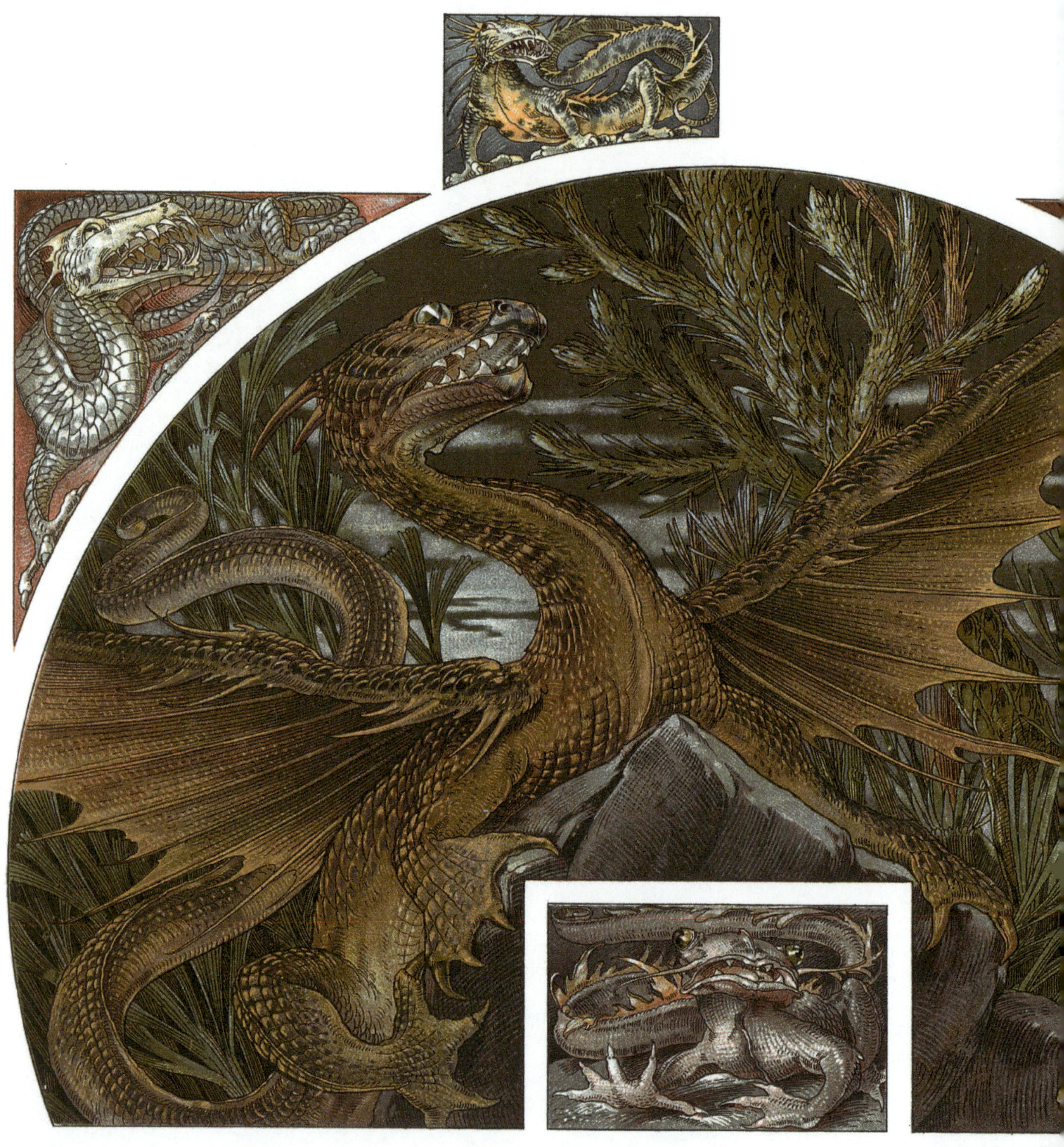

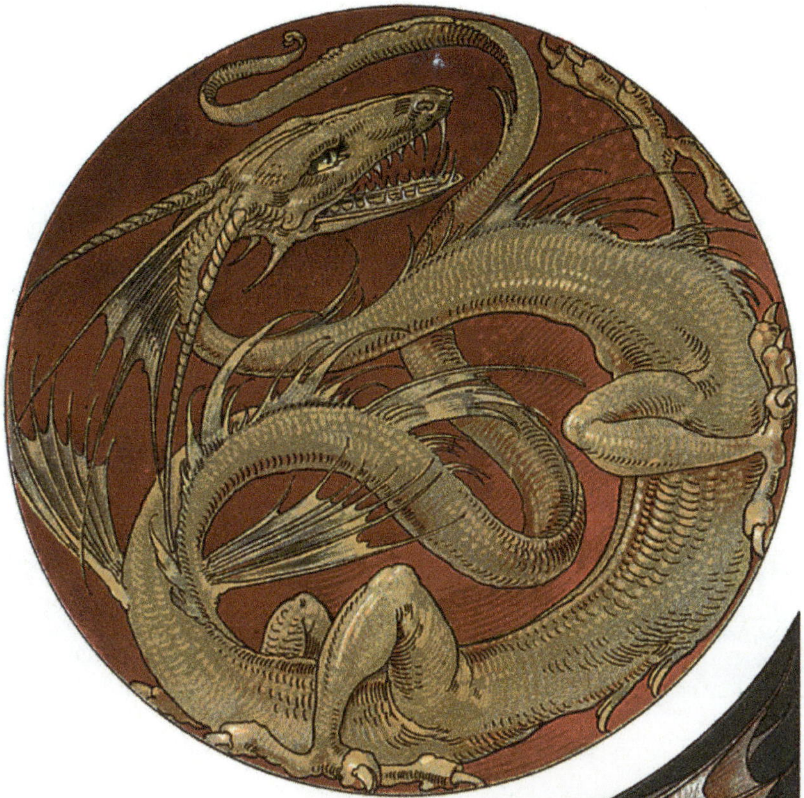

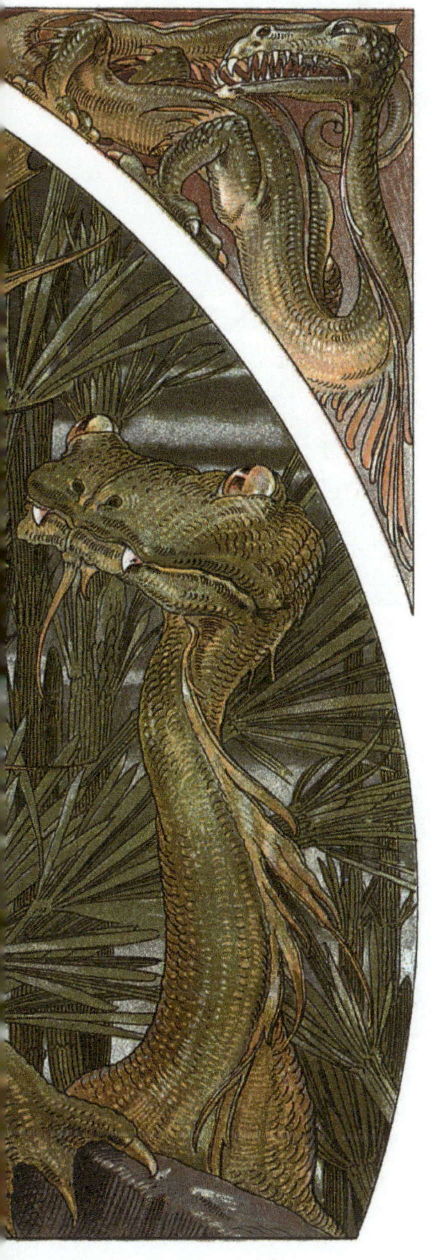

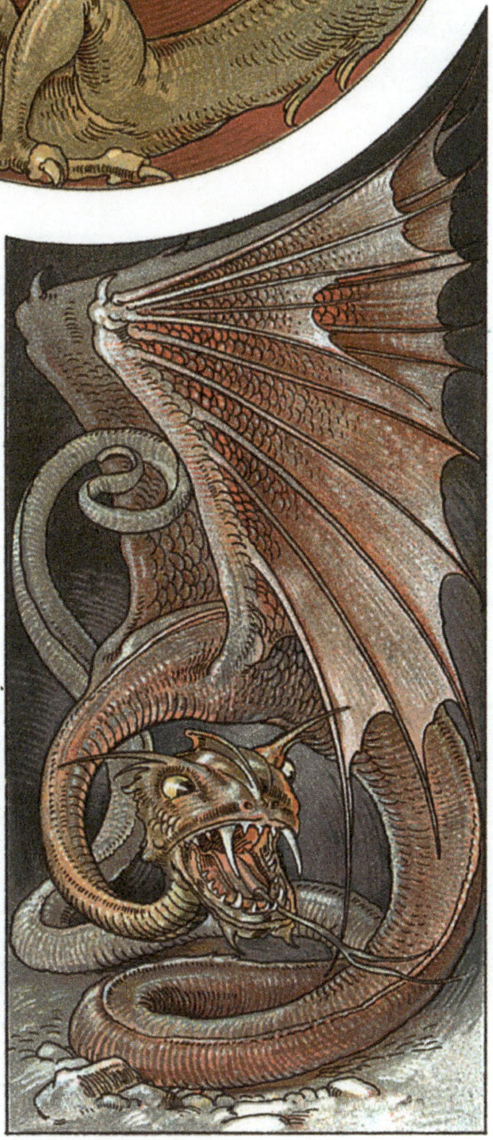

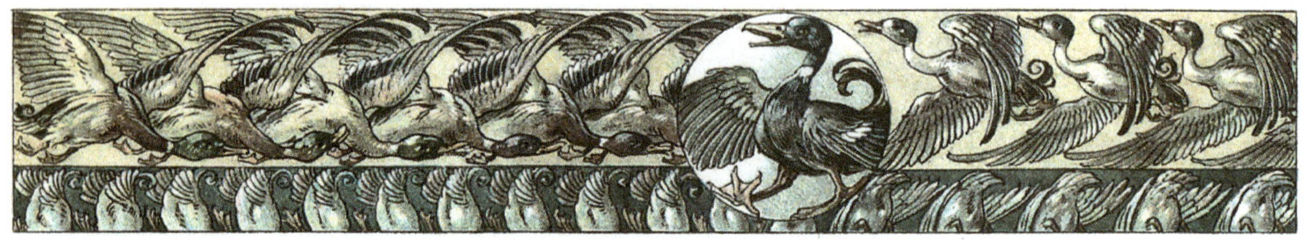

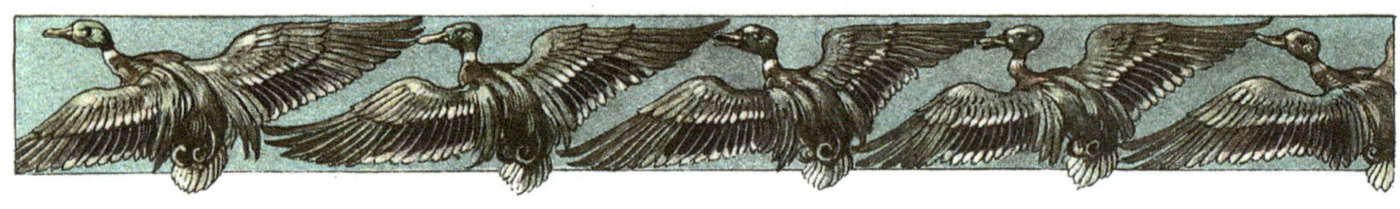

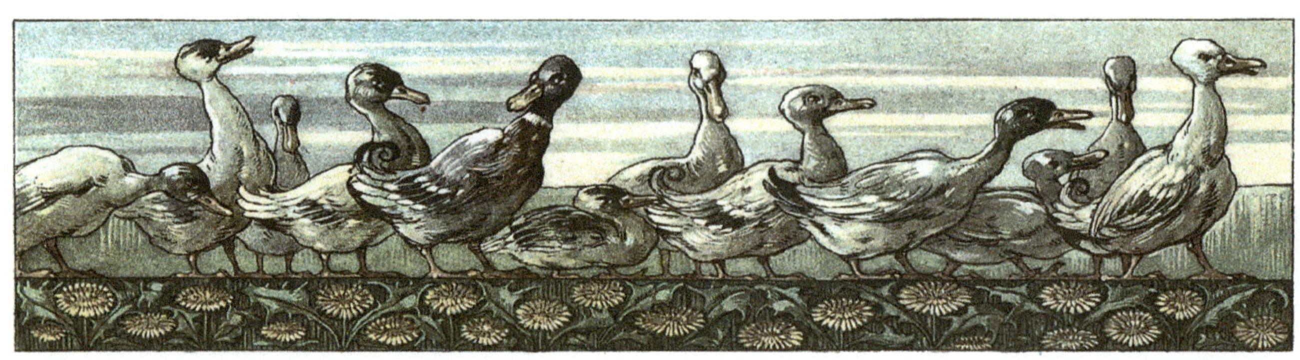

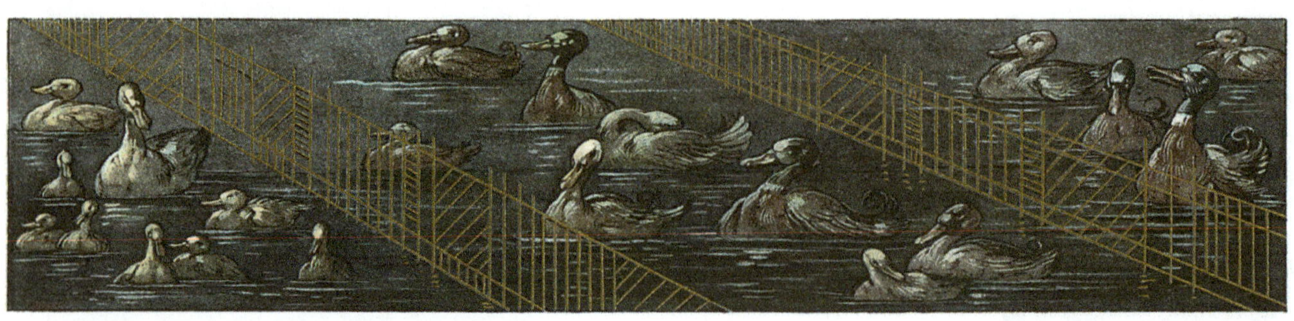

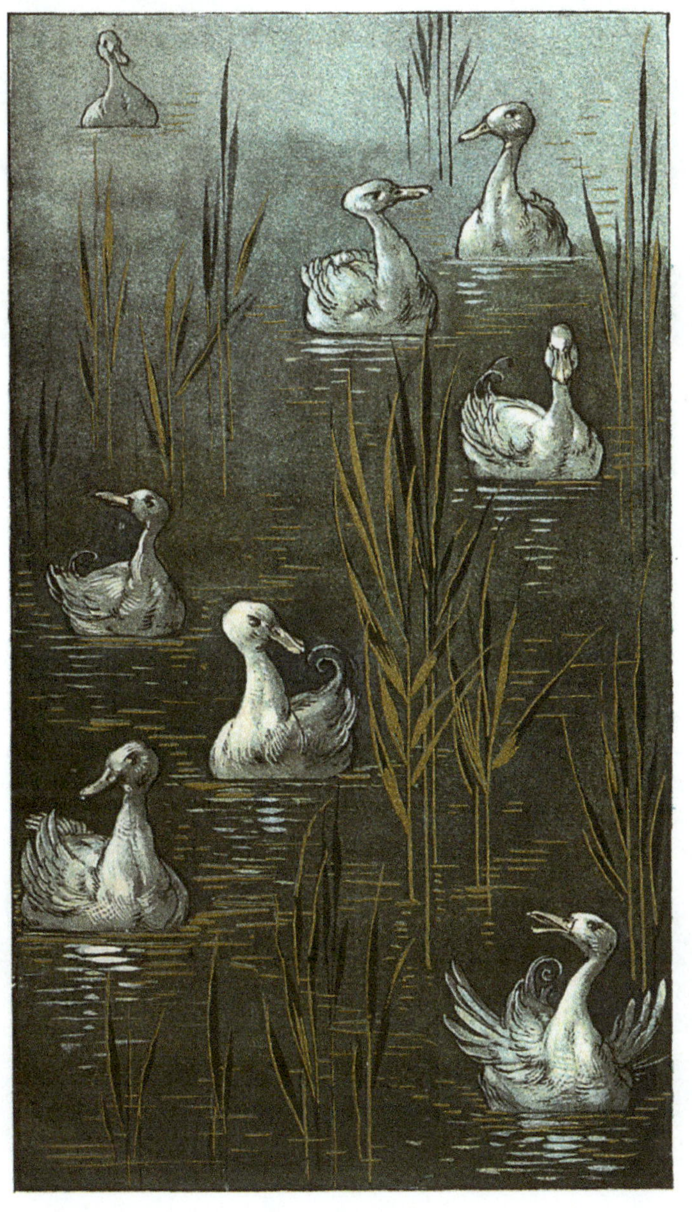
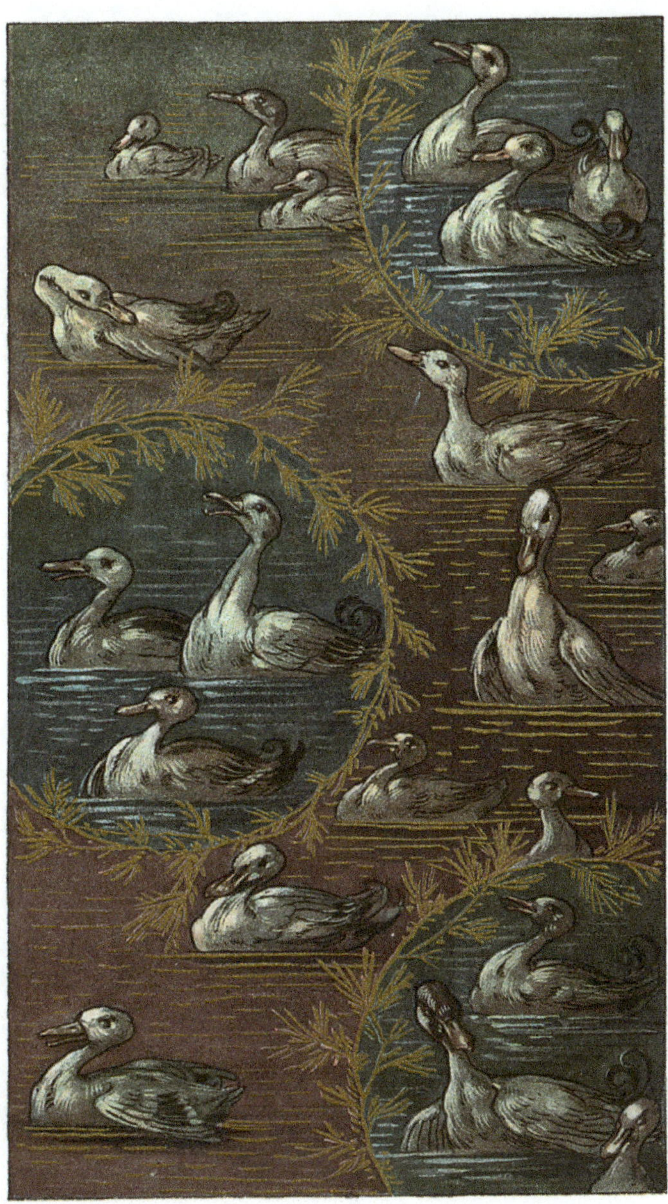

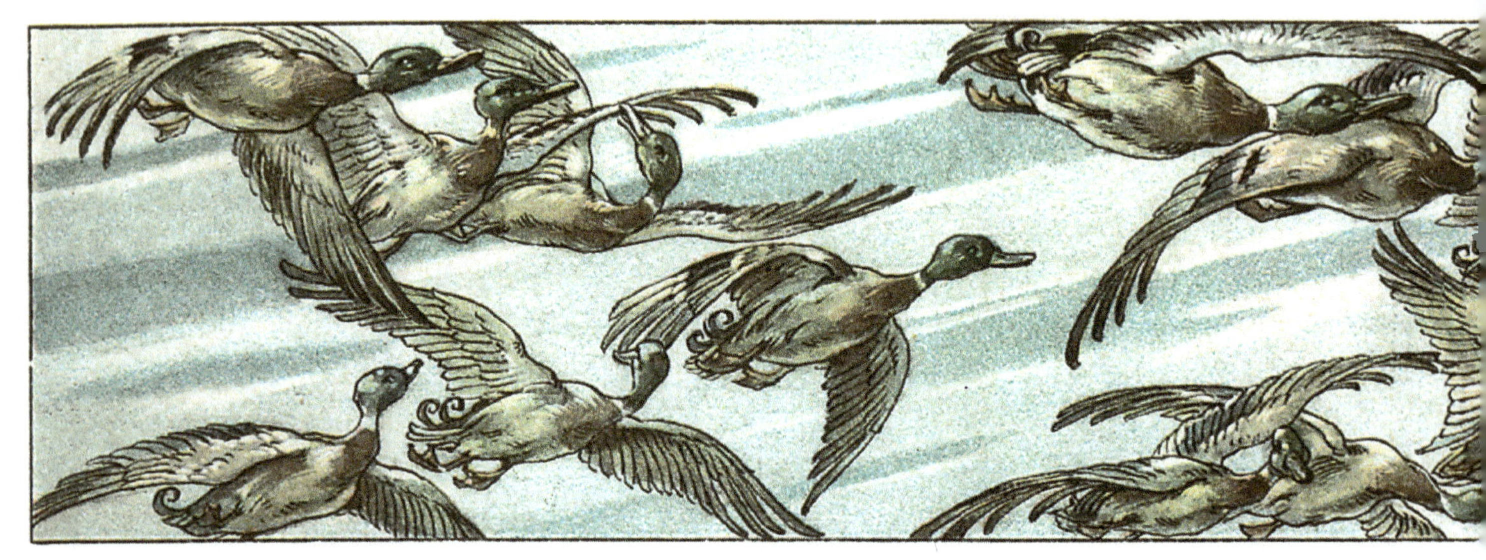

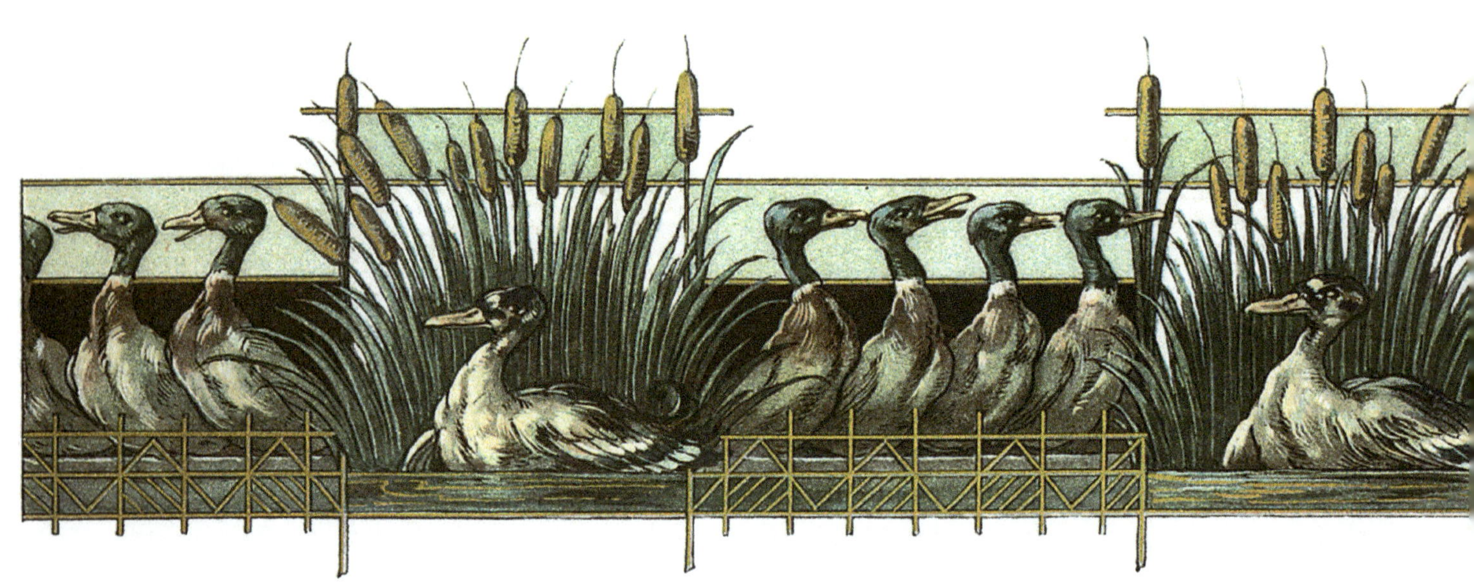

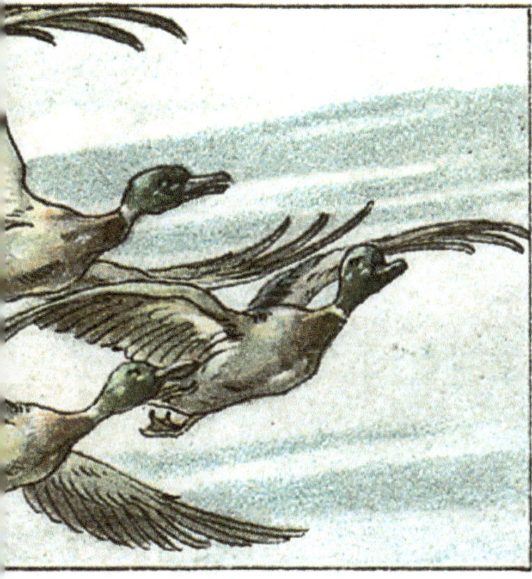

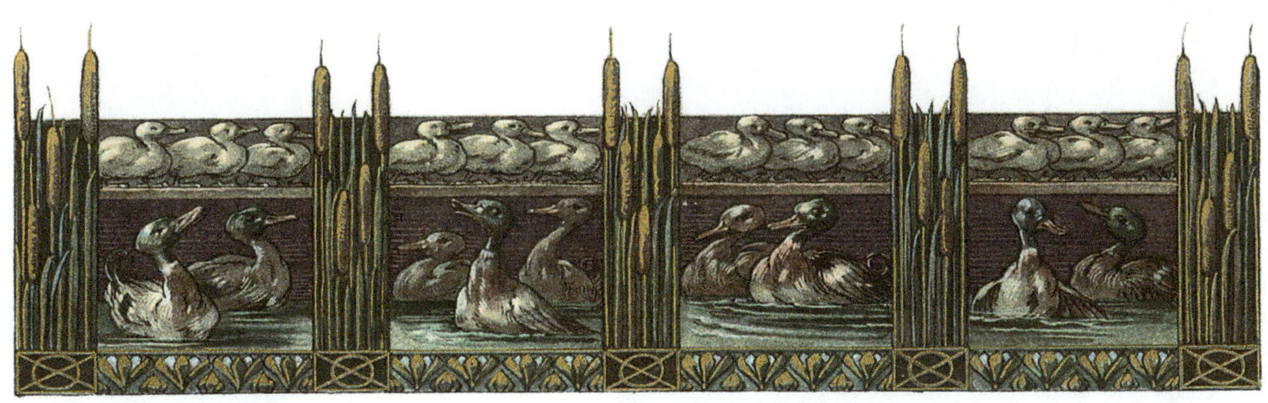

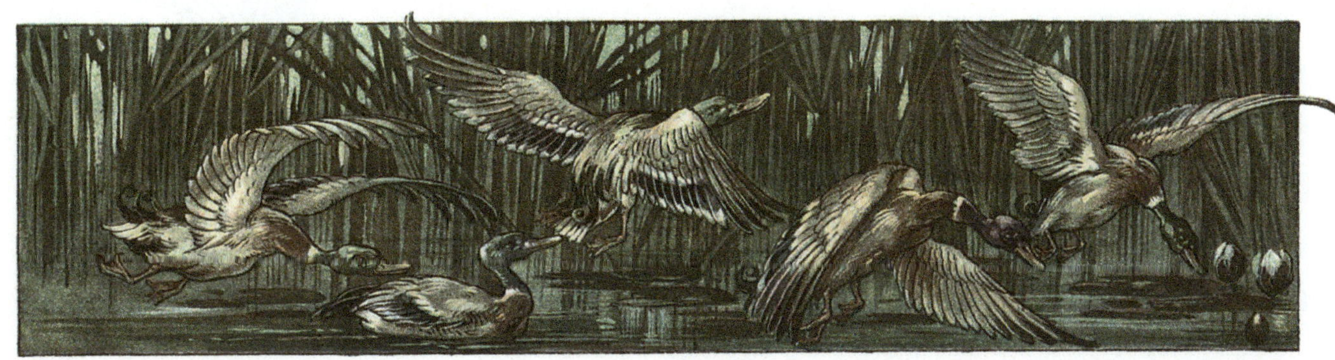

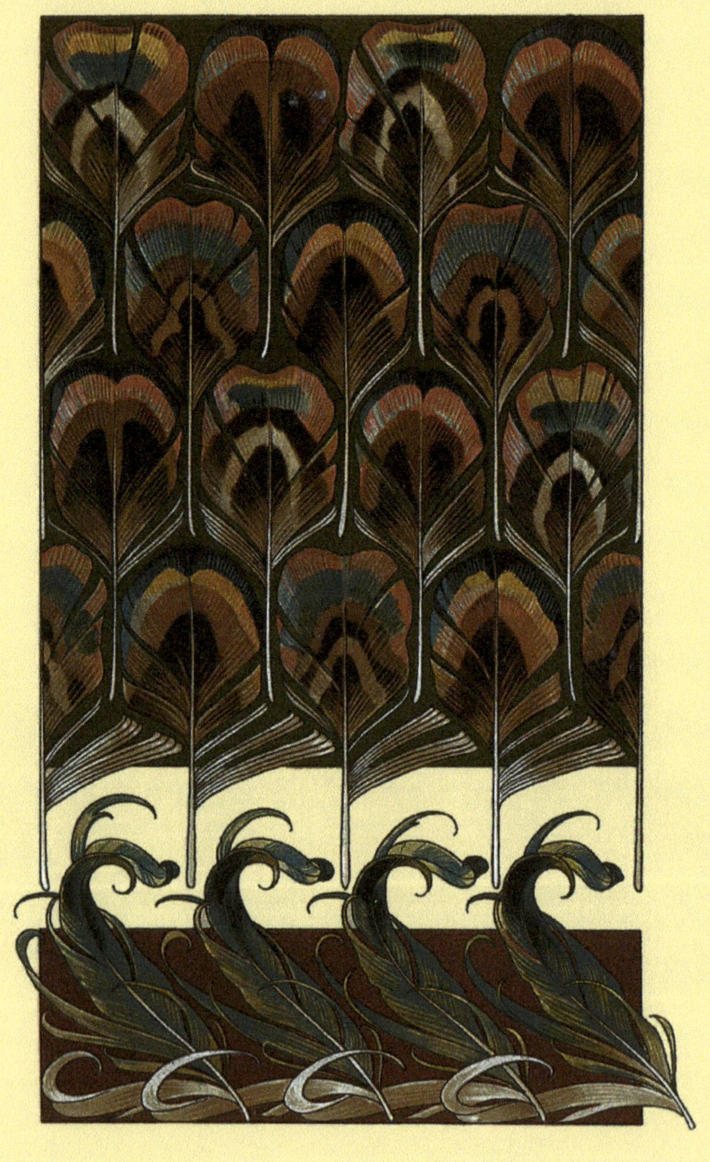

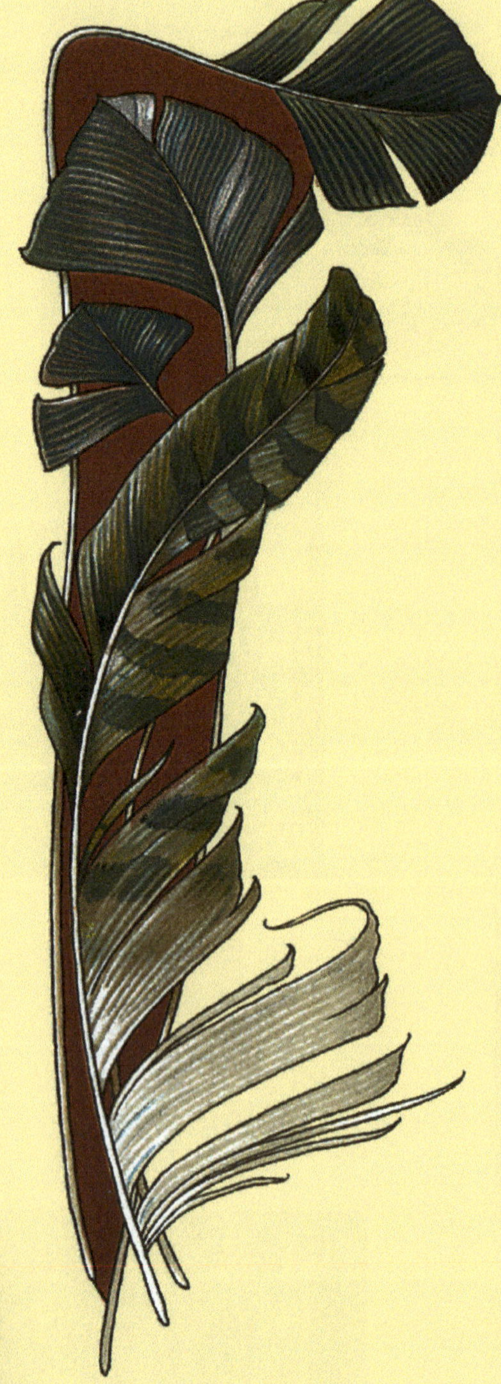

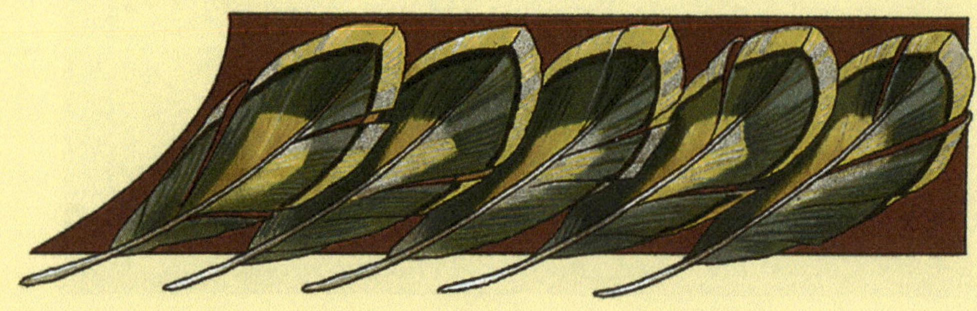

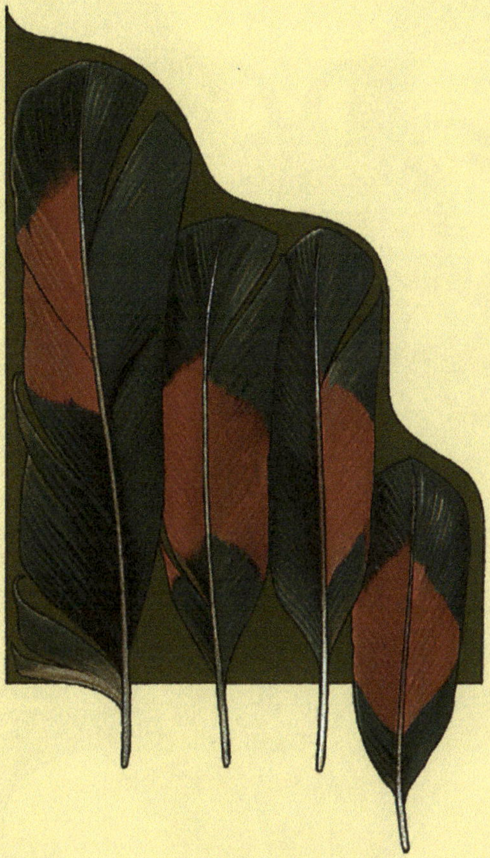

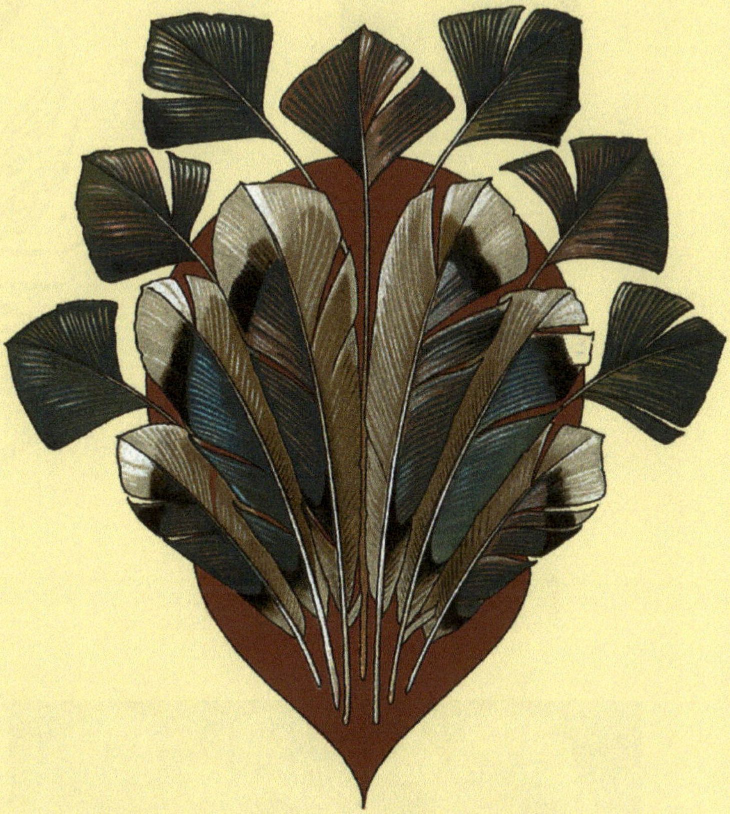

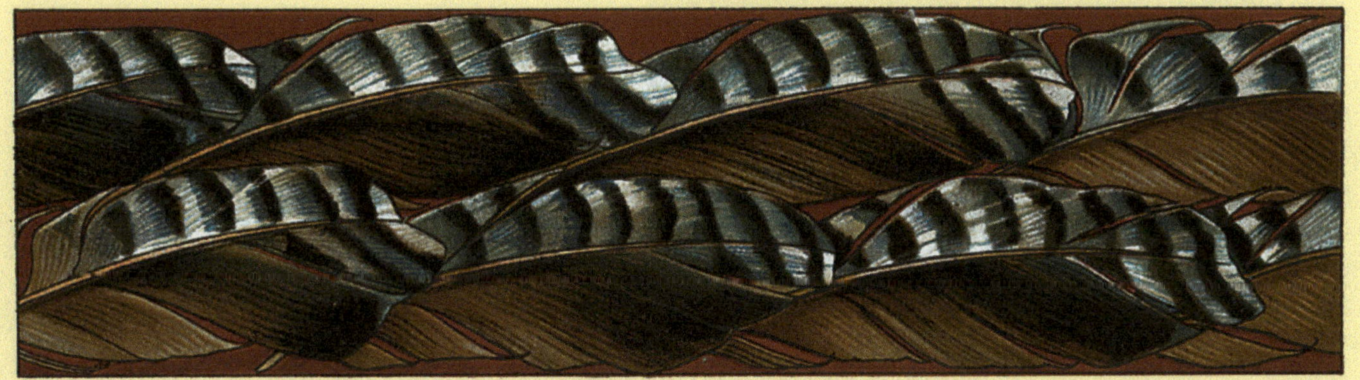

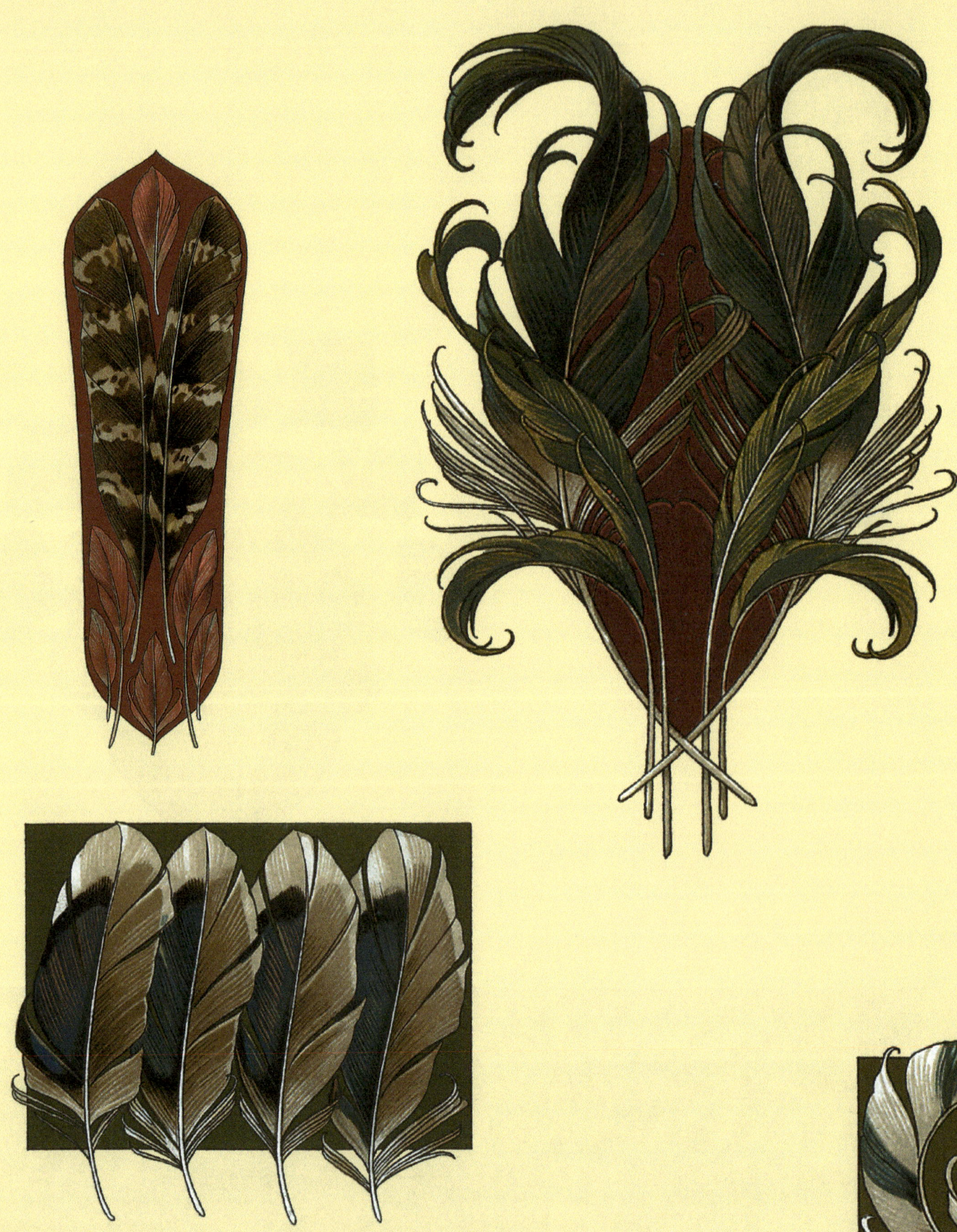

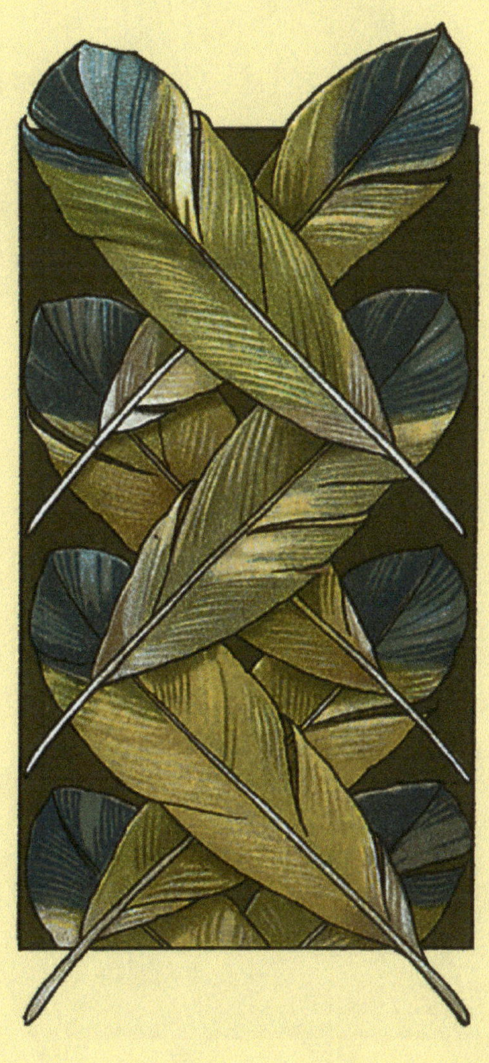

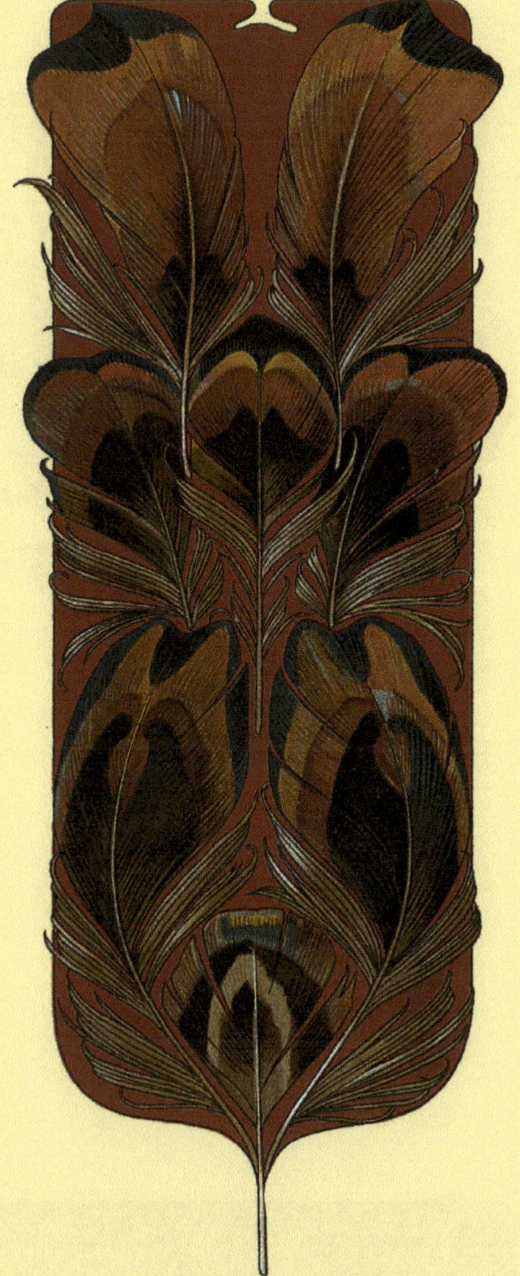

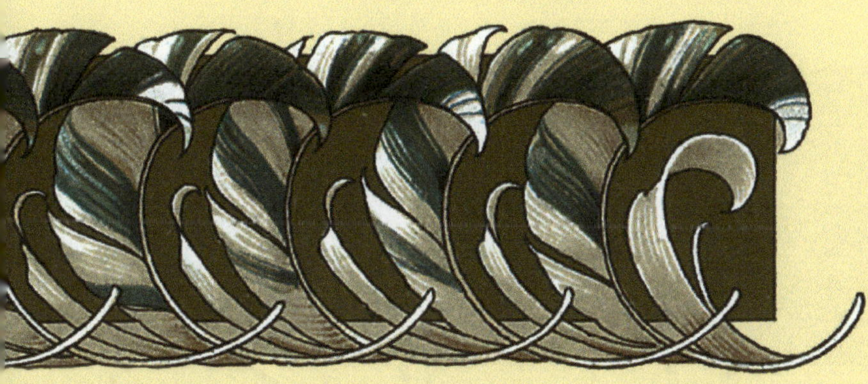

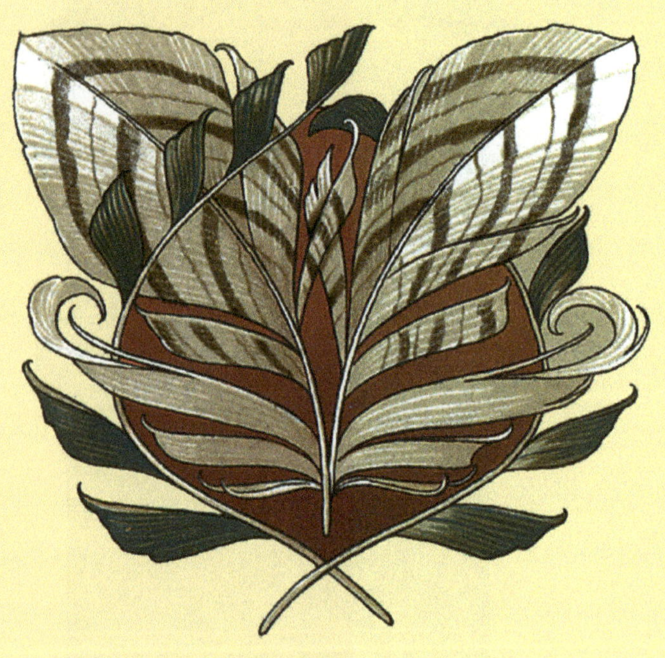

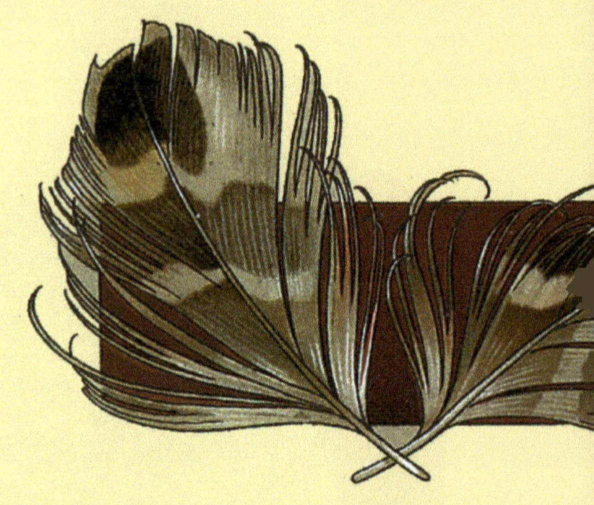

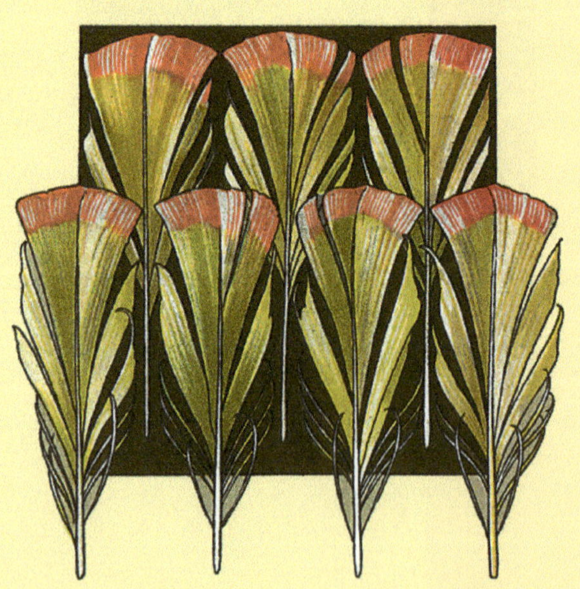

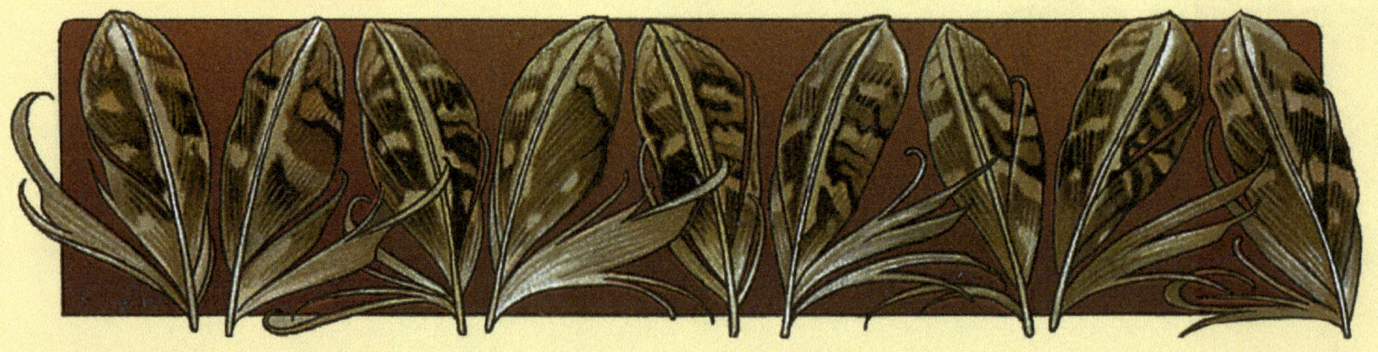

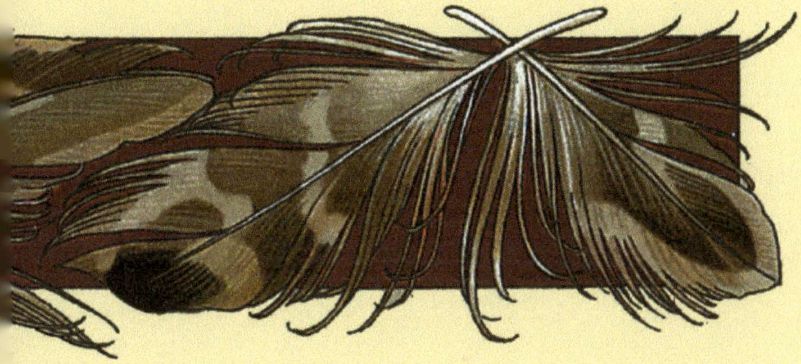

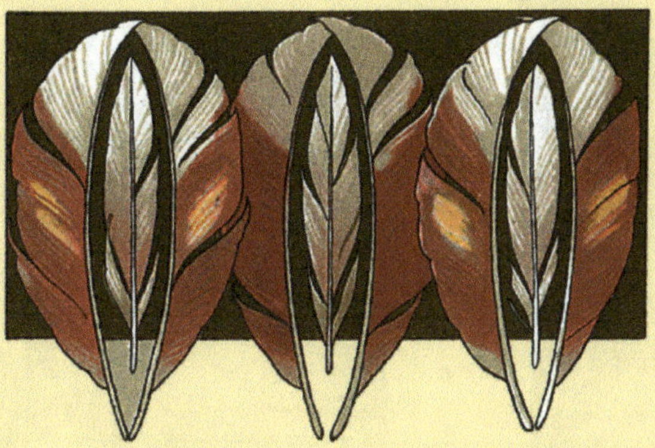

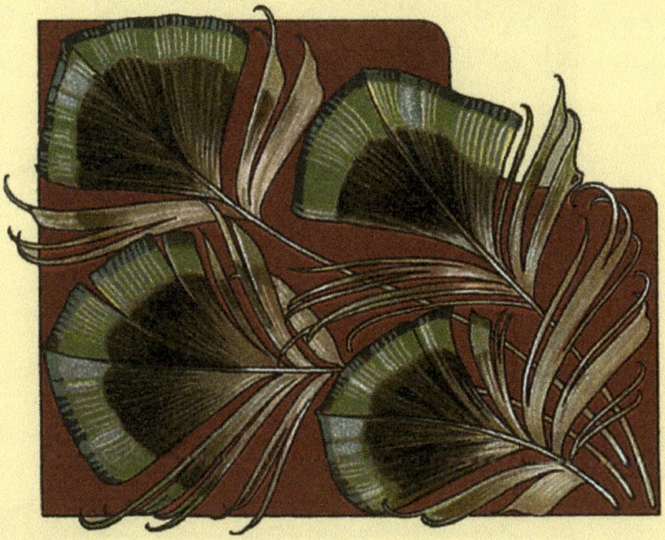

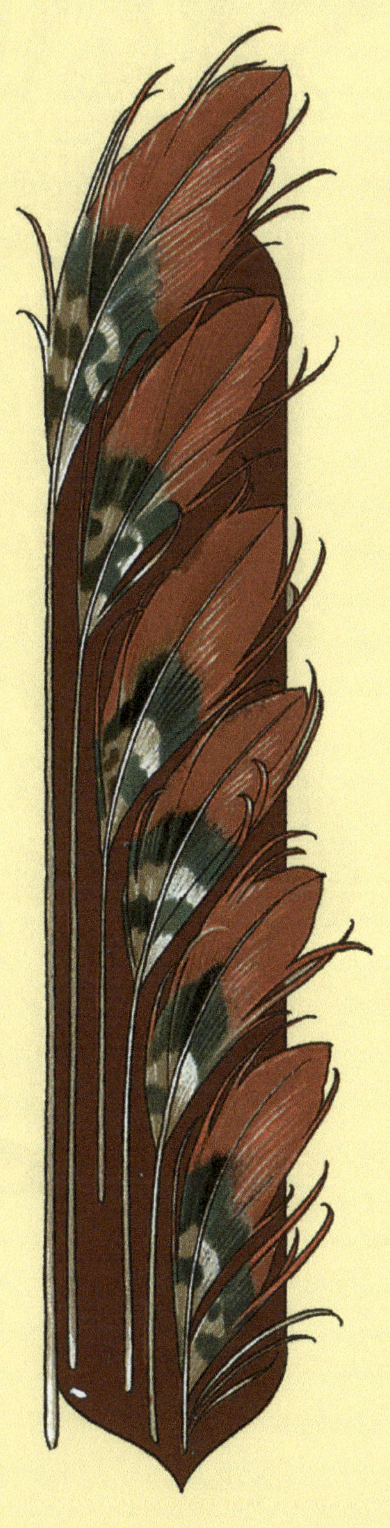

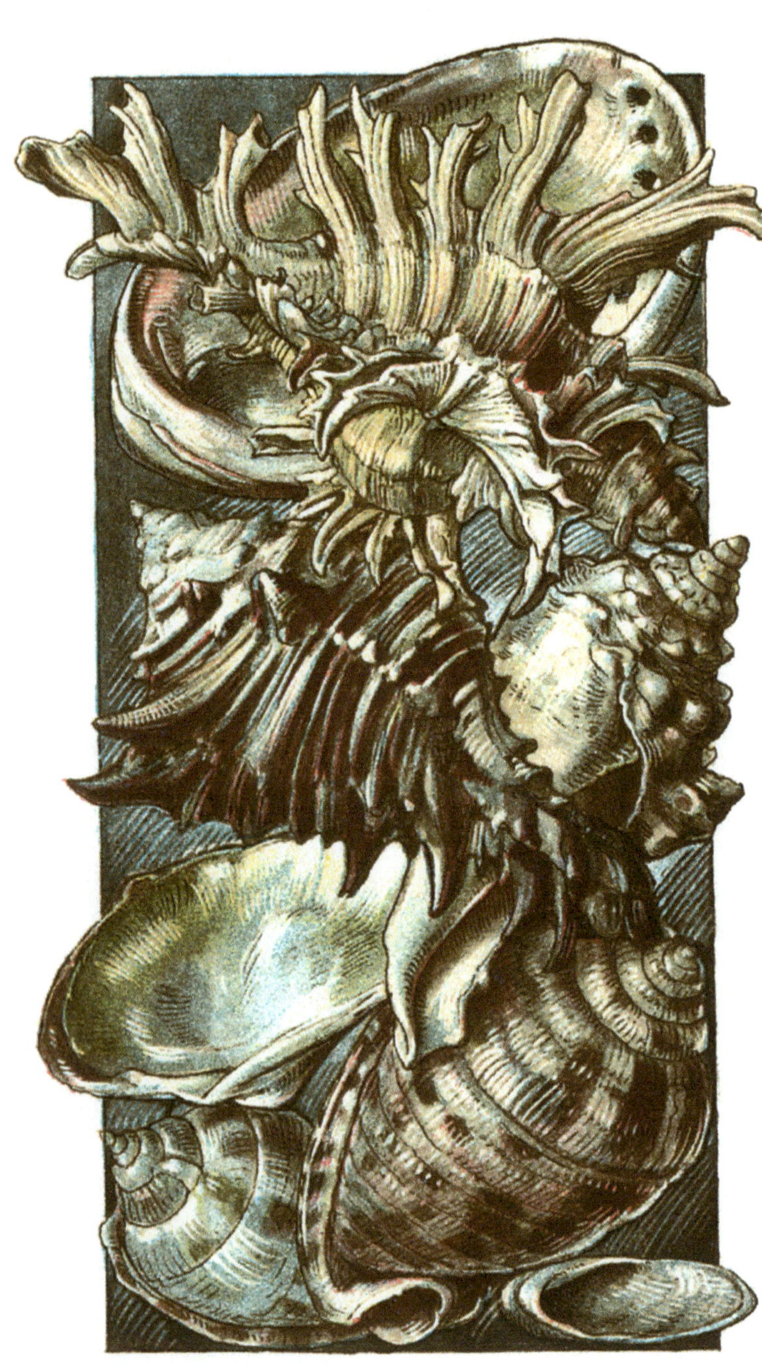
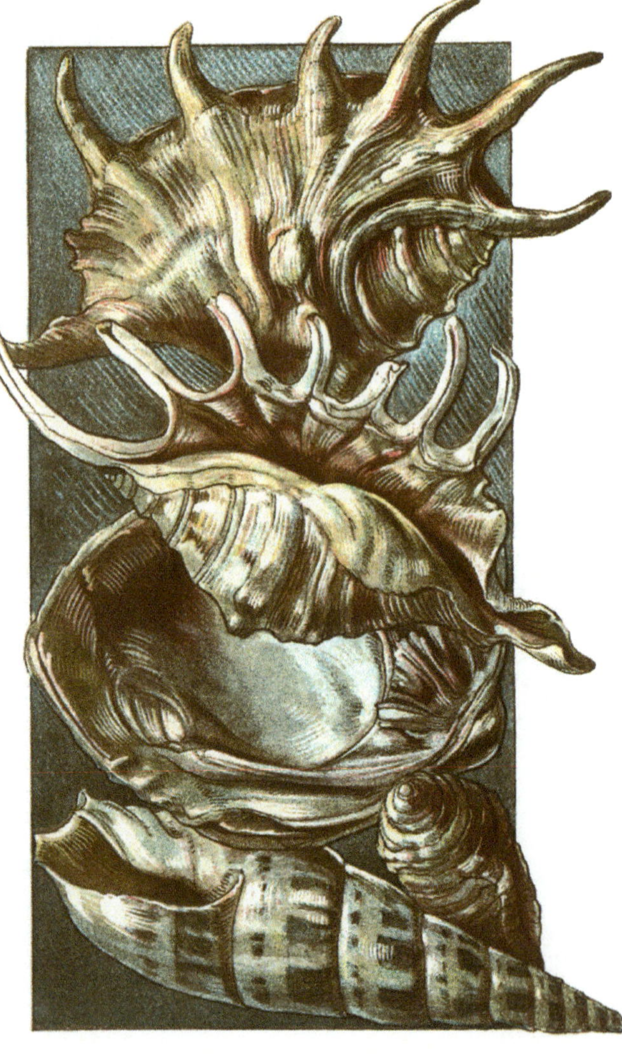

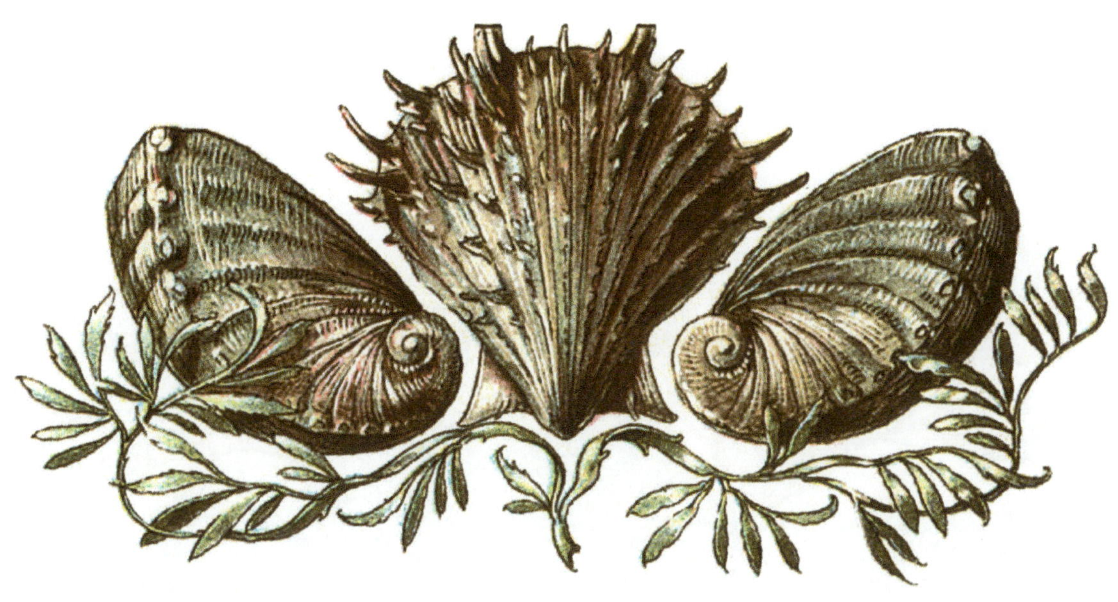

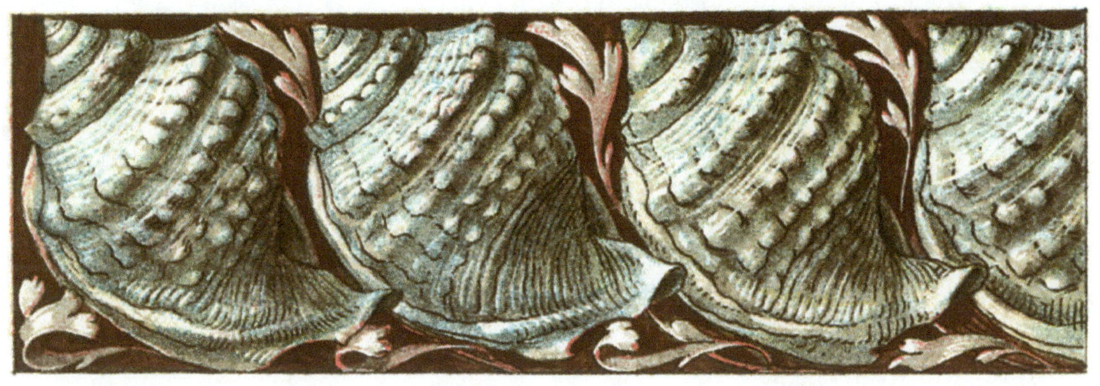

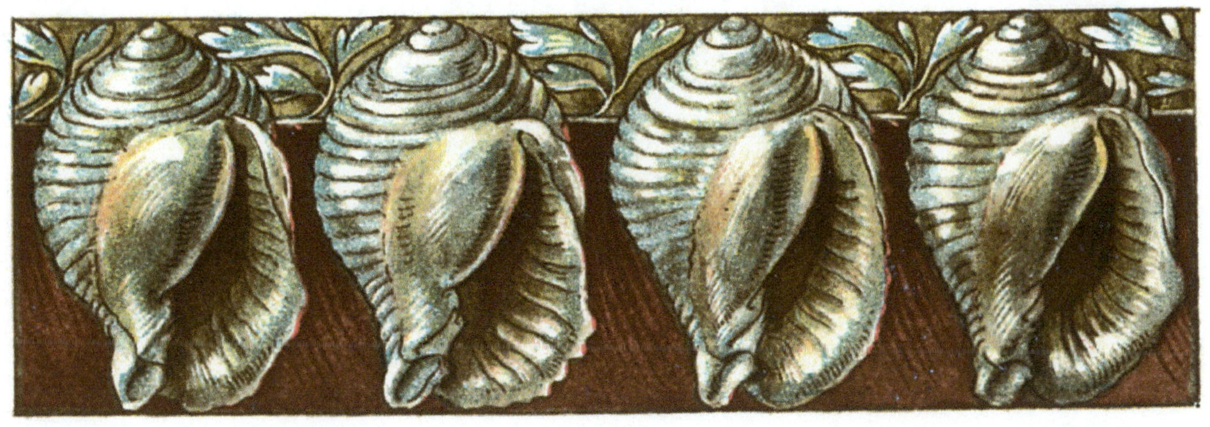

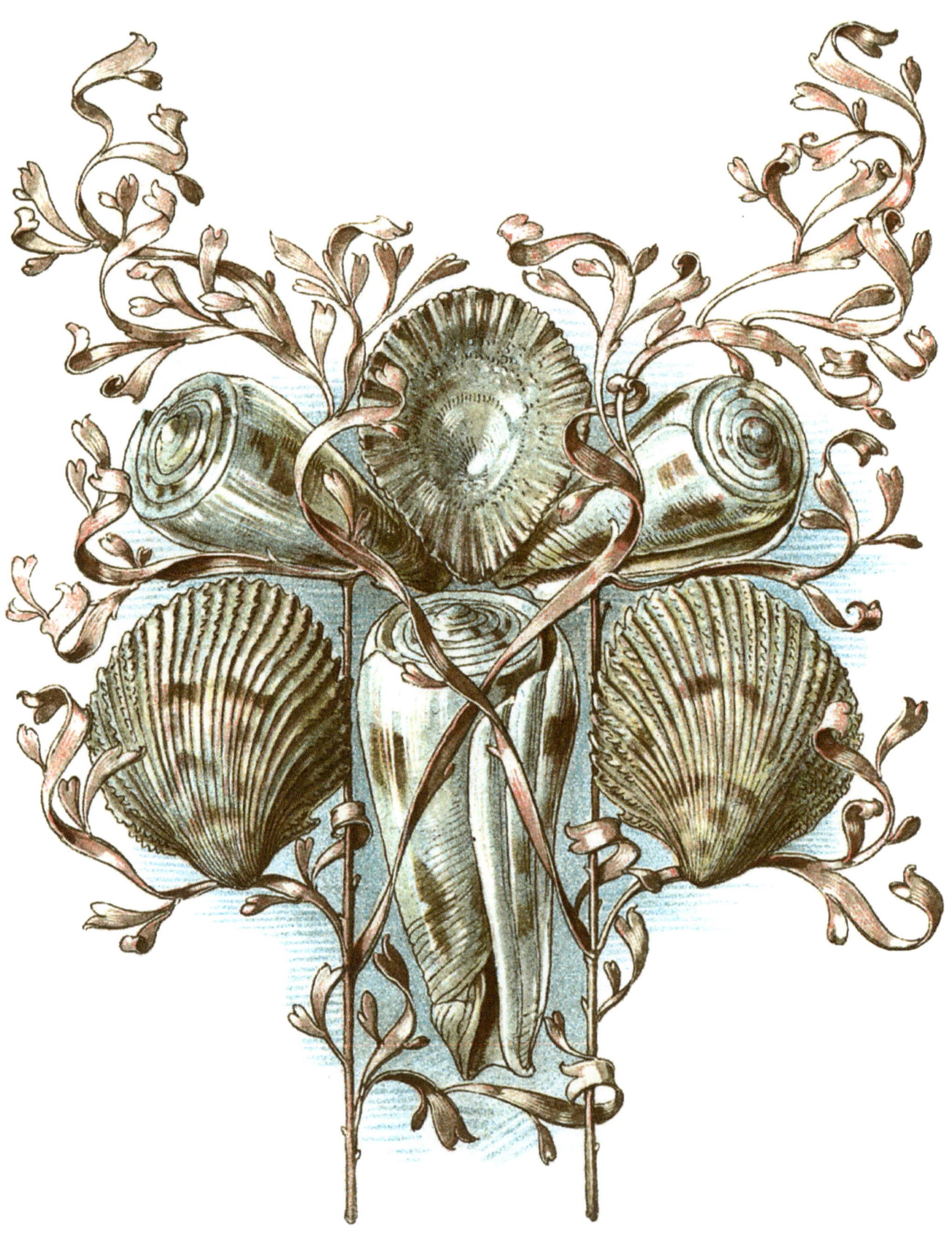

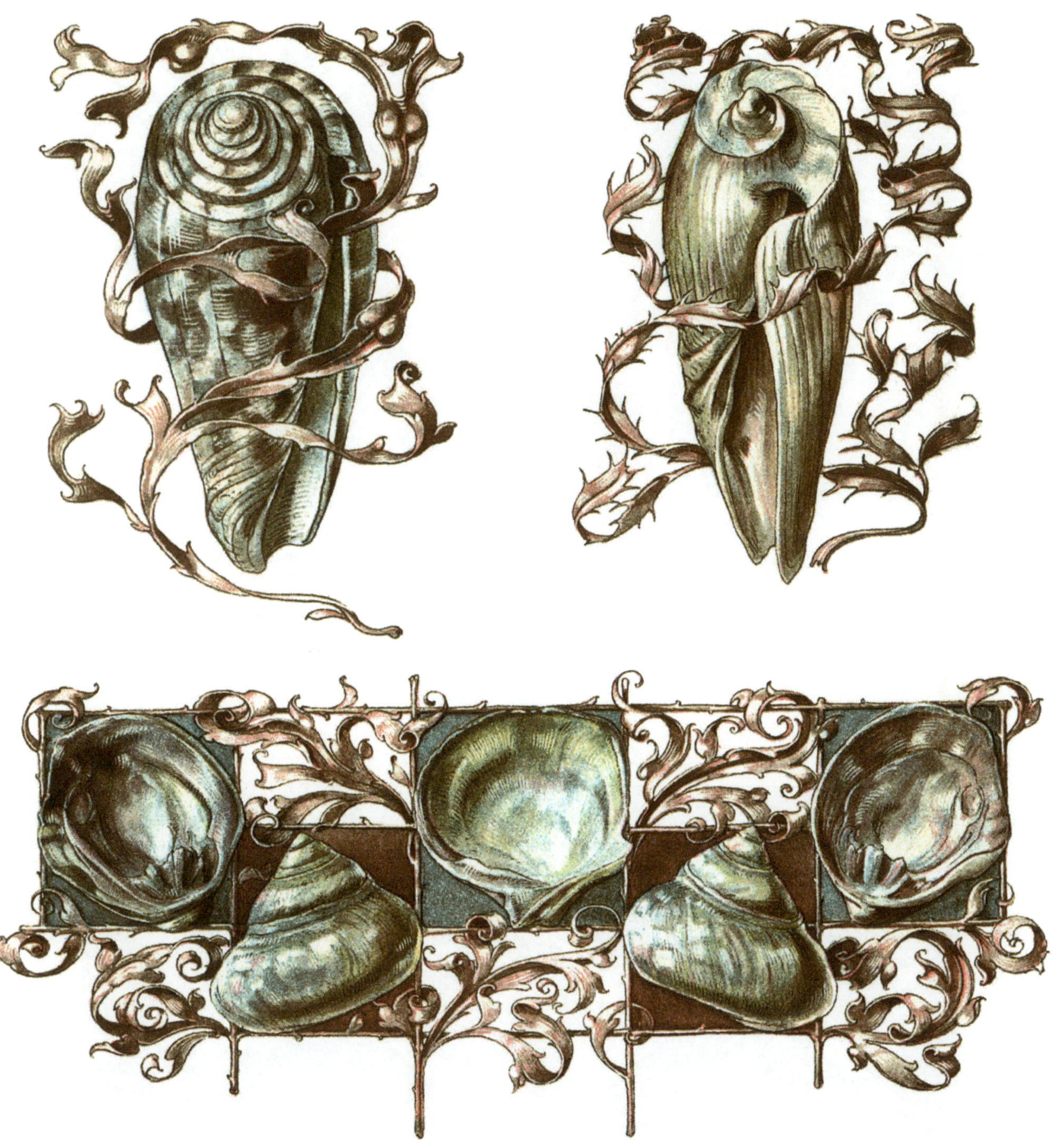

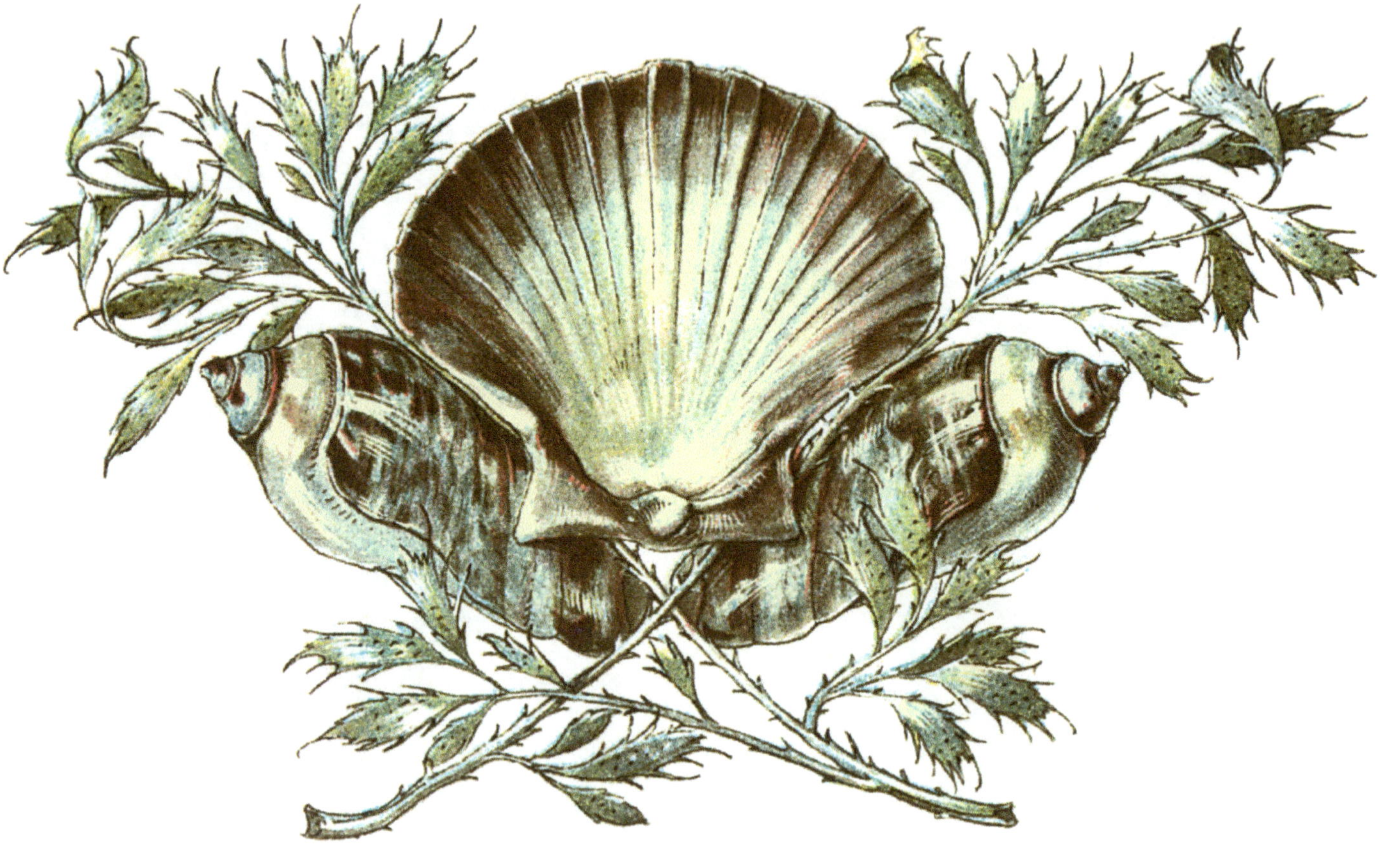

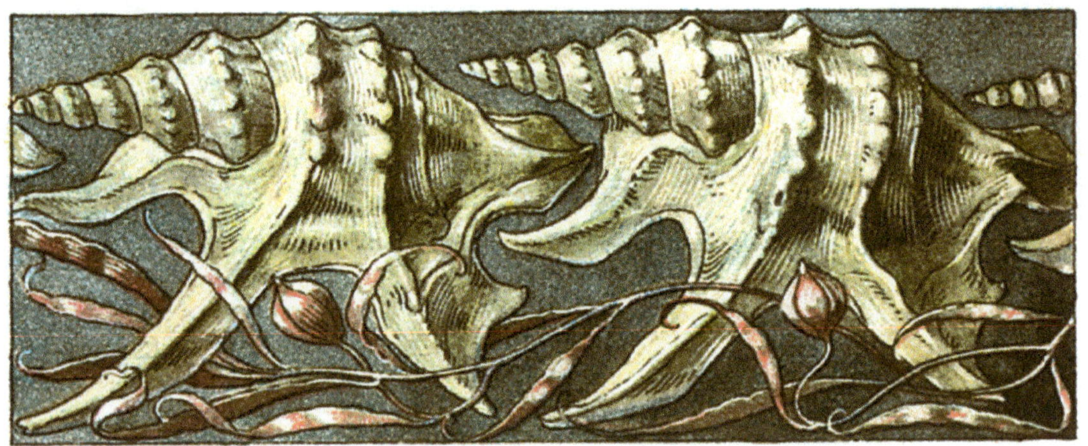

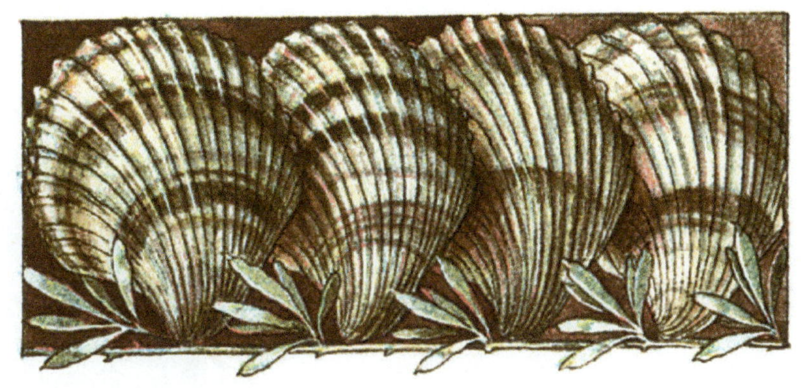

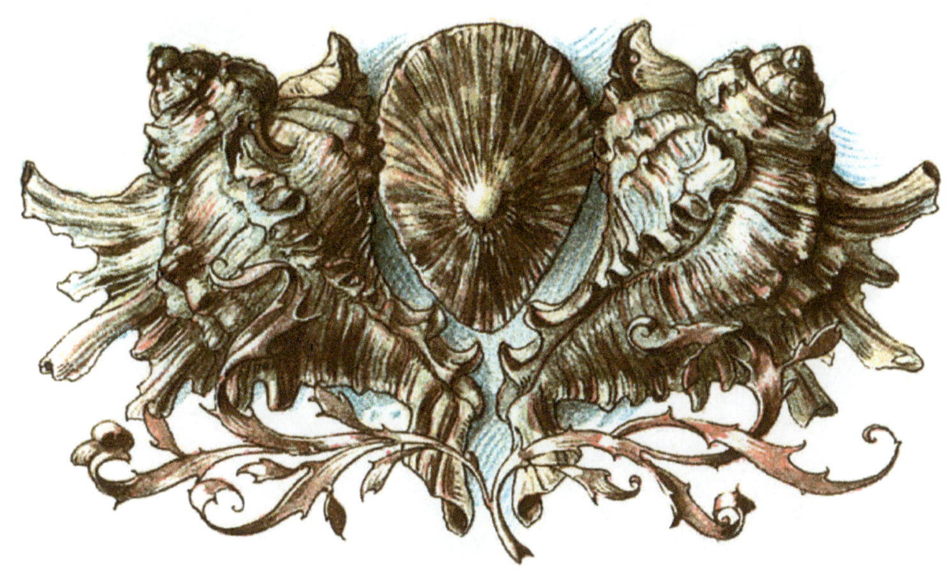

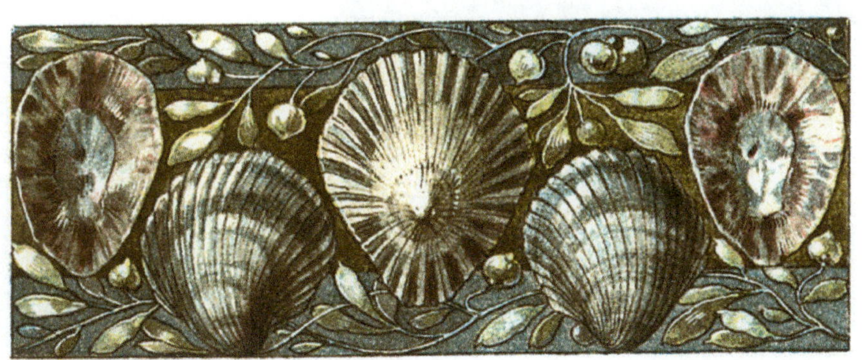

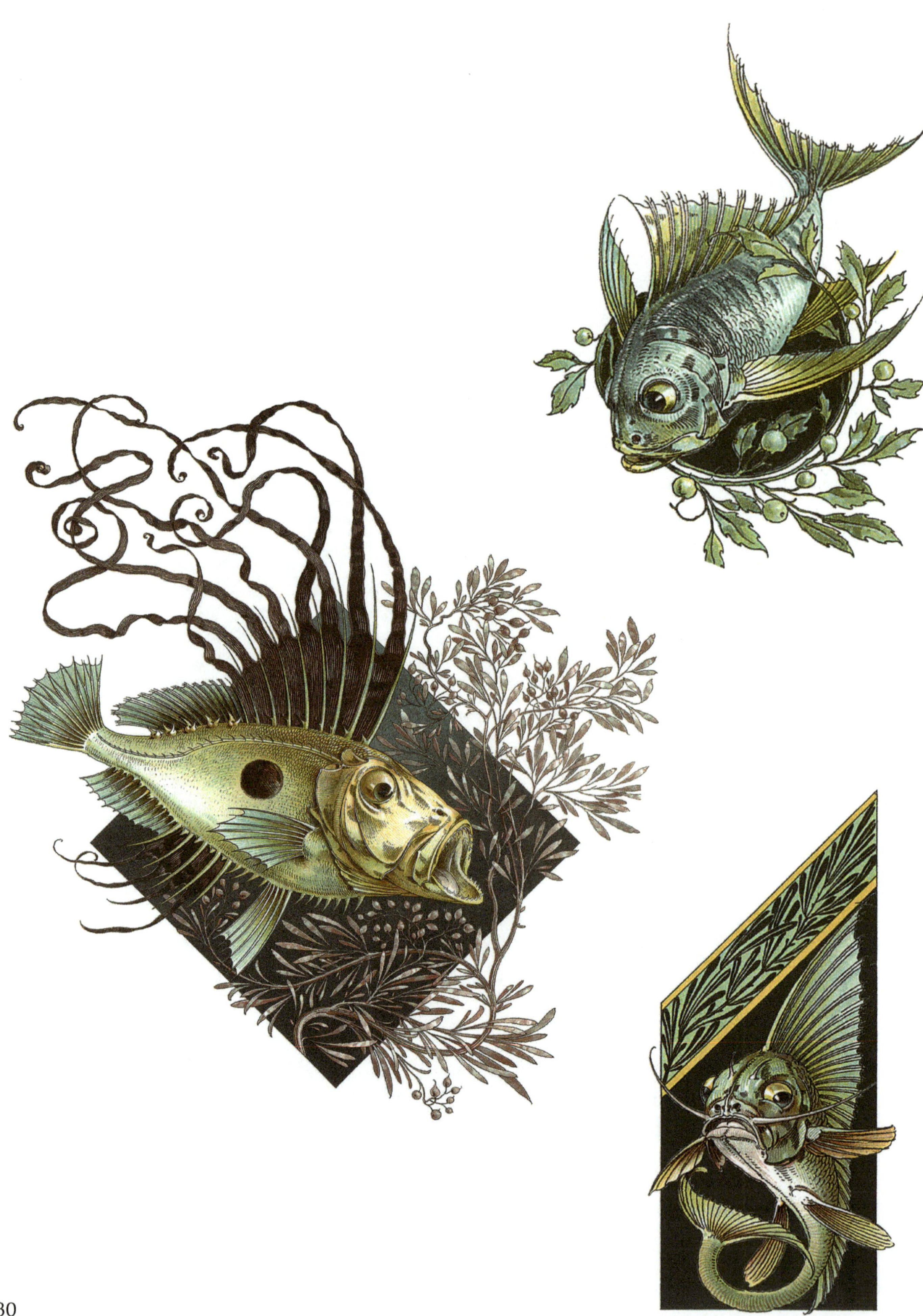

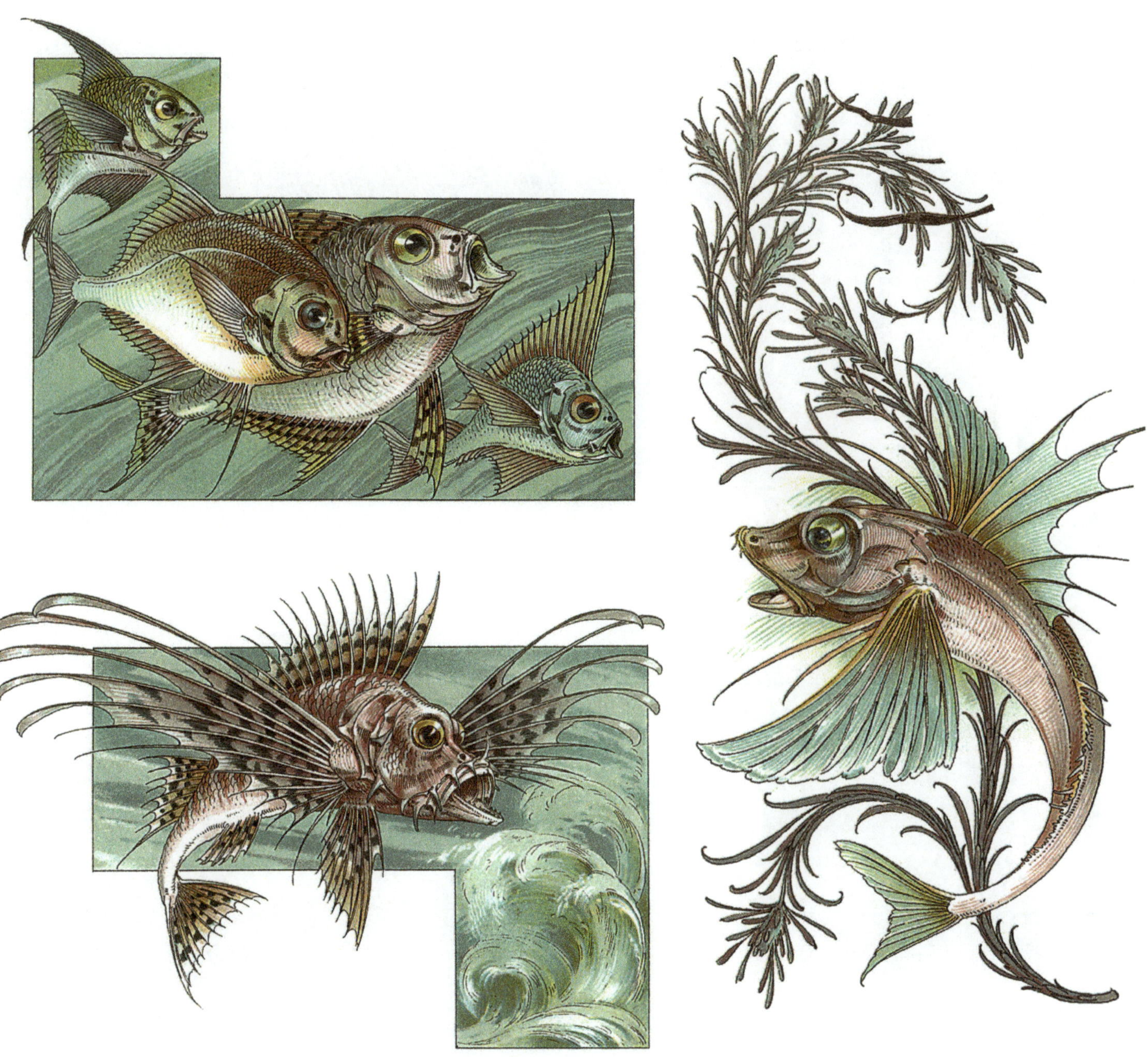

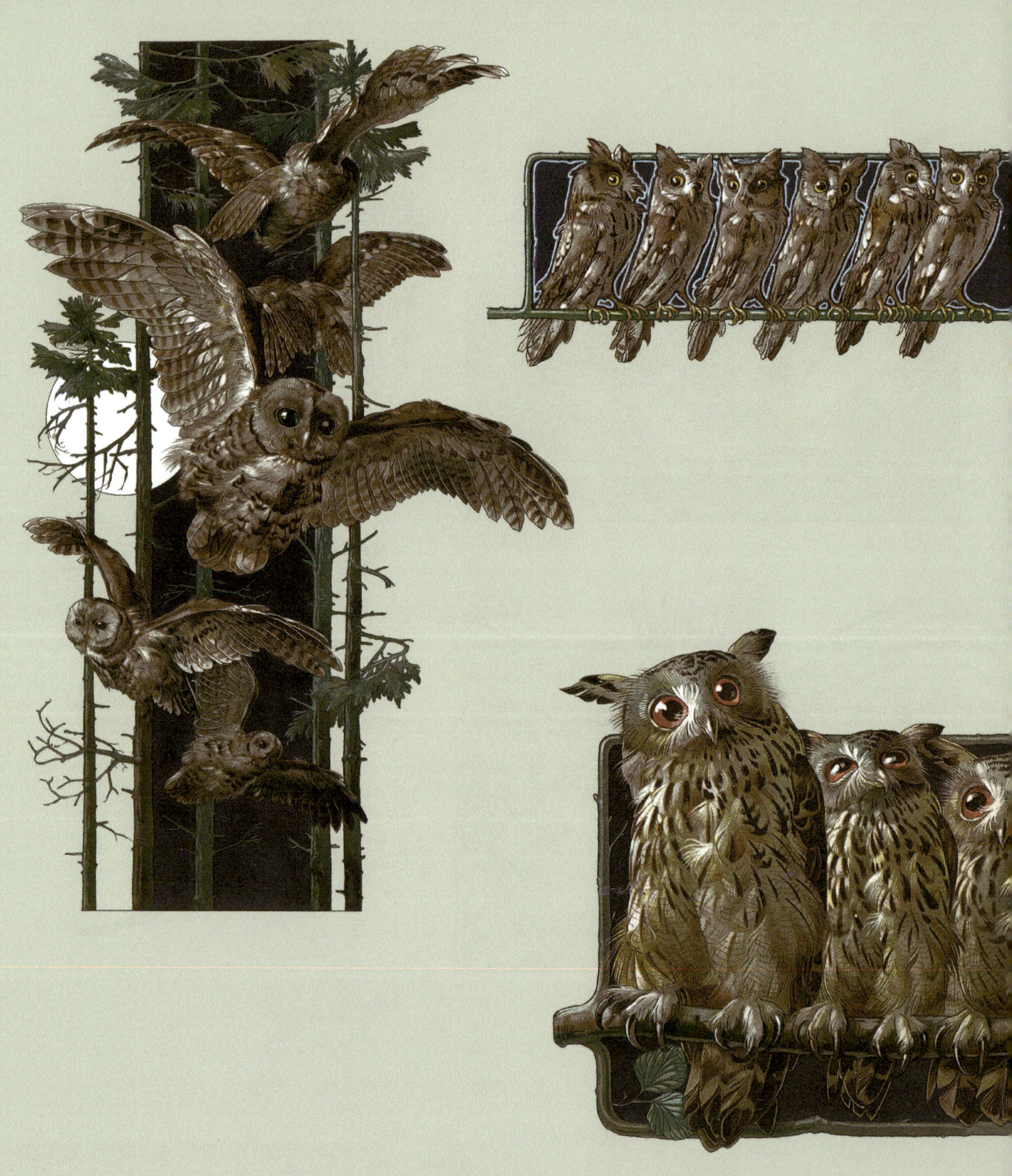

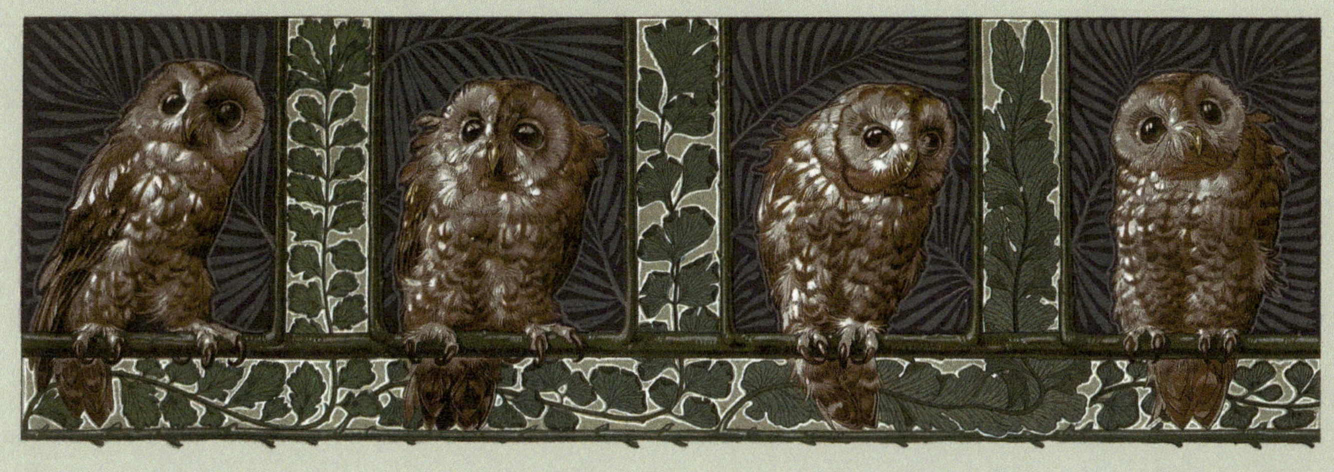

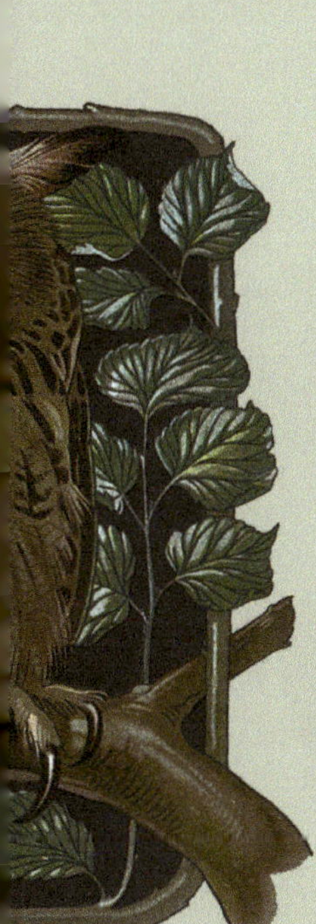

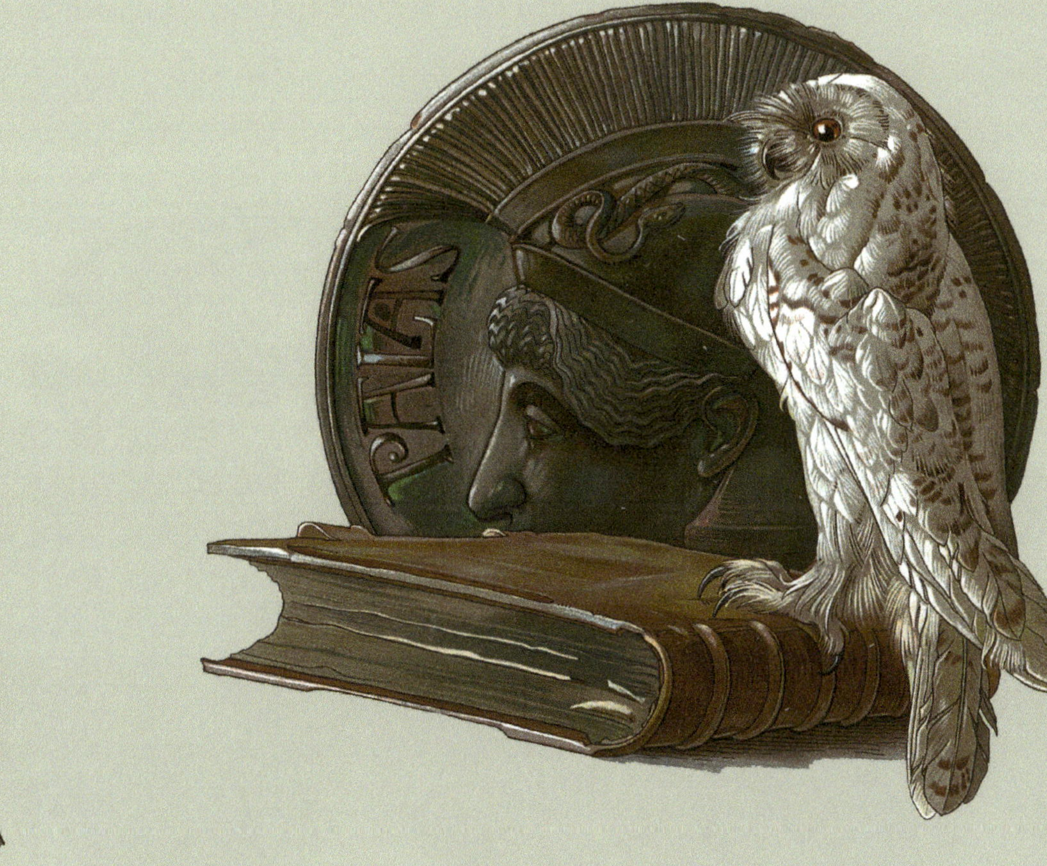

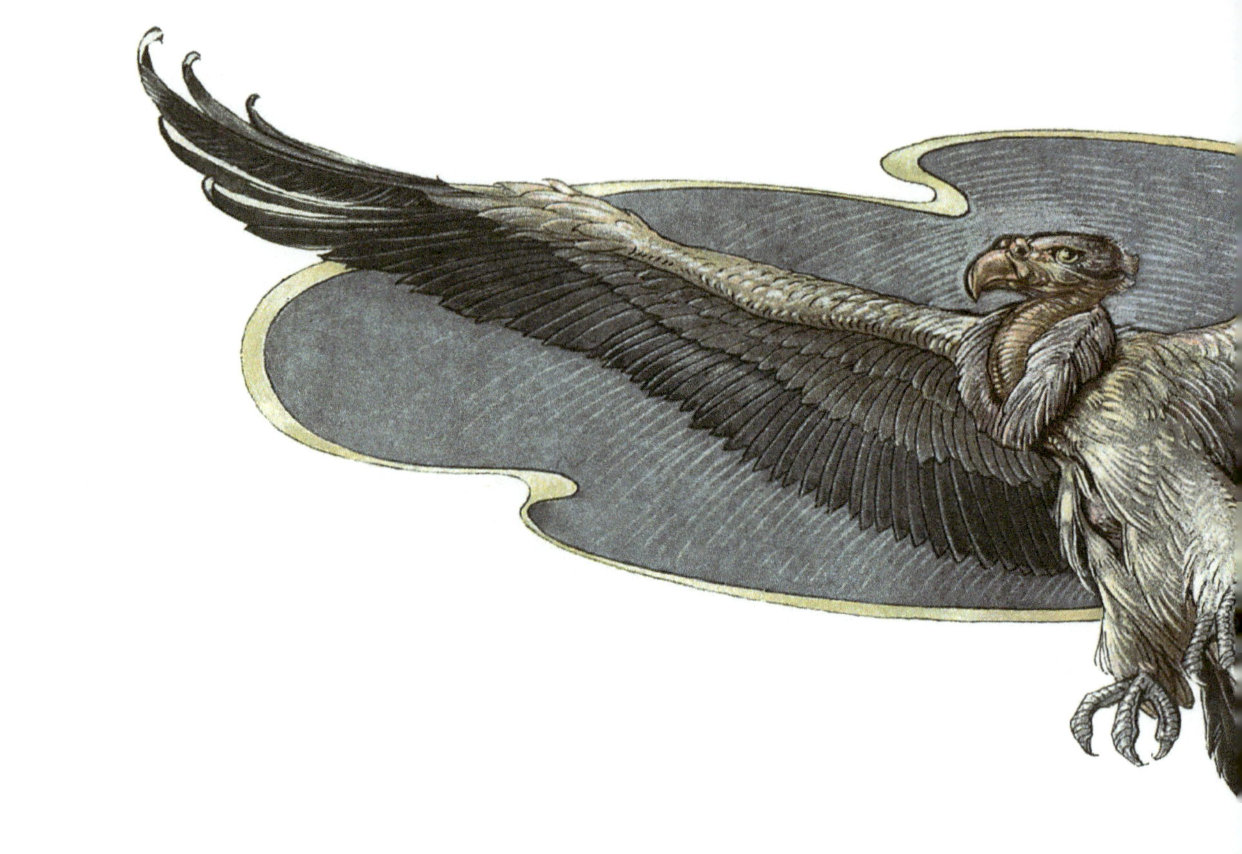

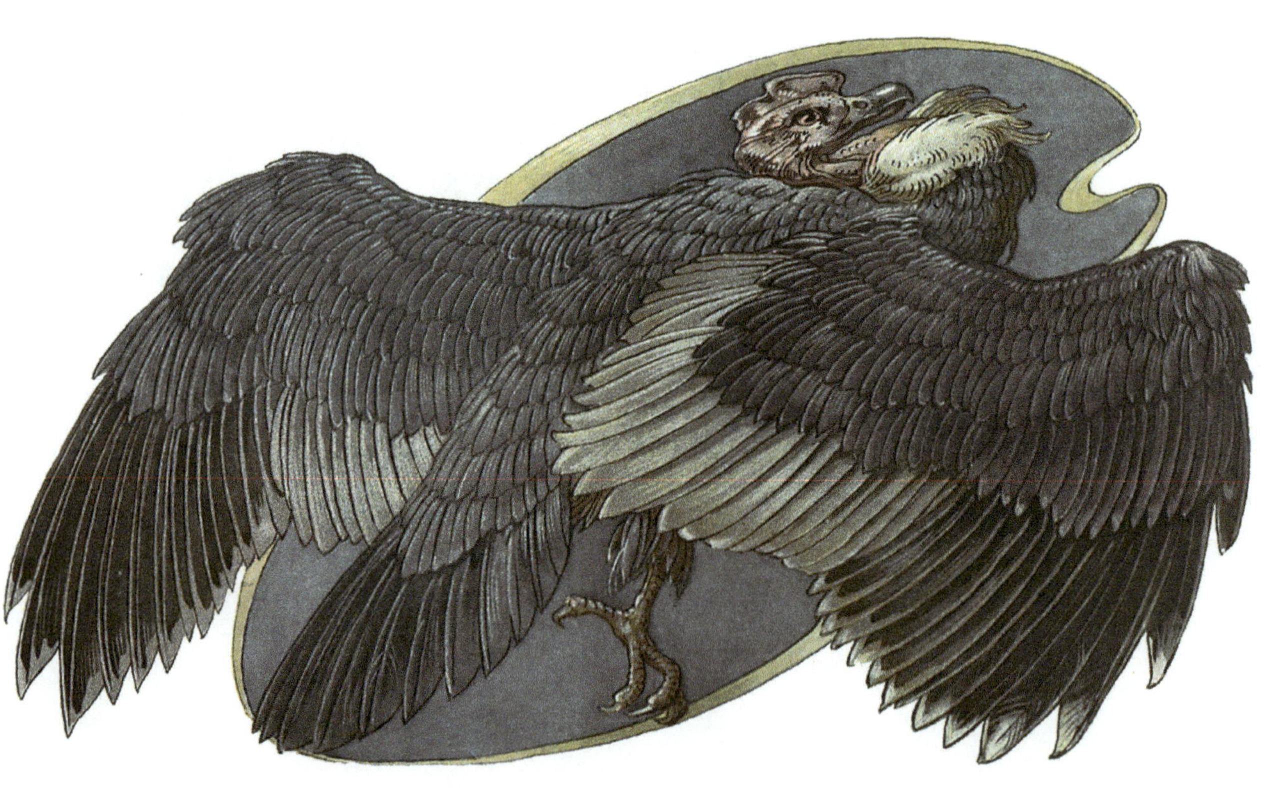

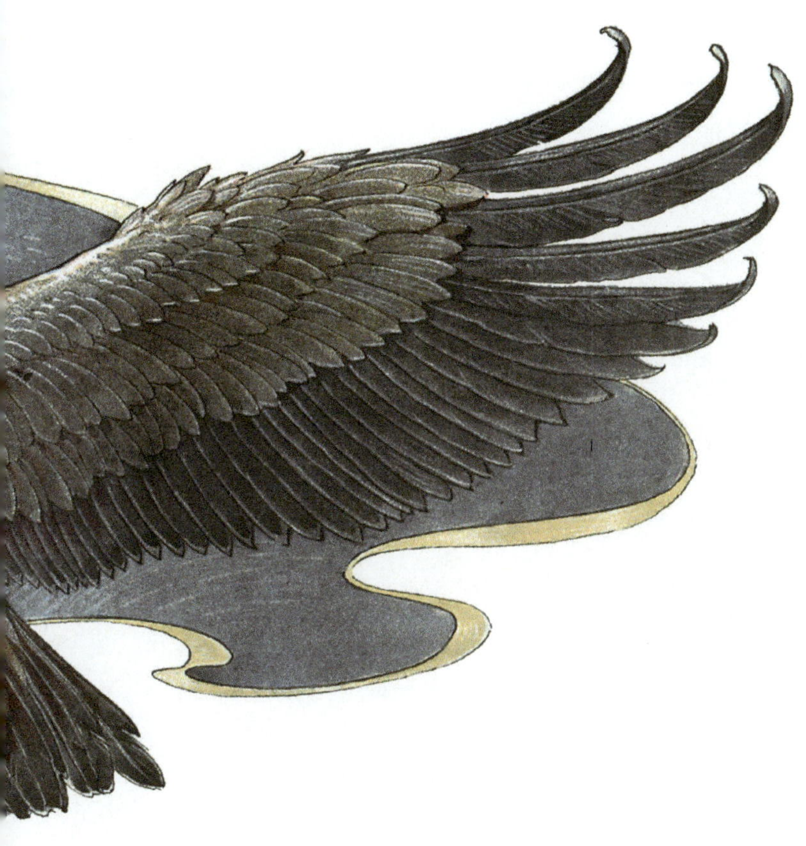

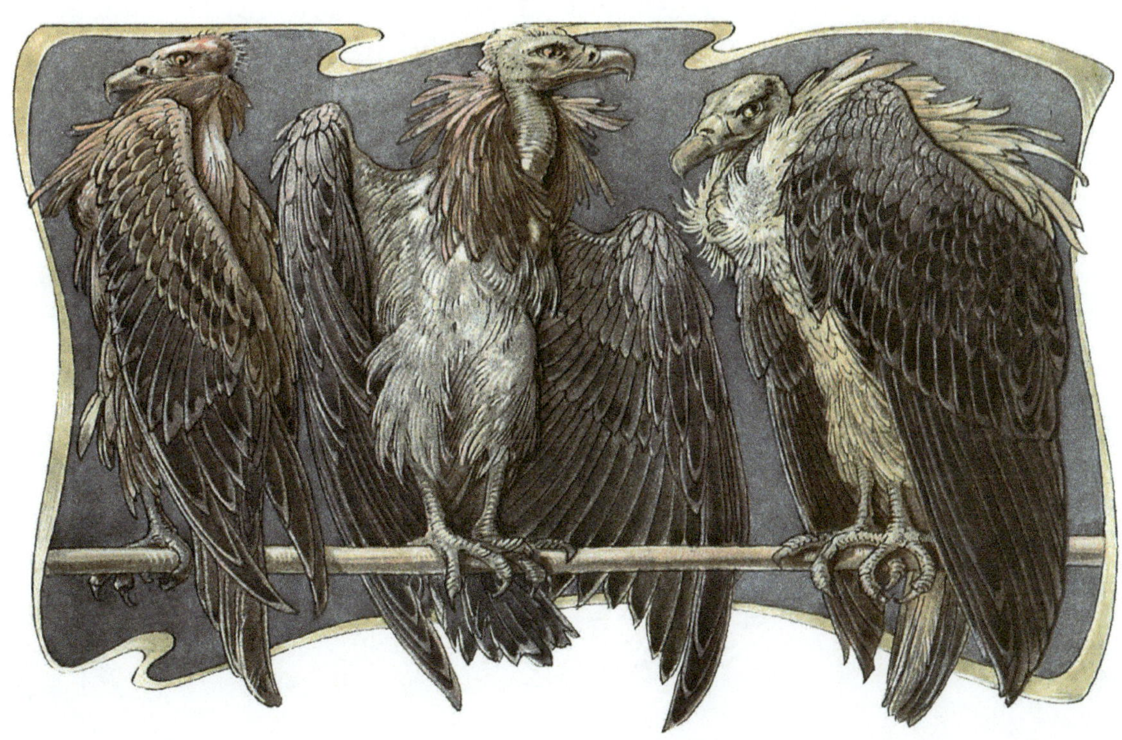

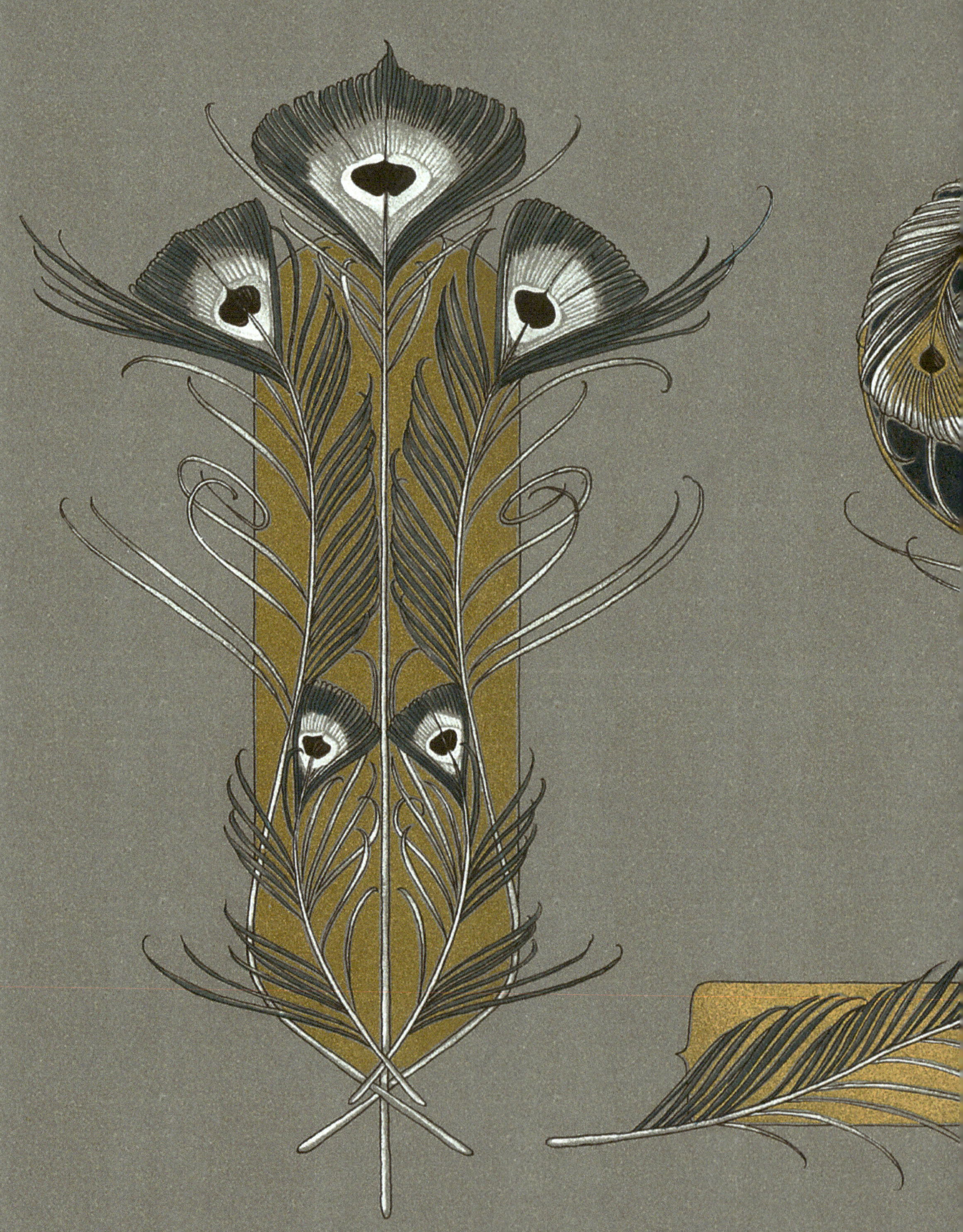

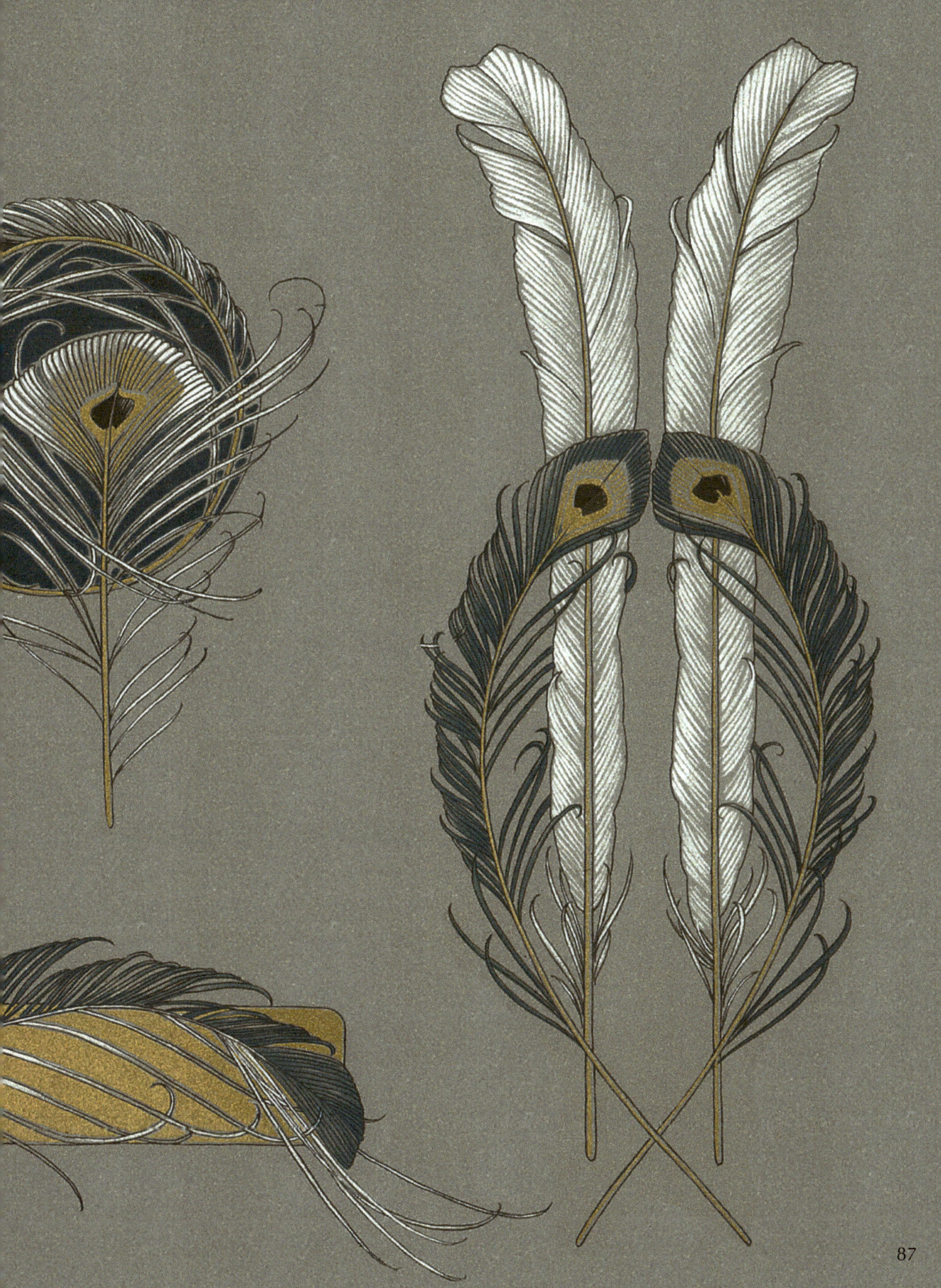

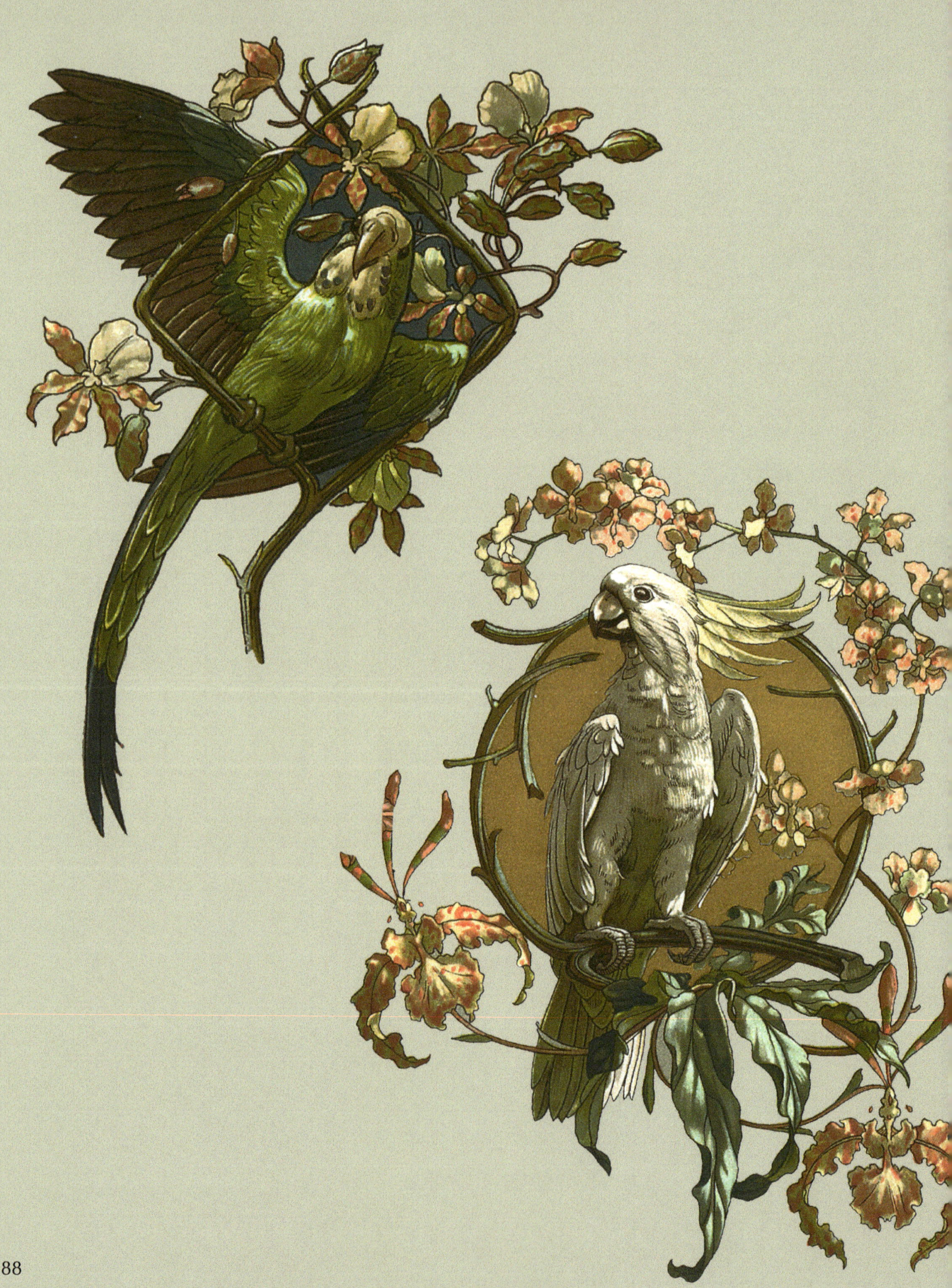

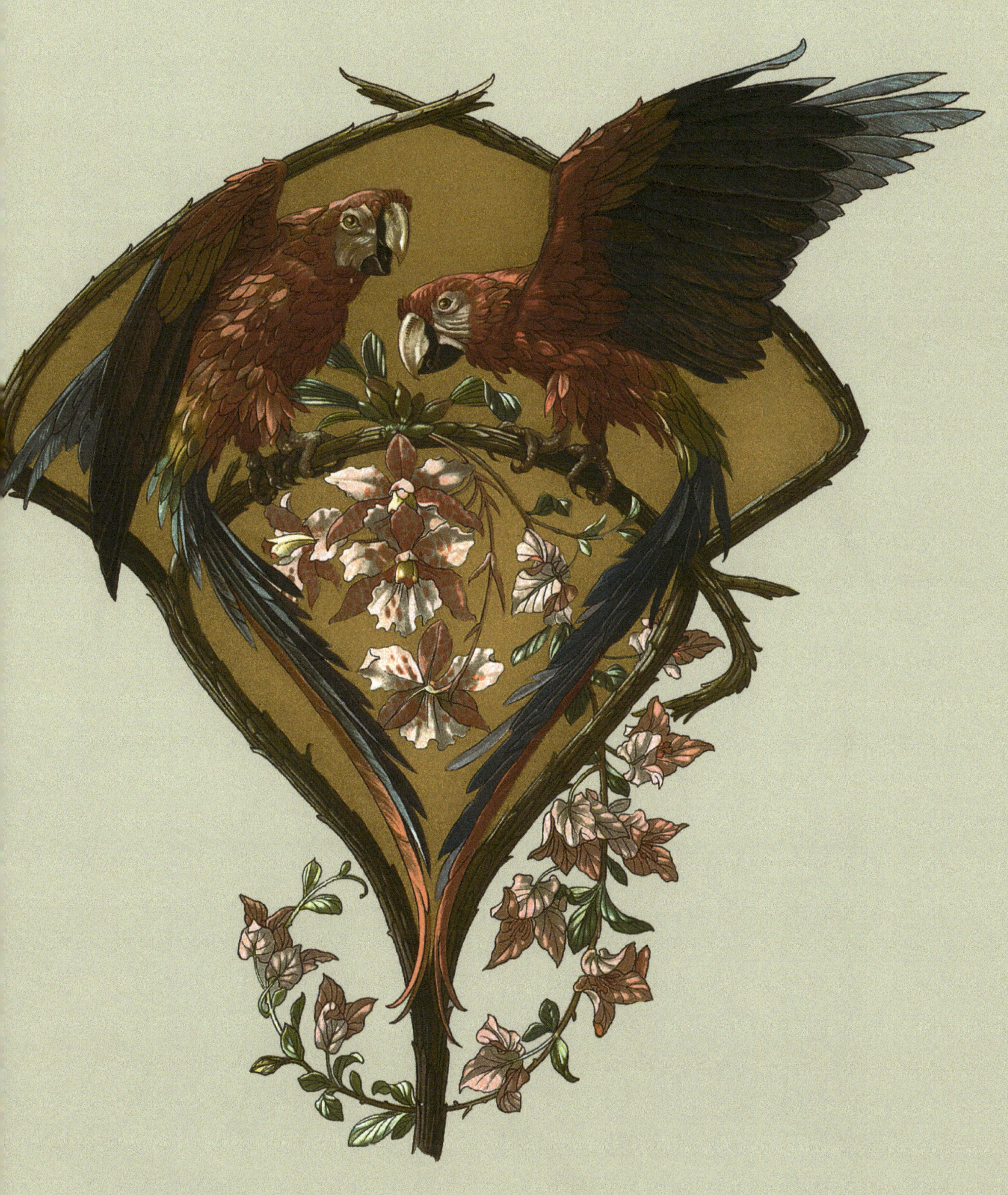

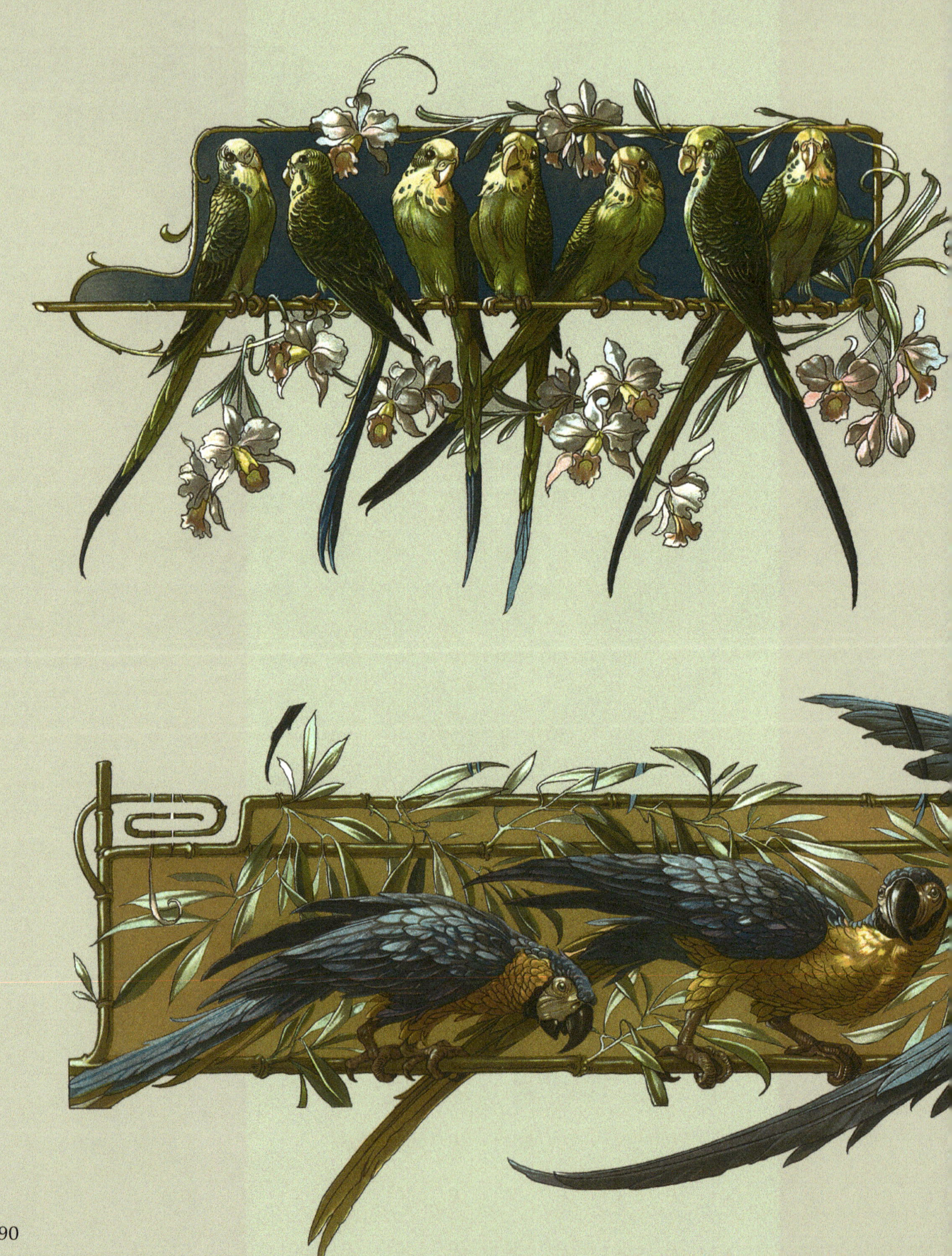

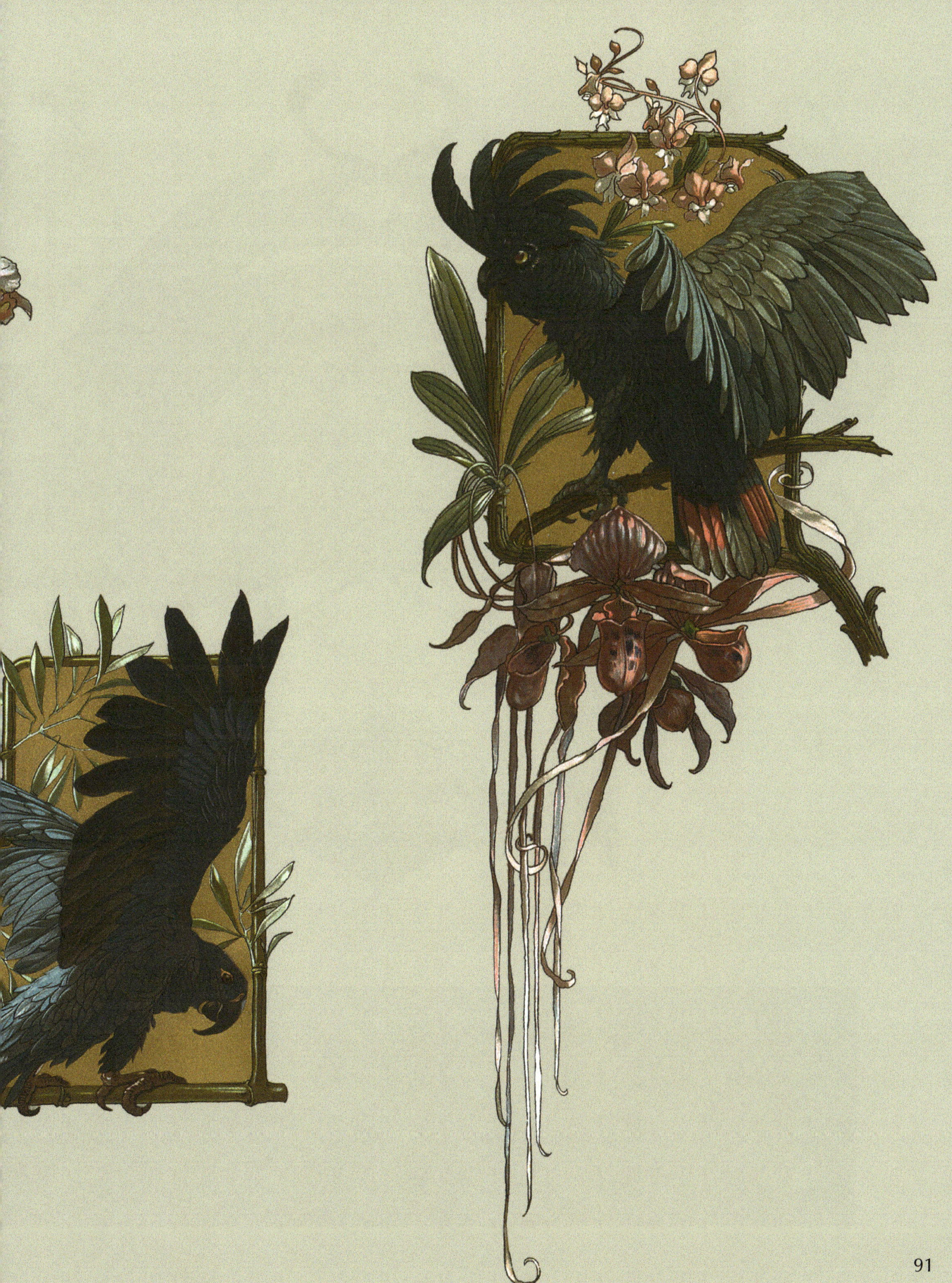

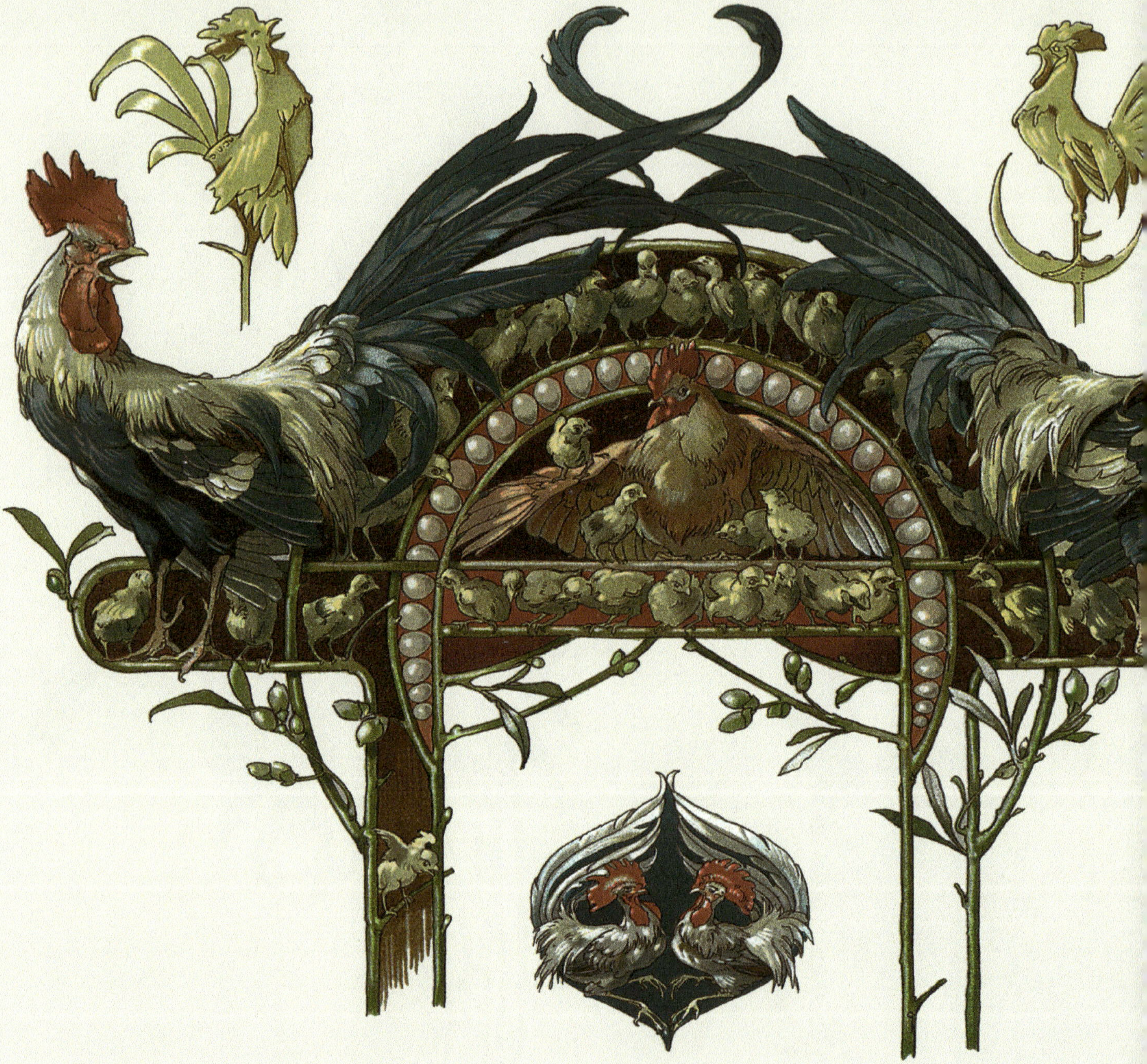

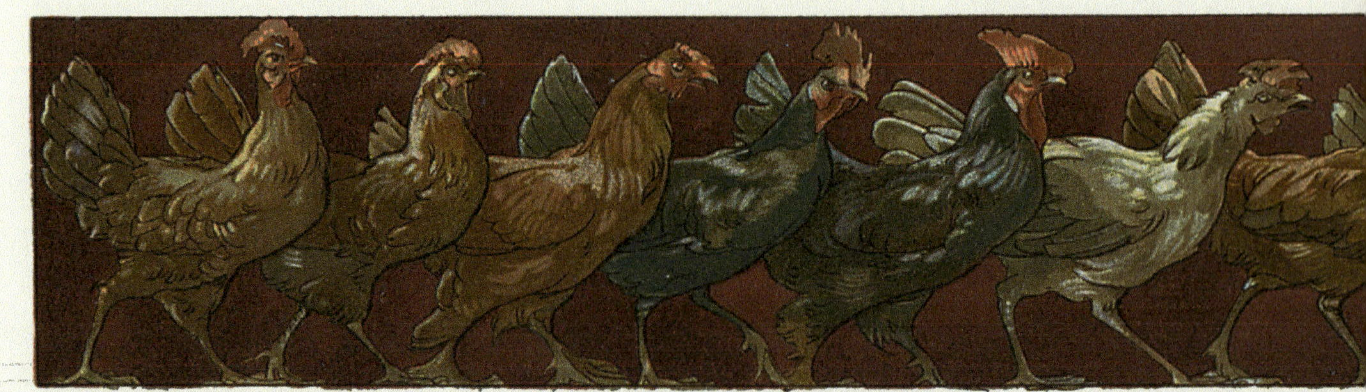

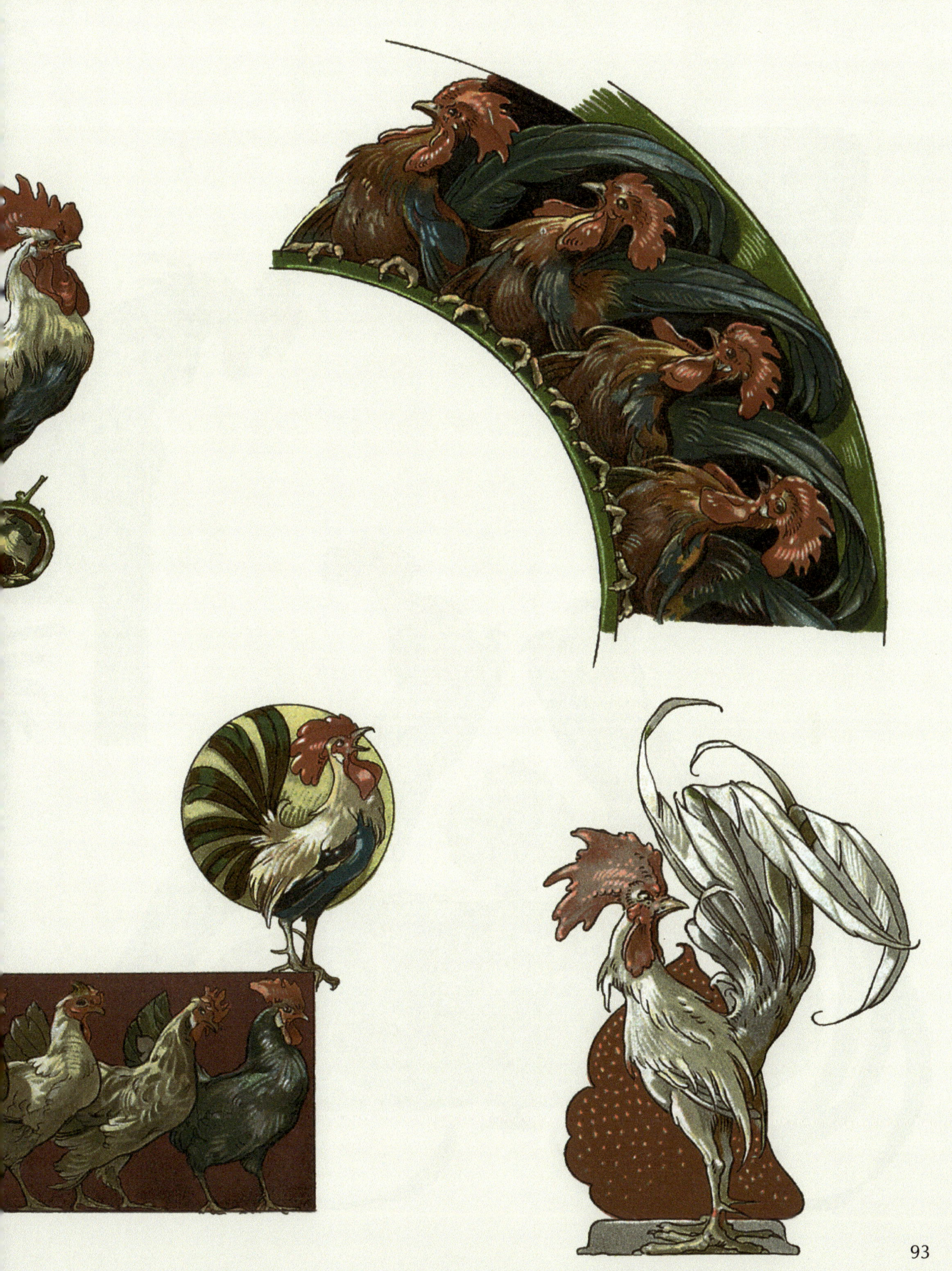

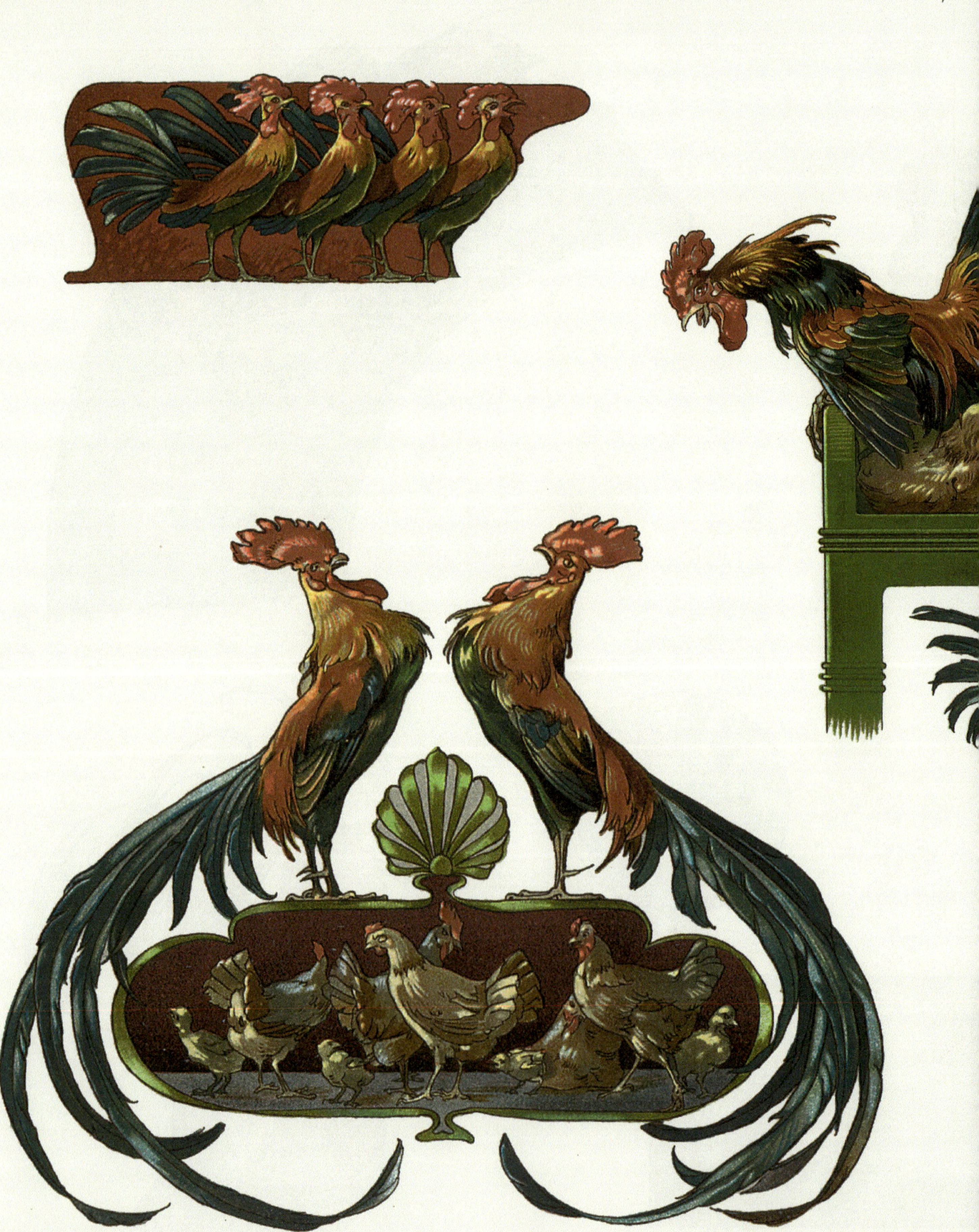

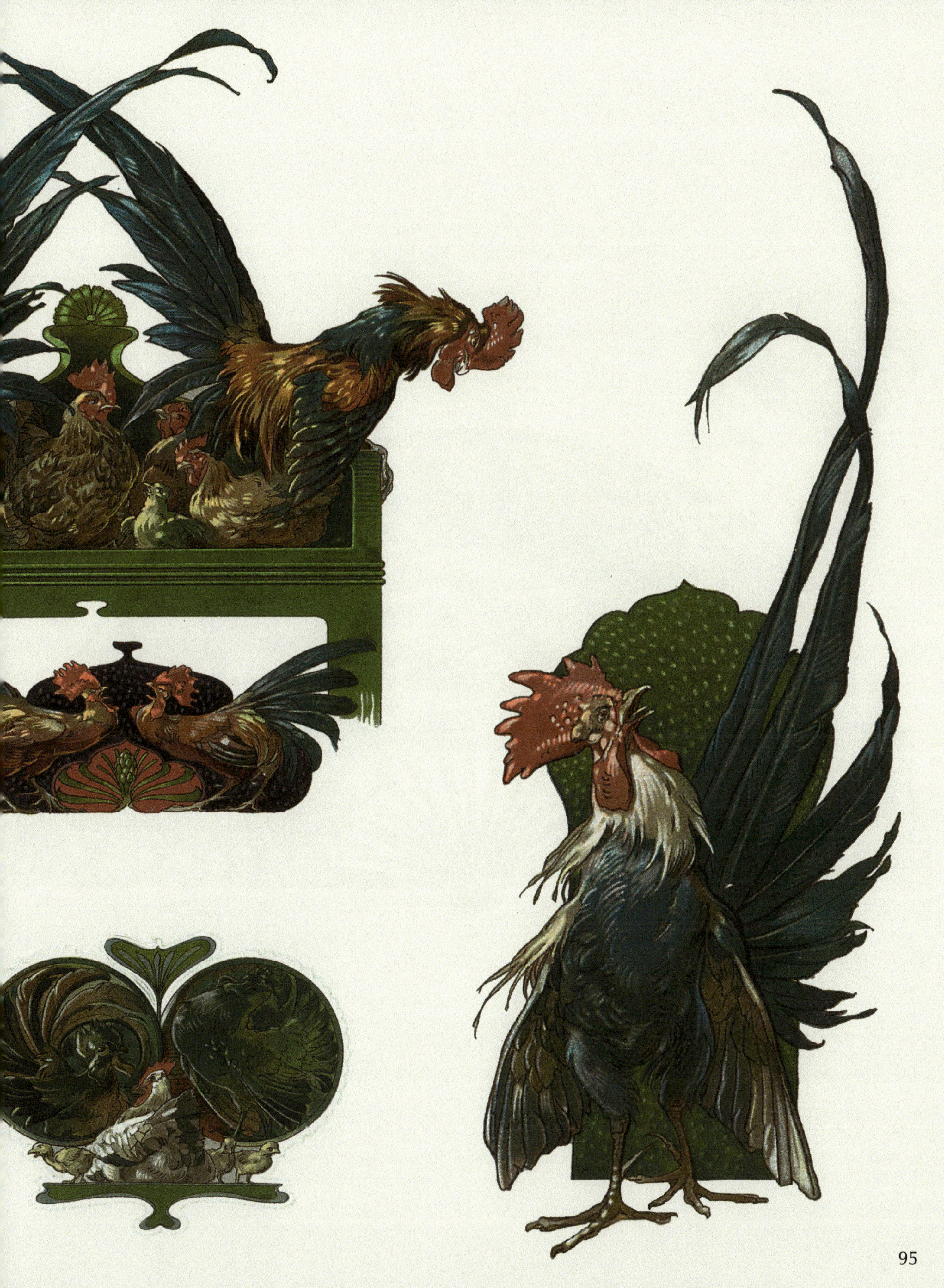

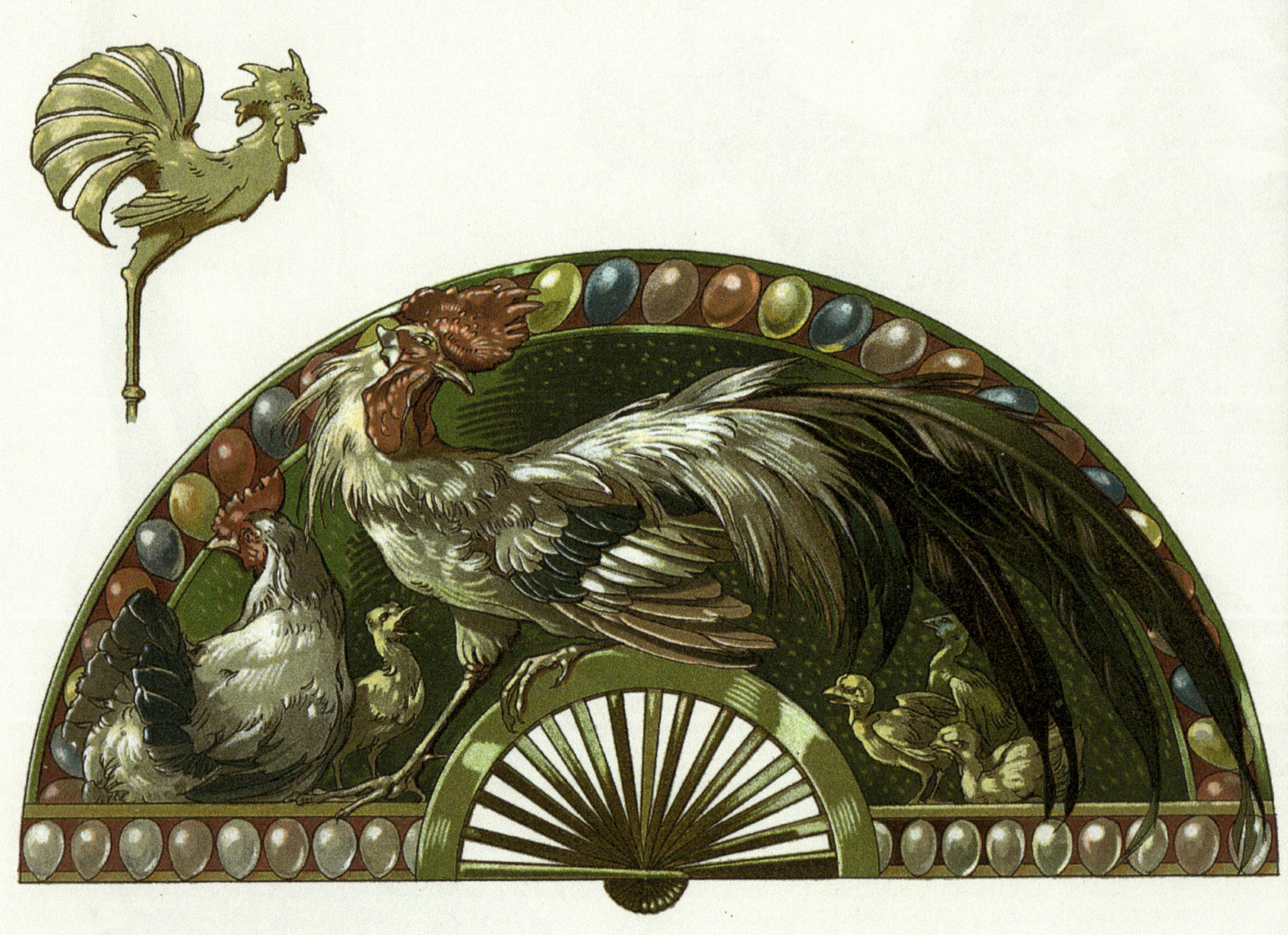